COORDINATION IN SYNTAX

Coordination in syntax is an important part of the analysis of sentence structure. Niina Ning Zhang addresses the issues raised by coordinate pairings and the implications of these structures, looking in particular at examples within English and Chinese. The volume covers the major questions regarding coordinates in syntax, providing a fresh perspective to arguments raised within previous literature. She explains how such coordinate complexes are structured, how some coordinators can be combined with conjuncts of various parts of speech, the fixed nature of some of these pairings and what changes exist between the coordinate and non-coordinate constructions. The theories raised are backed up by a rich variety of examples as well as providing a crosslinguistic perspective, contextualizing these ideas within current syntactic research.

NIINA NING ZHANG is Associate Professor and Director in the Graduate Institute of Linguistics at National Chung Cheng University. She previously co-edited *Ellipsis in Conjuction* (2000) and has written many journal articles on syntactic theory and practice.

In this series

CAMBRIDGE STUDIES IN LINGUISTICS

Coordination in Syntax

COORDINATION IN SYNTAX

NIINA NING ZHANG

National Chung Cheng University

CAMBRIDGE UNIVERSITY PRESS
Cambridge, New York, Melbourne, Madrid, Cape Town, Singapore,
São Paulo, Delhi, Dubai, Tokyo

Cambridge University Press
The Edinburgh Building, Cambridge CB2 8RU, UK

Published in the United States of America by Cambridge University Press, New York

www.cambridge.org
Information on this title: www.cambridge.org/9780521767552

First published 2010

Printed in the United Kingdom at the University Press, Cambridge

A catalogue record for this publication is available from the British Library

ISBN 978-0-521-76755-2 Hardback

This book is dedicated to my late parents
Zhang Guangbi 張光璧 and Fang Aiqi 方愛七.

Contents

Acknowledgments

It is more than nine years since I attended a summer school course called *The Syntax of Coordination* in Potsdam, 1999, taught by Chris Wilder. My interest in the topic started then. My initial work on coordination received help from Chris Wilder, of course, as well as other former colleagues at the Center for General Linguistics (Zentrum für Allgemeine Sprachwissenschaft, ZAS) and other linguists in Berlin, including Philippa Cook, Laura Downing, Werner Frey, Dieter Gasde, Hans-Martin Gärtner, Ljudmilla Geist, Andreas Haida, Silke Hamann, Daniel Hole, Manfred Krifka, Ewald Lang, André Meinunger, Kerstin Schwabe, Ben Shaer, and Arthur Stepanov. After I moved to Taiwan in the fall of 2003, the writing of this book has benefited from various kinds of help from the local linguistics community. I thank Henry Yungli Chang, Tzong-Hong Jonah Lin, Jowang Lin, Chen-Sheng Luther Liu, Miaoling Hsieh, Shuying Shyu, Chih-Chen Jane Tang, Tingchi Tang, Sze-Wing Tang, Jen Ting, and Wei-Tien Dylan Tsai. In the Linguistics Institute at National Chung Cheng University, I have been blessed with the kind support of my colleagues Jung-hsing Chang, Jim H. Y. Tai, Jane S. Tsay, and our administrative assistant Shu-Fen Hsu.

Early versions of most of the chapters have been presented at many conferences, including the 11th International Conference on Chinese Linguistics (Nagoya, Aug. 20–22, 2002), the 1st International Workshop on East Asian Linguistics (Kyoto, Aug. 23, 2002), the Conference on Null Subjects and Parametric Variation, Reykjavik (July 18–19, 2003), GLOW in Asia 4 (Seoul, Aug. 20–23, 2003), the 2nd Workshop on Formal Syntax and Semantics (Taipei, Sept. 27–29, 2003), the 16th North American Conference on Chinese Linguistics (Iowa, May 21–23, 2004), the 2nd International Workshop on Theoretical East Asian Linguistics (Hsinchu, June 12–13, 2004), GLOW in Asia 5 (New Delhi, Oct. 5–8, 2005), NELS 36 (Amherst, Oct. 28–30, 2005), GLOW 29 (Barcelona, April 5–8, 2006), the 4th Workshop on Formal Syntax and Semantics (Chiayi, April 14–15, 2006), the Symposium on Chinese Syntax and Semantics (Hong Kong, Aug. 18–20, 2007), and the 13th International Morphology Meeting

(Vienna, Feb. 3–6, 2008). I am grateful to the audience members of these conferences and readers of various parts of the book manuscript for their suggestions, encouragement, and challenges, especially Mark Baltin, Lisa Lai Shen Cheng, Norbert Corver, Wayne Cowart, David Adger, Jingqi Fu, Yang Gu, Anders Holmberg, Cheng-teh James Huang, Richard Kayne, Paul Kiparsky, Paul Law, Thomas Lee, Yen-hui Audrey Li, Danqing Liu, Feng-his Liu, Jianming Lu, Norvin Richards, Mamoru Saito, Yang Shen, Dingxu Shi, Peter Svenonius, Satoshi Tomioka, Juan Uriakereka, Henk van Riemsdijk, Akira Watanabe, Dan Xu, Hang-Jin Yoon, James Yoon, and Bojiang Zhang. Special thanks go to Neal Whitman, who wrote fifteen pages of comments on the manuscript, which helped me with the final revision.

I also want to thank Elizabeth Cowper and Diane Massam for teaching me formal syntax, and Jinguo Ding, Yucun Qi, Yili Xu, Dechun Wang, and Liejiong Xu for inspiring me to work on the puzzles of language.

Previous versions of parts of the book have been published in *Language and Linguistics* (2006, Vol. 7: 175–223), *Lingua* (2007, Vol. 117: 2134–2158), *Lingua et Linguistica* (2007, Vol. 1: 7–46), *Taiwan Journal of Linguistics* (2007, Vol. 5: 19–47), *Canadian Journal of Linguistics* (2009, Vol. 54), *Studia Linguistica* (2009, Vol. 63), and *Language Research* (2008, Vol. 44: 121–163). I am grateful to these journals for allowing me to include revised versions of the papers in this book. The suggestions from the reviewers and editors of the journals and from the reviewers and board members of Cambridge Studies in Linguistics have all helped improve the strength of the argumentation presented in this final version. I am indebted to these anonymous teachers. Needless to say, all remaining errors are mine.

Since the end of 2003, the writing of this book has been supported by grants from the National Science Council in Taiwan. In preparing for the publication of this book, I have also received tremendous assistance from Andrew Winnard, the Senior Commissioning Editor of Cambridge Studies in Linguistics, and the editorial and production team of Cambridge University Press.

I owe extremely special thanks to my husband James Myers. Without his insightful academic discussions and psychological support, as well as his editing of the English in the whole manuscript, this book would be uninterpretable.

Abbreviations

AC	Asymmetrical Coordination
AP	Adjective Phrase
ATB	the Across-the-Board dependency
CC	Conjunct Constraint (the first part of CSC)
CCe	No movement of external conjuncts (part of CC)
CCi	No movement of internal conjuncts (part of CC)
CCC	Coordinate Constituent Constraint
CED	Condition on Extraction Domains
CCH	Clausal Conjunct Hypothesis
CHC	the Coordinate-Head RC Construction
CLC	Coordination of Likes Constraint
CLC_{func}	CLC with respect to grammatical functions
CLC_{sem}	CLC with respect to semantic types
CSC	Coordinate Structure Constraint
DP	Determiner Phrase
EC	Element Constraint (the second part of CSC)
FM	Focus Marker
IDC	the Interwoven Dependency Construction
ID	Identification feature
IP	Infl Phrase
LF	Logical Form
Mod	Modifier
ModP	Modifier Phrase
MSC	the Modifier-Sharing Construction
NCC	Null Conjunct Constraint
NP	Noun Phrase
Num	Number
PF	Phonological Form
PP	Preposition Phrase
PPC	the Paired Pronoun *same* Construction

PR	Parallelism Requirement
QR	Quantifier Raising
QT	quotative morpheme
RC	Relative Clause
RNR	Right Node Raising
RPR	Relativized PR
SAC	the Split Argument Construction
SE	Similarity Expression
TLC	the Thematic Licensing *same* Construction
TP	Tense Phrase
UTAH	Uniformity of Theta-Assignment Hypothesis
VP	Verb Phrase
&P	Conjunction Phrase

In the Chinese examples:

CL	classifier
EXP	experiential aspect
INCH	inchoative aspect
PRF	perfect aspect
PRG	progressive aspect
PRT	sentence-final aspect particle
DE	associative particle
Q	sentence-final question particle
TOP	topic

1 *Introduction*

All languages have coordinate constructions. Although generative grammar, including recent work within the Minimalist framework, has made much progress in reducing various types of construction-specific syntax to the minimum, it has not answered the following four fundamental questions:

A. Does the derivation of coordinate constructions create any special syntactic configuration, other than the general binary complementation and adjunction configuration?
B. Does the derivation of coordinate constructions resort to any special syntactic category, other than NP, VP, and so on?
C. Is the derivation of coordinate constructions subject to any special constraint on syntactic operations, other than general conditions such as the Minimal Link Condition?
D. Does the derivation of coordinate constructions require any special type of syntactic operations, other than Merge and the step-by-step, one-tail-one-head chains of Move?

In this monograph, my answer to all of these four questions is negative. I argue against any special syntax of coordination. Consequently, NO SPECIAL SYNTAX is the real syntactic law of coordination, just as the Minimalist program would lead us to expect.

However, the standard answer to Question A is affirmative. Coordination has hitherto enjoyed the exclusive privilege of the flat multiple branching structure, as shown in (1.1a), which can be found in nearly all linguistics textbooks.

(1.1) a.

The binary-branching structure of coordination shown in (1.1b) has occasionally been proposed (Yngve 1960: 456; Thiersch 1985; Munn 1987; Kayne 1994; Zoerner 1995; Johannessen 1996; among others). However, the key arguments against the binary-branching structure summarized by Dik (1968) have never been refuted. For instance, if the combination of a coordinator and one conjunct is a constituent, excluding the other conjunct, why is it never able to undergo any regular movement? Since questions like this have not been answered, the two opposing analyses still co-exist in the literature. However, binary vs. not binary should be an issue of truth, rather than taste. In this monograph, I not only answer Dik's challenges to the binary structure analysis, but also present a variety of new arguments to show that coordinate complexes have a complementation structure, rather than any coordination-specific structure. My arguments thus indicate that the relationship between two conjuncts is that between a specifier (external conjunct) and a complement (internal conjunct), with the head realized by the coordinator. Unlike previous binary approaches (Munn 1993; Johannessen 1998; among others), I do not consider morphological agreement in my argumentation. Since Koutsoudas (1968), it has been noted that verbs may agree with the closest conjunct of a coordinate nominal, regardless of whether they precede or follow the nominal. This adjacency effect has been accounted for from a processing perspective (e.g. Lorimor 2007; Steiner 2008). Moreover, it has long been observed that the denotation of coordination also plays a role in agreement (e.g. McNally 1993: 363; Huddleston and Pullum 2002: 1283). Since in many cases morphological agreement in coordinate construction is a processing or semantic issue, it cannot be used to argue for any special structure of coordinate complexes. Instead, I use facts like the following to argue for the structure in (1.1b): the asymmetry of conjuncts in binding, in possessee pronominalization, in hosting coordinators, and in coordinator floating.

Question B concerns the syntax of the categorial makeup of coordinate complexes. In the literature, there are basically two approaches to this issue. In the traditional approach, it has been assumed that the category of a coordinate complex is simply that of the conjuncts. However, if the two conjuncts are of different categories, like the nominal and clause in (1.2a) and the nominal and PP in (1.2b), this approach does not tell us what the category of the whole coordinate complex is and where it comes from.

(1.2) a.   You can depend on [my assistance and that he will be on time].   (Sag
             et al. 1985: 165)
       b.   John eats only pork and only at home.   (Grosu 1985: 232)

The other approach is to claim that the category of all coordinate complexes is &P (or CoP, ConjP, BooleanP), a special category exclusively for coordinate constructions (Munn 1987; 1993; Zoerner 1995; Johannessen 1996; among others). I show that &P is both theoretically and empirically problematic. I argue that in coordinate complexes headed by coordinators without any intrinsic categorial features, like English *and*, the categorial features of a designated conjunct move and provide the category features for the whole coordinate complex. Thus, the category of a coordinate complex is always that of one of the two conjuncts. The category feature movement argued for here not only removes the problematic &P from the computation system, but also gives a simple answer to Question C.

The main issue of Question C is how to account for the effects of the Coordinate Structure Constraint (CSC, Ross 1967). This constraint is composed of two parts: no conjunct may be moved (the Conjunct Condition, CC), and no element may be extracted from conjuncts (the Element Condition, EC). The CC and EC are illustrated in (1.3a) and (1.3b), respectively.

(1.3) a. *Which boy did John kiss [_ and which girl]?   (CC violation)
       b. *What kind of herbs did you [[eat _] and [drink beer]]?   (EC violation)

On the one hand, the CSC has been regarded as "the most problem-free syntactic constraint ever discovered" (Postal 1998: 52), but on the other hand, it has remained as the only construction-specific constraint in generative syntactic theory. When Riemsdijk and Williams (1986: 28) introduce various constraints, they state "All the principles discussed here have since been modified, generalized, or replaced. The fate of the CSC has been somewhat different, however, because it has not interacted with the other constraints under these revisions." The CSC has survived for more than 40 years. It still challenges generative linguistics, including the Minimalist program, which aims to abolish all construction-specific constraints.

This monograph makes two contributions to syntactic theory with respect to the CSC.

First, I review data showing that both the CC and the EC may be violated. Representations that violate the CSC are fully acceptable if they satisfy a Relativized Parallelism Requirement, a processing filter. The Relativized Parallelism Requirement is satisfied if conjuncts are semantically related to each other, or if conjuncts show resemblance in semantic type and movement history.

Second, I propose a new account for the observed CSC effects. The observed EC effects are explained by deviation from the Relativized Parallelism Requirement alone, and the observed CC effects are explained by the combination of two factors: deviation from the Relativized Parallelism Requirement, and the special lexical properties of *and*-like coordinators. These properties are revealed when we compare such coordinators with those that have intrinsic categorial features, as in Chinese. Our proposed category feature movement, which answers Question B above, accounts for the CC effects in coordinate complexes headed by *and*-like coordinators. The categorial feature movement from the external conjunct (i.e. first conjunct, in English) to the coordinator brings about the effect that the conjunct may not move any more, since its moving carrier, i.e., its categorial features (Chomsky 1995: 265), have gone. Coordinators with c-selectional restrictions as well as null coordinators do not need this categorial feature movement, and consequently the external conjunct may move. By contrast, the internal conjuncts can never move away from coordinators, since the latter, like many other types of head elements, may not be stranded. This correctly predicts that internal conjuncts may move if the coordinators are null.

Evidence for my new explanation of CSC effects comes from a wide range of empirical studies, including detailed studies of comitative constructions, a study of other types of head elements that also have no intrinsic categorial features, and asymmetrical coordination in both English and Chinese.

Theoretically, this new account of the CSC is plausible. In the Minimalist program, movement is driven by morphological considerations (Chomsky 1995: 262). Logically, it is also possible that the blocking of movement is related to morphological properties of specific syntactic elements, in addition to the generally recognized locality restrictions.

Empirically, one sees in this monograph that removing the CSC from the computational system also enables us to understand the syntactic derivations of three apparently puzzling constructions: Split Argument Constructions in both English and Chinese, as in (1.4a) and (1.5a) (cf. (1.4b) and (1.5b)), Modifier-Sharing Constructions in English, as in (1.6), and Interwoven Dependency Constructions in both English and Chinese, as in (1.7).

(1.4) a. John married Jane.
　　 b. [John and Jane] married.

(1.5) a. Tudou   yijing   shao-le   niurou.   [Chinese]
　　　　potato already cook-PRF beef
　　　　'The potatoes have already been cooked with the beef.'
　　 b. Baoyu shao-le   [tudou gen niurou].
　　　　Baoyu cook-PRF potato and beef
　　　　'Baoyu cooked the potatoes and the beef.'   (either separately or together)

(1.6)　　John met a man and Mary met a woman who knew each other well.
(1.7)　　How many frogs and how many toads did respectively Greg capture and Lucilli train?

These constructions seem to be in conflict with certain basic syntactic laws observed elsewhere: theta-role licensing and the general semantics–syntax mapping stated in Baker's (1988; 1997) Uniformity of Theta-Assignment Hypothesis, the identification of the syntactic relation between modifiers and their split modified elements, and the identification of the launching site of certain movement operations. As stated in the final sentence of Postal (1998), the challenges brought by such constructions can be avoided only under pain of maintaining a theory that denies that these constructions actually occur in natural languages. In this monograph, I propose syntactic derivations for the three constructions that require us to set aside the CSC. Specifically, both Split Argument Constructions and Modifier-Sharing Constructions are derived by conjunct raising, and Interwoven Dependency Constructions are derived by element extraction from conjuncts. Thus, giving up the CSC may strengthen the explanatory power of syntactic theory.

Finally, Question D asks how the Minimalist program explains the derivation of Across-the-Board (ATB) constructions, as in (1.8a), which have motivated so-called ATB movement, illustrated in (1.8b) (Ross 1967; Williams 1977).

(1.8) a. Who did Jim like and Jane hate?
      b. Who did Jim like _ and Jane hate _?   (ATB movement)

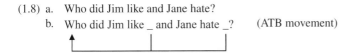

This alleged operation is specific to coordinate constructions. Unlike all other movement chains, the chain of ATB movement is forking, with two tail links. By contrast, I argue that ATB constructions are derived by the extraction of a relational expression from just one conjunct, with a binding dependency between the relational expression and a silent pronominal element in the other conjunct. Both the extraction operation and the pronoun binding dependency are motivated independently of coordinate complexes. Thus this proposed derivation does not require any ad hoc forking chains of movement.

In the course of addressing these four fundamental questions, many other empirical issues are investigated more deeply in this monograph than ever before, including certain conjunct-internal coordinators in Chinese and other languages, coordinators that cannot be used in collective contexts, the syntactic relationship between coordinate constructions and comitative constructions in Chinese, the derivation of the identity relation construction such as *The same man Mary helped and Jane ruined*, as well as the syntactic derivations of the constructions represented by (1.4a), (1.5a), (1.6), and (1.7).

This monograph, however, does not cover all properties of coordination. As noted above, morphological agreement is not discussed in this monograph, and neither are Right Node Raising, reduction forms such as gapping, VP ellipsis, and sluicing, or diachronic aspects of coordination.

The monograph has four main parts, in addition to this introduction and the final concluding chapter. Part I (Chapter 2) deals with question A; Part II (Chapter 3) deals with question B; Part III (Chapters 4, 5, 6, and 7) deals with question C; and Part IV (Chapters 8 and 9) deals with question D.

I No special syntactic configuration

2 The complementation structure of coordinate complexes

2.1 Introduction

A coordinate complex is a syntactic constituent consisting of two or more units (called conjuncts), and its category is identical to that of at least one of the conjuncts.[1] Generally, there is an element (particle, clitic, affix) to link the conjuncts. Such an element is called a coordinator, which can be further classified as a conjunctive (e.g. *and*), disjunctive (e.g. *or*), and adversative coordinator (e.g. *but*). How two (or more) conjuncts and a coordinator are organized in a coordinate complex has been an open question: do they form a flat multiple branching structure or any version of the basic binary-branching structure? The goal of this chapter is to answer this question.

In this chapter, I examine the structure of coordinate complexes that are composed of two conjuncts. This is the basic type of coordinate complex. I will leave my discussion of coordinate complexes that are composed of more conjuncts to Chapter 3. I will also leave discussion of the category of coordinate complexes to that chapter.

The following claims have been seen in the previous literature, but have not been generally accepted. This is why it is still necessary to argue for them in this chapter:

(A) Coordinate complexes have a binary-branching structure, and thus one conjunct is structurally closer to the coordinator than the other conjunct. This constituency is not captured by the traditional flat multiple-branching representations.

(B) The head of the structure is realized by a coordinator, and the conjunct that is structurally closer to the coordinator is the complement of the head, and the other conjunct is Spec of the head.

---

1 De Vries (2006: 239) states that the term *conjunct* is confusing, since it refers to one of the coordinated elements, regardless of whether the coordination is conjunctive, disjunctive, or adversative. However, the term conjunct is conventional in the syntactic literature on coordination.

(C) The semantic relation between conjuncts does not need to be symmetrical, and thus the asymmetrical syntactic relation between conjuncts is compatible with the possibility of an asymmetrical relation in semantics.

(D) Conjuncts, which are non-projecting elements in coordinate complexes, can be of any constituency level (word-fragment, word, phrase), and this freedom in conjuncts does not affect the complementation structure of coordinate complexes.

The above four claims will be made one by one in Sections 2.2 to 2.5. Section 2.6 is a brief summary.

2.2   The binary-branching constituency of coordinate complexes

This section discusses the constituency of coordinate complexes. I will advocate a binary-branching structure for such complexes, making a syntactic distinction between internal and external conjuncts.

The hypothesis that coordinate complexes are binary has been proposed in De Groot (1949: 66, 112–113), Nida (1949: 42 fn. 25), Yngve (1960: 456), Thiersch (1985), Schachter (1985: 46), and Munn (1987). It is in contrast to the assumption that such complexes have a flat structure in which conjuncts are on the same level, while the coordinator holds them together without being more closely connected with any one of them. The two assumptions are represented in (2.1a/a′) and (2.1b), respectively.

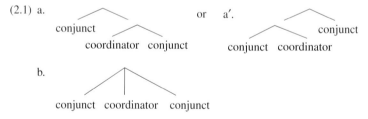

(2.1) a.   or   a′.

    conjunct   conjunct

       coordinator conjunct   conjunct coordinator

   b.

    conjunct coordinator   conjunct

The structure in (2.1b) has been assumed in many works, including Blümel (1914: 193, 205), Bloomfield (1933: 185), Bach (1964: 67–68), Chomsky (1965: 12–13, 196 fn.7), Dik (1968), Dougherty (1969), Gazdar *et al.* (1985: 170), Goodall (1987), and Muadz (1991). It is still quite popular in the current literature of coordination (e.g. Phillips 2003; Takano 2004; Peterson 2004; Wurmbrand 2008; Johnson 2008). However, the cross-linguistic facts to be presented in this section do not support this assumption. Theoretically, the binary structures in (2.1a) and (2.1a′) are also superior to the multiple-branching structure in (2.1b) under economy considerations (Yngve 1960: 453; Collins 1997: 77).

I will first present evidence for the binary-branching structure in 2.2.1 through 2.2.4, and then answer Dik's (1968) challenges against the binary-branching analysis in Section 2.2.5.

Various arguments for the binary-branching structure of coordinate complexes have been seen in the literature. Among them, I choose a representative one, namely the asymmetry between conjuncts in binding, and then add three more myself: the asymmetry between conjuncts in possessee pronominalization, in hosting regular coordinators, and in hosting floating coordinators. These arguments show the structural closeness of the coordinator to one of the two conjuncts, and thus indicate that the coordinator forms a constituent with the conjunct, as in the two structures in (2.1a) and (2.1a′).

2.2.1   The asymmetry between conjuncts in binding

A well-cited argument for the binary-branching constituency of coordinate complexes is Blümel's (1914: 164) observation of a binding asymmetry in coordination. The first conjunct as a whole can be the antecedent of a pronoun in the second conjunct, but the second conjunct as a whole cannot be the antecedent of a pronoun in the first conjunct. Relevant English data appear in Dik (1968: 36, 57) and Moltmann (1992a: 28, 45, 50). For instance, in the coordinate complex *every man and his dog* in (2.2a), the first conjunct *every man* can be the antecedent of the pronoun *his* in the second conjunct. However, in the coordinate complex *his dog and every man* in (2.2b), the second conjunct *every man* cannot be the antecedent of the pronoun *his* in the first conjunct.

(2.2) a. Every man$_i$ and his$_i$ dog left.
      b. *His$_i$ dog and every man$_i$ left.

Likewise, in each of the following examples, the second conjunct contains a pronoun which is co-referential with the first conjunct.

(2.3) a. [That Himmler appointed Heydrich] and [the implications
         thereof] frightened many observers.   (Bayer 1996: 580)
      b. Pat is [a Republican] and [proud of it].   (Sag *et al.* 1985: 117)

In (2.3a), the word *there* is combined with the preposition *of*. In this usage, *there* is co-referential with the first conjunct *that Himmler appointed Heydrich*. In (2.3b) the pronoun *it* pronominalizes the whole first conjunct *a Republican*, which is a predicate nominal here (see Déchaine and Wiltschko 2002: 410 for a discussion of NP pronouns, in addition to the more familiar DP pronouns).

If we reversed the order of the two conjuncts in the above data, the resulting forms would not allow the binding relation. We can see that the two conjuncts are asymmetrical in binding: the first conjunct is structurally higher than the second one, as in the structure in (2.1a). Accordingly, the structure of coordinate complexes cannot be a flat multiple-branching one.[2]

2.2.2   *The asymmetry between conjuncts in possessee pronominalization*

The binary-branching constituency of coordinate complexes is also supported by the asymmetry between conjuncts in possessee pronominalization. A possessee in the first conjunct can take part in pronominalization in the second conjunct, but no possessee in the second conjunct may take part in pronominalization in the first conjunct. In (2.4a), the semantics of the possessee NP *mother* in the first conjunct takes part in the pronominalization of *yours*, which is the second conjunct. However, in (2.4b), the semantics of the possessee NP *mother* in the second conjunct may not take part in the pronominalization of *yours*, which is the first conjunct.

(2.4) a.   Sally's mother and yours have turned vegetarian.
     b.   *Yours and Sally's mother have turned vegetarian.

The contrast indicates that the two conjuncts are asymmetrical. Such an asymmetry is also observed between subjects and objects:

(2.5) a.   Sally's mother praised yours.
     b.   *Yours praised Sally's mother.

Subjects c-command objects. Data like (2.5) lead us to the generalization that no c-commanded element may take part in possessee pronominalization. The NP *mother* is c-commanded by *yours* in (2.5b), but not in (2.5a). If first conjuncts c-command the second conjuncts, the contrast in (2.4) is accounted for by the same generalization.

---

2 Another type of binding asymmetry between two conjuncts can be found between an element in one conjunct and an element in another conjunct, for example the nominal *one bottle of wine* in one conjunct and *it* in the other conjunct in the following data.

(i)   John bought just [one bottle of wine]$_i$ and served it$_i$ with the dessert.
(ii)   *John bought (just) it$_i$ and served [one bottle of wine]$_i$ with the dessert.

For relevant discussions, see Mittwoch (1979), Munn (1993), Collins (1988a; 1988b), Wilder (1994; 1999: Section 4.4 and Section 3.4), Heim and Kratzer (1998: 280–297), Progovac (1998a; 1998b), Camacho (2003: 16).

Note that the possessee nominal that takes part in the pronominalization is not referential. Thus the contrast seems not to be covered by binding Principle C, which considers pronominalization of referential nominals. The above generalization captures both Principle C and the possessee pronominalization.

The asymmetry in possessee pronominalization suggests that the first conjunct is structurally higher than the second one. Accordingly, the structure of coordinate complexes cannot be a flat multiple-branching configuration.

2.2.3 *The asymmetry between conjuncts in hosting coordinators*
Coordinators are not hosted by every conjunct equally. Coordinators can be to the left (prepositive), or right (postpositive) of a conjunct. Even in the same language, one coordinator can be prepositive and another one can be postpositive (Dik 1968: 47; Haspelmath 2004: 6). Ross (1967: 90–91) observes that coordinators like Japanese *-to* or *-si* form a phonological unit with the preceding conjunct whereas a coordinator like English *and* forms a phonological unit with the following conjunct (see also Schachter 1985: 47 and McCawley 1988a: 523). The prepositive position of *and* is shown in (2.6a), and the postpositive position of *-si* is shown in (2.6b).

(2.6) a. The son graduated // and the daughter got married.
      b. musuko-ga sotugyoo sita-si //musume-ga yome-ni itta
           son-NOM graduation did-and daughter-NOM bride-DAT went
           'The son graduated and the daughter got married.'

If the two conjuncts of a coordinate complex were syntactically equal, it would be possible for the coordinator to be merged with either conjunct and thus be grouped with either conjunct phonologically, so long as its position relative to the conjuncts is consistent. We would then predict the following forms to be acceptable:

(2.7) a. *and the son graduated // the daughter got married.
      b. *musuko-ga sotugyoo sita //musume-ga yome-ni itta-si
           son-NOM graduation did daughter-NOM bride-DAT went-and

The fact that such forms are not acceptable indicates that the two conjuncts are not syntactically symmetrical, and only one of them is consistently grouped with the coordinator. The acceptability contrast between (2.6) and (2.7) clearly shows that coordinate complexes have a binary structure and *and*-coordinate complexes are right-branching, whereas *si*-coordinate complexes are left-branching.

One might use a certain iconicity principle to ascribe the unacceptability of (2.7) to the edge positions of the coordinators, assuming coordinators must occur between the linked elements. However, the Latin coordinator *-que* almost always occurs after the first word of a conjunct, and if the conjunct is a single word, *-que* does not occur in the middle of a coordinate complex. Data like (2.8) falsify the alleged iconicity principle.

(2.8)   Marcus Julius-que   [Latin]
         Marcus Julius-and
         'Marcus and Julius'

It is true that in some languages, a coordinator may occur with each conjunct. However, in such cases, the deletable coordinator and the undeletable one are grouped with different conjuncts. If we consider the undeletable one only, we see the same asymmetry of conjuncts in hosting coordinators (see Zoerner 1995: 23 and Zhang 2006: 179). Deletable coordinators have been argued to be focus particles parasitic on the real coordinators (Hendriks 2002; de Vries 2005; Zhang 2008a).

2.2.4   The asymmetry between conjuncts in coordinator floating

In this subsection, I report that in Mandarin Chinese and Hungarian, certain coordinators can occur either between two conjuncts, or inside the second conjunct, but they never occur to the left of or inside the first conjunct. I call such coordinators floating coordinators.

In Chinese, the adversative coordinator *ke(shi)* 'but' and the conjunction *yushi* 'and thus' conjoin clauses. They either precede the second conjunct or immediately follow the subject (or topic) of the second conjunct (Shi 1986; Lü *et al.* 1999). In (2.9), the subject of the second conjunct is *wo* 'I.' In (2.9a), *ke(shi)* precedes the second conjunct, i.e., to the left of *wo*. In (2.9b), it follows *wo*. (2.9c) and (2.9d) show that *ke(shi)* cannot occur in the first conjunct, regardless of its position relative to the subject there.[3]

(2.9) a. Baoyu yao tiaowu, **ke(shi)** wo yao hui-jia.
          Baoyu want dance   but   I   want return-home

      b. Baoyu yao tiaowu, wo **ke(shi)** yao hui-jia.
          Baoyu want dance   I   but   want return-home
          Both a and b: 'Baoyu wants to dance, but I want to go home.'

      c. *Baoyu **ke(shi)**) yao tiaowu, wo yao hui-jia.
           Baoyu but   want dance   I   want return-home

      d. ***Ke(shi)**) Baoyu yao tiaowu, wo yao hui-jia.
           but   Baoyu want dance   I   want return-home

---

3 The word *ke(shi)* is not an adverb. Adverbs may not precede a nominal in Chinese. See Zhang (2006: 183) for more arguments against the adverb analysis of this word.

If the coordinator *ke(shi)* floats in the second conjunct only, we can conclude that the coordinator has a closer relation to the second conjunct than to the first conjunct.

The same restriction on the floating scope is seen in another coordinator *yushi* 'and thus.' This coordinator is used if the eventuality expressed by the second conjunct is a consequence of the eventuality expressed by the first conjunct. It can be regarded as the Chinese counterpart of *and* in (2.10) (or the Malagasy coordinator *dia* 'and then'; see Payne 1985: 24 for similar asymmetrical coordinators in other languages). In (2.10a), for instance, the event denoted by the second conjunct *broke down in tears* is a consequence of the event denoted by the first conjunct *heard the news*.

(2.10) a. The child heard the news and broke down in tears.
      b. John drank the poison and died.

The distributions of *yushi* are similar to that of *keshi*. It either precedes the second conjunct, as in (2.11a) below, or follows the subject of the second conjunct, as in (2.11b). Moreover, no other coordinator may precede the conjunct in which *yushi* occurs. Importantly, *yushi* never precedes any element of the first conjunct, as shown by (2.11c).

(2.11) a. Baoyu yi   guli,   **yushi** Daiyu huifu-le   xinxin.
        Baoyu once encourage and   Daiyu recover-PRF confidence
      b. Baoyu yi   guli,   Daiyu **yushi** huifu-le   xinxin.
        Baoyu once encourage Daiyu and   recover-PRF confidence
        Both a and b: 'Baoyu encouraged her, and thus Daiyu recovered her confidence.'
      c. (***yushi**) Baoyu (***yushi**) yi   guli,   Daiyu huifu-le   xinxin.
         and   Baoyu   and   one encourage Daiyu recover-PRF confidence

My syntactic analysis of the floating of the two coordinators will be presented in Section 2.3.3.

Parallel Hungarian data can be found in Bánréti (1994: 356ff.). In this language, coordinators are divided into three groups, according to their distributions. Coordinators such as *és* 'and' must occur between two conjuncts. Coordinators such as *azonban* 'however,' called right-shifted coordinators, occur either between two clausal conjuncts or within the second clausal conjunct (following the topic or subject of the clause). Finally, coordinators such as *meg* 'and' must occur within the second conjunct, specifically, they must follow the topic or subject of the second conjunct. In (2.12a), the conjunction *meg* follows the subject of the second conjunct, *Péter*. In (2.12b), *meg* precedes the whole conjunct and the sentence is unacceptable (Bánréti 1994: 357).

(2.12) a. János a televiziót nézte, Péter **meg** a rádiót hallgatta.
      John the TV-ACC watched Peter and the radio-ACC listened
      'John watched the TV, and Peter listened to the radio.'
   b. *János a televiziót nézte, **meg** Péter a rádiót hallgatta.

In this language, although coordinators such as *meg* must occur within the second conjunct, no coordinator may occur within the first conjunct. The asymmetry between the two conjuncts is obvious (conjunctions that must follow the topic of the second conjunct are also observed in Nupe; see Kandybowics 2006, Section 2).

The restricted floating scope of the coordinators suggests that in a coordinate complex, the two conjuncts do not have an equidistant relation with the coordinator. One of them is closer to the coordinator and is thus able to interact with it. The scope of the interaction divides a coordinate complex into two parts: (i) the first conjunct; (ii) the combination of the coordinator and the second conjunct. The constituency of a coordinate complex in Mandarin Chinese is thus [[conjunct [& conjunct]].[4]

2.2.5   Conclusion and Dik's challenges

The above four arguments show that coordinate complexes do not have a flat or multiple-branching structure. Instead, they show a binary-branching structure, where the coordinator and one conjunct form a constituent, excluding the other conjunct. I will call a conjunct that forms a constituent with a coordinator an *Internal Conjunct*, and the one that does not an *External Conjunct*. A binary structure can be either right-branching, as in (2.13a) (= (2.1a)), or left-branching, as in (2.13b) (= (2.1a′)). I will concentrate my study to the pattern of (2.13a) only.

(2.13) a.

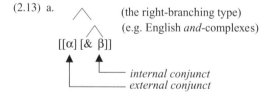

internal conjunct
external conjunct

---

4 Ross (1967) uses the distribution of the German word *aber* 'but' to argue that coordinators must be grouped with the second conjunct in this language. See Zhang (2006: fn 6) for a critical comment on this *aber* argument, although my discussion here and Ross's argument lead to the same conclusion.

b.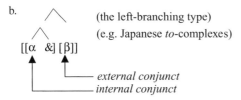

(the left-branching type)

(e.g. Japanese *to*-complexes)

Note that in these structures, what is shown is the constituency of sub-components of a coordinate complex, rather than the surface position of the elements within a constituent. Specifically, I care about which conjunct belongs to the same constituent as the coordinator. Where the coordinator surfaces with respect to this particular conjunct is a separate issue: it can be to the left (prepositive), as seen in (2.6a), or right (postpositive) of the conjunct, as seen in (2.6b), or align with a certain prosodic unit within the conjunct (e.g. Latin -*que*). Even in the same language, one coordinator can be prepositive and another one can be postpositive (Dik 1968: 47; Haspelmath 2004: 6).

Dik (1968: 53–55) argues against the binary-branching structure of coordinate complexes, advocating a flat multiple-branching structure where all conjuncts and coordinators are structurally on the same level.

I address his four challenges as follows.

(a) Assuming that there must be a parallelism between conjuncts, Dik claims that the parallelism "is spoiled" by the binary-branching analysis (p. 53). However, we have seen in the arguments in 2.1 that conjuncts are intrinsically asymmetrical. Therefore, I do not accept Dik's assumption that there must be a syntactic parallelism between conjuncts. In addition to the binding asymmetry presented above, data like (2.14a), which he also cites (p. 28), do not show a categorial parallelism, and data like (2.14b) (Lakoff 1986) do not show any movement chain parallelism.

(2.14) a. John walked slowly and with great care.   (Adv and PP)
       b. What kind of cancer can you eat herbs and not get _?

In general, not all coordinate complexes show syntactic parallelism. Indeed, no binary-branching representation requires conjuncts to be parallel to each other. Rather than "spoiling" anything, binary branching actually captures the facts.

Chapter 7 of this book will show that parallelism is a processing filter on representations of syntactic complexes rather than a constraint on syntactic operations, and thus it has no effect on the structure-building of syntactic complexes. In other words, under certain conditions, parallelism may lead to the rejection of certain representations; however, no structure-building operation needs to follow a parallelism constraint. Data like (2.14) are well-formed exactly because they are derived without the enforcement of parallelism.

(b)   Dik claims that only the flat multiple branching structure is "able to connect the difference between coordination and subordination with different hierarchical descriptions" (p. 54). The difference, in my analysis, is between the complementation structure of coordination and the adjunction structure of subordination. In Section 2.3, I will argue for the Spec-Complement relation between conjuncts and show how conjuncts are syntactically different from adjuncts.

(c)   Some early advocates of the binary-branching approach, such as van der Lubbe (1958: 80), claimed that the closer connection between coordinators and second conjuncts is evident from the following contrast: coordinators may be separated from first conjuncts by other elements, whereas they may not be separated from second conjuncts. Dik presents the data below to show that their claim is wrong:

(2.15) a. John will come today but, as he said to me yesterday, he will not be able to stay for the weekend.
       b. I want you to know that he will come today and also that he will not be able to stay for the weekend.

Dik is right in pointing out that insertion before the second conjunct is possible. However, this only reveals sub-constituency inside the constituent formed by a coordinator and the second conjunct. It does not show that they themselves cannot form a constituent that excludes the first conjunct. The possibility of insertion in examples like (2.15) does not rule out alternatives to his flat structure.

(d)   Dik's strongest argument, in my judgment, is the following (p. 54):

> If it were really true that the coordinator and the following member constitute a unit with greater freedom of combination, we would expect, e.g., that this unit could be shifted to the front of the whole construction, as is indeed possible with subordinating coordinators and certain adverbial modifiers . . . With coordinators, however, this is always excluded; a fact which is at least partly accounted for if the coordinator and the following member are not treated as a single constituent.

Dik's challenge is based on a contrast observed by Sledd (1959: 101) and others. Sledd states that the cluster formed by a subordinator like *when* and a clause may appear either initially or finally, as shown in (2.16), whereas the cluster formed by *and* and a clause does not have this freedom, as shown in (2.17):

(2.16) a. The Yankees and the Indians finished the second game of their double-header, when the rain stopped.
       b. When the rain stopped, the Yankees and the Indians finished the second game of their double-header.

(2.17) a. The rain stopped and they finished the second game.
       b. *And they finished the second game the rain stopped.

Dik uses the constraint that coordinators cannot be moved together with the second conjunct to argue that they do not form a constituent. He concludes that coordinate complexes must have a flat structure, as in (2.1b). Recently, Dik's argumentation and conclusion reappear in Bánréti (2003: Section 1). Unfortunately, advocates of the binary structure of coordinate complexes make no comment on this challenge of Dik. I will answer this challenge in Section 2.3.2. Briefly speaking, the immobility of the constituent comes from its projecting level: it is an intermediate projection. This property itself distinguishes coordinate structure, which I will argue to be a complementation structure, from adjunction structure (cf. (b) above).

I end this section with the following claims. Coordinate complexes have a binary-branching structure. A coordinator forms a constituent with only one of the conjuncts, the internal conjunct. The asymmetry between external and internal conjuncts has an important impact on the computation of coordinate complexes. Thus any multidaughter structure is problematic. Finally, all of Dik's challenges can be refuted.

In this section, I have focused my attention on the constituency issue of coordinate complexes. I leave the issue of configuration to the next section.

2.3   The complementation structure of coordinate complexes

I have not yet discussed the syntactic status of the sister of the external conjunct in (2.13a), [&β]. There are three possibilities. The first two are adjunction structures, as shown in (2.18a) and (2.18b).

(2.18)

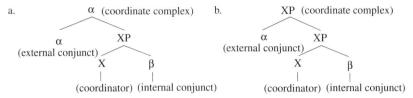

In (2.18a), [&β] is an adjunct to the external conjunct α. This structure is proposed in Munn (1992; 1993) and adopted in Bošković and Franks (2000) and Hartmann (2000). Munn's (1992; 1993) structure for (2.19a) is shown in (2.19b). In this structure, the projection headed by a coordinator is a right-adjunct to the external conjunct. Consequently, it is the external conjunct that is c-selected by the sister of the coordinate complex.

(2.19) a. Hobbs and Rhodes

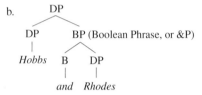

In (2.18b), the external conjunct is an adjunct to the constituent formed by the coordinator and the internal conjunct.

Both (2.18a)/(2.19b) and (2.18b) can be rejected if there is evidence to show that the external conjunct and the internal conjunct are in a Spec-Complement relationship. This is the third possibility. In this section, I advocate this possibility. The complementation structure is shown in (2.20):

(2.20)

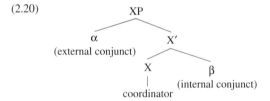

This structure has been previously proposed by Munn (1987), Larson (1990), Johannessen (1998), and Zoerner (1995). One of Zoerner's arguments will be introduced below in Section 2.3.3A. My arguments for (2.20) are the following:

> No stranding of external conjuncts (Section 2.3.2);
> The existence of interactions between coordinators and internal conjuncts (Section 2.3.3);

The possibility of extraction from either internal or external conjuncts (Section 2.3.4).

Unlike the works cited above, I do not consider agreement in my analysis. I justify the exclusion of agreement in Section 2.3.1 (for critical comments on other unreliable arguments for the structure in (2.20), see Chaves 2007: 23).

2.3.1   *The dubious status of agreement in the syntax of coordination*

Although conjuncts can be asymmetric in their nominal and verbal inflections (e.g. agreement, case, and finiteness morphology; see Payne 1985: 27), inflection patterns are not directly related to the complementation structure. Since Koutsoudas (1968), it has been noted that verbs may agree with the closest conjunct of a coordinate nominal, regardless of whether they precede or follow the nominal (also see Sadler 1999; 2003; Marušic *et al.* 2006). This adjacency effect has been accounted for from a processing perspective (Lorimor 2007; Steiner 2008). Moreover, it has long been observed that the denotation of coordination also plays a role in agreement (e.g. McNally 1993: 363; Huddleston and Pullum 2002: 1283; see also Section 5.2.3B of this book). Since in many cases the contrast between singular and plural agreement is a semantic issue in English (Humphreys and Bock 2005), using singular conjunct agreement to argue for any special structure of coordinate complexes is misleading. Even simplex plurals can trigger singular agreement, as seen in (2.21b) (Sag *et al.* 1985: 154) and (2.21c) (Bernard Comrie p.c. to Miao-Ling Hsieh):

(2.21) a. Ham and eggs is my favorite breakfast.
　　　　b. Flapjacks is my favorite breakfast.
　　　　c. Two bottles of wine {were/was} thrown into the soup.

Sag *et al.* (1985: 154 fn. 23) correctly point out that coordination is not relevant to the verbal inflection in examples like (2.21a). Sobin (2004: 507) also finds it problematic to use inflection as a diagnostic of the syntactic structure of coordinate complexes. Inconsistency in the manifestations of inflection has even led Peterson (2004: 650f.) to argue that coordinate complexes have a headless structure. This conclusion seems unwarranted given that Lorimor's (2007) experimental study concludes that "notional information, lexical plurality, adjacency, and linear (surface) word order play significant roles in the computation and production of agreement" (cf. Cowart & McDaniel 2008).

2.3.2   *The impossibility for external conjuncts to be stranded*

My first argument for the complementation structure of coordinate complexes is the immobility of the combination of a coordinator and the internal conjunct.

A coordinate complex can move as a whole, as seen in (2.22a), whereas the constituents that are composed of a coordinator and an internal conjunct cannot, as seen in (2.22b).

(2.22) a. [Tall and slim]$_i$ though Helen is $_{-i}$, . . .
     b. *[And slim]$_i$ though Helen is [tall $_{-i}$], . . .   (Postal 1998: 191)

The following data from McCawley (1988a: 267) show that clefting is possible for adverbials but not for the combination of the coordinator and the internal conjunct. If clefting involves movement, the contrast in (2.23) is parallel to the contrast presented above.

(2.23) a. It was before Jane arrived that Tom left.   (McCawley 1988a: 267)
     b. *It was and Jane arrived that Tom left.

Recall that Dik (1968: 54) uses the immobility of the combination of the coordinator and the internal conjunct to challenge the binary-branching analysis of coordinate complexes (Section 2.2.5). Dik's challenge has not been answered in the literature. McCawley (1988a: 267) states that "*and S* is not a constituent of a type that allows the mobility that time adverbs such as *before S* have," but he does not give any explanation. Kehler (2002: 61) also uses this constraint to distinguish coordination constructions from adjunction (or "subordination") constructions.

The constraint is explained when one realizes that the combination of a coordinator and its internal conjunct is an intermediate projection, which is the sister of a Spec element, as seen in the structure in (2.20). As generally recognized in generative syntax (Chomsky 1994; 1995: 253), no intermediate projection may move. The illegal movement of an intermediate projection can be illustrated by the following examples. In (2.24a), there is an I′ topicalization, stranding the subject, which is at Spec of IP. In (2.24b), similarly, there is a P′ wh-movement, assuming *directly* is in Spec of PP. In (2.24c), there is a P′ wh-movement, adopting the general assumption that *right* is at a Spec position if it precedes a spatial or temporal PP (see Emonds 1972; among others) (I thank Chris Wilder for providing examples (2.24a) and (2.24b)).

(2.24) a. *[Will see John]$_i$, (she thinks that) [Peter $_{-i}$].
     b. *[Under which book]$_i$ was it [directly $_{-i}$]?
     c. *[To which town]$_i$ did you take the car [right $_{-i}$]?

If an intermediate projection is not able to move, the constituent composed of a coordinator and an internal conjunct can never move together, stranding the external conjunct. The immobility of such constituents makes the structure of coordinate complexes significantly different from that of adjunction constructions. As is well known, adjuncts introduced by words like *after, before, since*, etc. enjoy the freedom of A-bar movement. We have seen such examples in (2.23a). The mobility of the adjuncts indicates that they are not intermediate projections.

The above analysis might be challenged by the hypothesis that (2.25a) is derived from (2.25b) by the raising of [*and he is an expert*]:

(2.25) a. The professor [and he's an expert], thinks the recession will continue.
       b. The professor thinks the recession will continue [and he's an expert].

We have, however, two doubts about this derivation relation between (2.25a) and (2.25b). First, it seems that no phrasal movement in English lands to the right of a subject. The syntactic status of this landing site in the language is not clear. Second, the alleged movement cannot land to the left-peripheral position, the default landing site for A-bar movement in English:

(2.26)   *[And {he/the professor} is an expert], {he/the professor} thinks the recession will continue.

I thus do not adopt this movement approach to data like (2.25a). Borsley (1994: 240) states that [*and he is an expert*] in (2.25a) is a parenthetical expression. I further assume that this parenthesis contains an implicit external conjunct. Parentheses could be analyzed as adverbials, in the spirit of Potts (2002). Importantly here, the complex does not undergo any movement. In contrast, in (2.25b), the external conjunct is the clause *The professor thinks the recession will continue*, and the internal one is [*he is an expert*].

I argue not only against any leftward movement of the sister of the external conjunct, but also against any rightward movement of such a constituent. Data like the following (2.27) have been cited to show that constituents that are composed of a coordinator and a conjunct can be extraposed in English, stranding the other conjunct (Collins 1988a; 1988b; Munn 1992: 19; 1993: 15; Zoerner 1995: 10, 85; Progovac 1998a; 1998b; Cowper and Hall 2000: 33; see also Huddleston and Pullum 2002: 1277; Fromkin *et al.* 2007: 149):

(2.27) a. John bought a book yesterday, and a newspaper.
       b. Tomorrow he will come, I think, or the day after.

Such data are called Split Coordination in Höhle (1990: 141 fn.). Similar examples can be found in German, as in (2.28), and in many other languages (see Johannessen 1998: Section 6.2.1).

(2.28)   Hans hat gestern   ein Buch gekauft, und eine Zeitung.
          Hans has yesterday a   book bought   and a   newspaper
          'Hans bought a book yesterday, and a newspaper.'

The extraposition analysis is not conclusive. Cross-linguistically, we have not seen any similar constructions in languages that unambiguously allow extraposition. For instance, Amele, a Papuan language from New Guinea, allows extraposition of adverbial clauses, but not of constituents that are composed of a coordinator and a conjunct. This is shown in (2.29) and (2.30) (Roberts 1988: 55). (TOD.P = today's past tense)

(2.29) a. [Ija ja hud-ig-en   fi] uqa sab man-igi-an.
          1s fire open-1s-FUT if 3s   food roast-3s-FUT
          'If I light the fire she will cook the food.'

       b. Uqa sab man-igi-an [ija ja hud-ig-en   fi].
          3s   food roast-3s-FUT 1s fire open-1s-FUT if
          'She will cook the food if I light the fire.'

(2.30) a. [Ija ja hud-ig-a   qa] uqa sab man-i-a.
          1s fire open-1s-TOD.P but 3s   food roast-3s-TOD.P
          'I lit the fire but she cooked the food.'

       b. *Uqa sab man-i-a   [ija ja hud-ig-a   qa].
          3s   food roast-3s-TOD.P 1s fire open-1s-TOD.P but

In this language, the coordinator *qa* is attached to the end of the left-conjunct, which should be the internal conjunct, and thus the internal structure of the complex is left-branching. Roberts uses (2.29b) to show that the combination of the *fi* 'if' and its complement can be extraposed, and uses (2.30b) to show that the constituent formed by the coordinator *qa* 'but' and the first conjunct cannot.

An alternative analysis of data like (2.27) is available. This is the Bare Argument Ellipsis analysis (Hudson 1976; Neijt 1979; Moltmann 1992a: 22, 48, 228; Johnson 1996; Schwarz 1999: 354–355). Bare Argument Ellipsis leaves only one non-verbal element in the elided sentence. In this analysis, the second conjunct is regarded as a reduced sentence fragment (see Lang 1984: 21 for a review of early studies following this approach). (2.27a) thus can be analyzed as follows:

(2.31)   John bought a book yesterday, and ~~he also bought~~ a newspaper ~~yesterday~~.

In Heim and Kratzer (1998: 249), it is assumed that in Bare Argument Ellipsis, "the 'remnant' argument always has been topicalized (adjoined to

S) before the deletion." The above sentence, for instance, should have the following representation:

(2.32)   John bought a book yesterday, and [[a newspaper]$_i$ ~~he also bought t$_i$ yesterday~~].

Johnson (1996) argues against the extraposition analysis based on the semantic type of the predicate involved. He observes that the analysis fails to predict the pattern of grammaticality illustrated in (2.33) below (Johnson 1996: 69; see Neijt 1979 for arguments against the extraposition analysis from an agreement perspective):

(2.33) a. I introduced Carrie and Will to each other.
          b. *I introduced Carrie to each other and Will.
          c. *I introduced Carrie to each other and I introduced Will to each other.

In the extraposition analysis, the ungrammaticality of (2.33b) requires the ad hoc restriction that a DP coordinate complex with a group interpretation may not be discontinuous at S-structure. Later in Chapter 4, we will see that the situation is just the opposite: a group interpretation allows conjuncts to be separated, whereas a distributive one does not. On the other hand, if (2.33b) is derived from the illegal (2.33c) through gapping, the ungrammaticality of (2.33b) follows automatically. It is indeed the case that neither gapping nor Bare Argument Ellipsis may have a collective predicate, as pointed out by Moltmann (1992a: 49) (see also Section 5.2.3D of this book):

(2.34) a. *John shared the coffee and Bill the cake.
          b. *John met and Bill (too).

Another restriction shared by Bare Argument Ellipsis and gapping is that they cannot occur in embedded clauses (Carlson 2002: 11):

(2.35) a. Bill ordered beans and Sam rice.   (Gapping)
          b. *Bill ordered beans and I think Sam rice.   (Gapping)

(2.36) a. Bill ordered beans for supper and Sam too.   (Bare Argument Ellipsis)
          b. *Bill ordered beans for supper and I think Sam too.   (Bare Argument Ellipsis)

The word *too* in data like (2.36a) has also been analyzed as an anaphoric element, referring back to the VP in the first conjunct. If so, there is no ellipsis (Goodall 1987: 28). However, as stated in Heim and Kratzer (1998: 259), not all examples of ellipsis include such a particle. In the cases where no *too* occurs, ellipsis is still possible.

I conclude that the plausibility of the deletion analysis casts doubt on the extraposition analysis. In the deletion analysis, the constituent that is composed of the coordinator and the internal conjunct is built independently of the preceding clause, and therefore it is not moved from the preceding clause.

It needs to be mentioned that Reinhart and Rooth (1991) propose an LF right-adjunction approach to Bare Argument Ellipsis. Exactly the same arguments are used in Cowper and Hall (2000) for an overt rightward movement of the *and*-DP cluster. The approach is convincingly argued against by Moltmann (1992a: 229).

I conclude that the immobility of the combination of a coordinator and an internal conjunct suggests that the combination is an intermediate projection. If so, the relation between an external conjunct and internal conjunct is a Spec-Complement relation.

2.3.3   *The possible interactions between coordinators and internal conjuncts*

The proposed complementation relation is also supported by the interactions between coordinators and internal conjuncts. Such interactions are impossible if one is an adjunct of the other as Moltmann (1992a) has claimed. I present two types of syntactic interactions between coordinators and internal conjuncts, one involving the launching site of head raising from internal conjuncts (used by Zoerner 1995: 41 to argue, as I do, that coordinators and second conjuncts have a head-complement relation), and the other involving the syntactic positions of floating coordinators in languages such as Chinese.

Head raising from internal conjuncts to the positions of coordinators

One case showing an interaction between coordinators and internal conjuncts is found in the Uto-Aztecan language Papago (O'odham). In this language, we see an instance of head raising from Infl of the internal conjunct to the position of coordinators. The canonical word order of the language is S-Aux-V, as seen in (2.37a) and (2.37b). However, when two clauses conjoin, the Aux of the second conjunct precedes the subject of the second conjunct, as seen in (2.37c) (Zepeda 1983: 25–27) (the second auxiliary verb in (2.37c) has lost its initial vowel through an independent phonological operation):

(2.37) a. 'Uwi   'o cipkan   (Papago)
        woman is working
        'The woman is working.'

b. 'A:ñi 'añ ko:s
   I   am sleeping
   'I am sleeping.'

c. 'Uwi   'o cipkan   ñ   'a:ni ko:s
   woman is working am I   sleeping
   'The woman is working and I am sleeping.'

Zoerner (1995: 41) analyzes this phenomenon as head raising from Infl of the second conjunct to the position of the coordinator. If this head raising analysis is right, the second conjunct must be the complement of the coordinator (contra Moltmann 1992a; Chaves 2007), since head movement may neither launch from nor land in an adjunct.

The syntactic positions of floating coordinators

Another case showing an interaction between coordinators and internal conjuncts is found in Mandarin Chinese.

Earlier I presented the fact that the coordinators *ke(shi)* 'but' and *yushi* 'and thus' can either immediately precede internal conjuncts or immediately follow the subjects (or topics) of internal conjuncts (Section 2.2.4). One pair of relevant data is repeated here:

(2.38) a. Baoyu yao   tiaowu, **ke(shi)** wo yao   hui-jia.
          Baoyu want dance   but   I   want return-home

       b. Baoyu yao   tiaowu, wo **ke(shi)** yao   hui-jia.
          Baoyu want dance   I   but   want return-home
          Both: 'Baoyu wants to dance, but I want to go home.'

The floating coordinators have two possible positions with respect to internal conjuncts. The availability of the two positions for the coordinators indicates that the coordinators and internal conjuncts interact. I have already showed that a coordinator and the internal conjunct are merged as sisters (Section 2.2). We also know that if there are interactions between sisters, they are in a head-complement relation. Accordingly, internal conjuncts must be the complement of the coordinators. If internal conjuncts were adjuncts, the dependency relation between the two positions would be impossible. The floating phenomenon thus supports the complementation configuration proposed in (2.20).

One property of floating coordinators is that they may not follow any non-topic element. Adverbs, which are not able to function as topics, cannot precede any coordinator. In (2.39), for instance, the manner adverbial *buxiaoxin* 'carelessly' is not a topic and it cannot precede *keshi*.

(2.39) a. Ta jijimangmang de qie cai,   <u>keshi</u> buxiaoxin qie-po-le   shouzhi.
        he hurriedly   DE cut vegetable but   carelessly cut-broken-PRF finger
        'He cut the vegetable hurriedly, but he cut his finger carelessly.'

   b. *Ta jijimangmang de qie cai, buxiaoxin <u>keshi</u> qie-po-le shouzhi.

In order to capture this property, I assume that floating coordinators have an unvalued [topic] feature, which can be valued by a topic of the internal conjunct (the topic in (2.39) is null). The valuation can be accomplished by either of two ways, namely by the Agree relation between the coordinator and the topic of the internal conjunct, as in (2.38a), or by the movement of the topic to a Spec position, as in (2.38b) (this point will be elaborated below).

Another property of floating coordinators is that when one follows the topic of the internal conjunct, the external conjunct is a background topic, whereas the topic of the internal conjunct is a contrastive topic. In (2.38b), for instance, the first conjunct *Baoyu yao tiaowu* 'Baoyu wants to dance' is a background topic, and *wo* 'I' is a contrastive topic.

Multiple topics, like multiple fronted wh-elements in certain Slavic languages, and multiple verbs in serial verb constructions, can be represented by tucking-in structures, based on the Minimal Link and Local Move conditions (see Collins 2002b: 10 for an implementation of Richards 1997). Accordingly, I propose the following derivation for the multiple topic constructions. If two CPs are coordinated, the head of the whole coordinate complex is also C (further discussion of the categorial issue is given in Chapter 3). When the coordinator *ke(shi)* or *yushi* is the realization of this C, the base-position of the whole internal conjunct is the complement of this C, as shown in (2.40a). In contrast to this, I claim, when the coordinator follows the topic of the internal conjunct, the topic has tucked in to an inner Spec position, as shown in (2.40b).

(2.40)

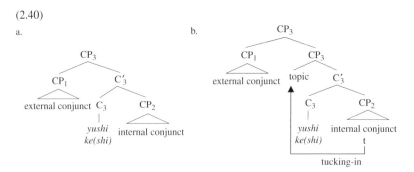

Note that in multiple-fronted wh-constructions and serial verb constructions, all of the relevant elements move, whereas in (2.40b), the outer Spec element is base-generated there. This difference does not affect the tucking-in analysis, however. This is because the Local Move condition forces the mover to land in the inner Spec position if the outer Spec is realized by an element of the same type, regardless of whether the latter element is base-generated there or not.

Topic movement across a C-element is also seen in clausal subordination in Chinese, where complementizers such as *yaoshi/ruguo* 'if,' *yinwei* 'because,' *suiran/suishuo* 'although,' *jiran* 'since' can also follow the subject/topic of the selected clause (Shi 1986: Section 3.7; McCawley 1988b: 181; Tsao 1996: 174; Zhou 2002: Chapter 5). In the following data, the two sentences are near synonymous.⁵

(2.41) a. <u>Ruguo</u> qingkuang shushi, najiu jianjue   geiyi   zhicai.
   if   case   true   then resolutely enforce punishment
   'If the case is true, then (we) must enforce punishment resolutely.'

   b. Qingkuang <u>ruguo</u> shushi, najiu jianjue geiyi zhicai.

The topics to the left of the complementizers are background topics rather than contrastive topics. Presumably, such complementizers also have an unvalued topic feature, to be valued by a topic of the selected clause.

As in the coordinate complex (2.39a), adverbs, which cannot be topics, cannot precede a complementizer. In (2.42), for instance, the adverb *jingchang* 'often' cannot precede *ruguo* 'if.'

(2.42) a. <u>Ruguo</u> jingchang xiayu, najiu bu yao   jiaoshui le.
   if   often   rain   then not should water   PRT
   'If it rains often, do not water (the plants) any more.'

   b. *Jingchang <u>ruguo</u> xiayu, najiu bu yao jiao shui le.

We can see that the behavior of coordinators patterns with that of typical complementizers. This fact shows that coordinators are head elements. I have assumed that the observed floating phenomenon is an indication of topic movement. Since syntactic movement starts from complement rather than adjunct, the floating phenomenon suggests that internal conjuncts are complements rather than adjuncts.

---

5 In classical Chinese, the conjunction *er* could also occur between the subject/topic and the predicate of the second conjunct of a coordinate complex. In Classical Latin poems and prose, subordinators such as *cum* 'when' can also be "shifted" inside the relevant subordinate clause; this inversion has been called topicalization (see Huttar 2004). In Nupe, conditional *gá* 'if' also follows the subject of the conditional clause, and like Hungarian *meg*, the conjunction *ma* and *ci* must follow the topic of the second conjunct (Kandybowics 2005: Section 2.2).

In 2.2.4 I introduced the Hungarian fact that *meg* 'and' must follow the topic of the second conjunct. If we extend the above analysis to the Hungarian coordinate complexes headed by *meg*, we can claim that the topic movement launching from the second conjunct to the left of *meg* is obligatory, assuming that there are certain edge features involved (see Chomsky 2007; 2008).

2.3.4   Extraction from both internal and external conjuncts

The fact that phrasal extraction is possible from both internal and external conjuncts distinguishes coordination from any adjunction structure.

This possibility is not expected given the Coordinate Structure Constraint (CSC, Ross 1967: 89), which states: "In a coordination structure, no conjunct may be moved, nor may any element contained in a conjunct be moved out of that conjunct." Since Grosu (1973), the CSC has been split into two parts. The first part is that no conjunct may be moved, and the second part is that no element may be extracted from conjuncts. Following Grosu (1973), I call the first part of the CSC the Conjunct Constraint (CC), and the second part the Element Constraint (EC). The CC and EC are illustrated in (2.43a) and (2.43b), respectively.

(2.43) a. *Which boy did John kiss [_ and which girl]?   (CC violation)
       b. *What kind of herbs did you [[eat _] and [drink beer]]?   (EC violation)

Unlike the CC, the status of the EC is controversial. Grosu (1973), Goldsmith (1985), and Lakoff (1986) present quite a lot of English data to show that the EC can be violated. Postal (1998), however, claims that none of Lakoff's data can challenge the CSC, since some of the data do not have typical coordination readings, or they are constrained in various ways. One weakness of this argument is highlighted by the relation between the CC and the EC. Both parts of the CSC have been supposed to apply only to coordinate constructions. Therefore, if Lakoff's data cannot be regarded as coordination data, they should not be subject to the other part of the CSC either. Yet as correctly pointed out by Postal, "The Conjunct Constraint is almost never questioned; nothing in Lakoff 1986 is intended to challenge it" (p. 83). Postal then shows how exactly the same data used by Lakoff to challenge the EC must obey the CC. If Lakoff's data strictly obey the CC, and if non-conjuncts are not constrained by either the CC or the EC, the conclusion must be that his data are indeed coordination data, and therefore the EC can indeed be violated in certain cases. I therefore accept Grosu (1973), Goldsmith (1985), and Lakoff's (1986) conclusion that the EC can be violated (see also Levine 2001: 161; Kehler 2002).

In (2.44), extraction from either conjunct is possible (Lakoff 1986):

(2.44) a. What kind of cancer can you eat herbs and not get _?
       b. What kind of herbs can you eat _ and not get cancer?

The data in (2.44) represent so-called Asymmetrical Coordination (AC; Ross 1967; Schmerling 1975; Lakoff 1986; Levin and Prince 1986).[6] The violation of the EC is also found in other languages (see Chapter 5). Summing up, there are good reasons to believe that the EC can be violated.

The extractability of conjunct-internal elements shows that AC does not have an adjunction structure. As presented in Culicover and Jackendoff (1997: 209), extraction from AC conjuncts is possible, whereas it is impossible from adjunct subordinate clauses, which are islands. This contrast supports the structure in (2.20), where neither conjunct is in an adjunct position. They cannot be hosted in an adjunct, either, suggesting that neither (2.18a) nor (2.18b) is likely.

In my proposal, external conjuncts are Spec elements. The fact that elements can be extracted from external conjuncts might cast doubt on this proposal, given the observations that subjects are Spec elements and that no element can be extracted from subjects (the Condition on Extraction Domains, or CED; Huang 1982). However, Takahashi (1994), Stepanov (2001), and Sabel (2002) have argued that elements can be extracted from subjects when the subjects remain *in situ*. In other words, the CED is effective only when subjects have been raised. Returning to coordination, then, note that in all of the data above, conjuncts are not in a derived position. Accordingly, extraction of elements out of external conjuncts is as legal as extraction of elements out of *in situ* subjects.

The fact that elements may be extracted from conjuncts does not mean that such an extraction is always possible. I will account for observed EC-like effects, as seen in (2.43b), in Chapter 7. Nevertheless, the fact that extraction is possible at all argues against an adjunction analysis of coordination.

2.3.5   *The syntactic relation between conjuncts: conclusions*
I have presented the following three arguments to show that external and internal conjuncts are in a Spec–Complement relation, and coordinators are realizations of the head of the projection, namely the immobility of the constituent composed of a coordinator and internal conjunct (Section 2.3.2), the existence of

---

6 Note that the term asymmetrical coordination is used here in a semantic sense. Such coordination is also called "fake coordination" (e.g. Szabolcsi and den Dikken 1999). Syntactically speaking, all conjuncts are syntactically asymmetrical (see Section 2.2).

interactions between coordinators and internal conjuncts (Section 2.3.3), and the possibility of extraction from either conjunct (Section 2.3.4).

My conclusion rules out both the structure in (2.45a) (= (2.18b)), where the external conjunct is an adjunct, and Munn's (1992; 1993) structure in (2.45b) ($\approx$ (2.18a), (2.19b)), where the sister of the external conjunct is an adjunct.[7]

(2.45) a.

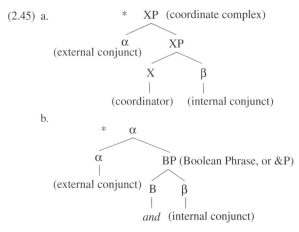

My conclusion does not support Moltmann's (1992a: 52) claim that "coordinators are formal adjuncts of (at least) one of the conjuncts." This claim fails to capture the interactions between coordinators and internal conjuncts (Section 2.3.3). The interactions instead show a complementation relation between coordinators and internal conjuncts.

Furthermore, in both Moltmann's (1992a, especially p. 54 (87b)) and Munn's approaches, the constituents that are composed of coordinators and internal conjuncts are regarded as maximal projections. The immobility of the constituents (Section 2.3.2) cannot be accounted for by these approaches.[8]

I conclude that the relationship between external and internal conjuncts is a Spec–Comp relationship, and that coordinators are the heads that integrate them. Thus neither conjuncts nor coordinators are adjuncts. The Spec–Comp relation is fundamentally different from an adjunction relation. In Chomsky's (2000) terminology, the former is built via Set-Merge, while the latter is built via Pair-Merge.

---

7 Cowart and McDaniel's (2008) experimental study also argues against an adjunction approach to coordination in English.

8 Kandybowics (2005) claims that clausal coordination has an adjunction structure. See Zhang (2006: 208) for critical comments on his arguments.

The complementation structure of coordinate complexes follows general phrase structure. The structure is built by the regular operation Merge (also Remerge; see Chapter 6). No special operation such as coordinate-α (Johannessen 1998) or union of phrase markers (Goodall 1987: 36) is called for, nor is any special mode of merger needed, such as the multiple-dimensional phrase marker structure proposed in Muadz (1991), Moltmann (1992a), and de Vries (2005). The syntax of coordination as second-order syntax (Lang's 1984 term) uses no new tools that are not found in first-order syntax, in integrating the sub-components of coordinate complexes.

One important implication of this conclusion is that coordination is not an independent syntactic relation. Very often, coordination is contrasted with subordination (e.g. Dik 1968: 63; Huddleston and Pullum 2002: 1275). If the definition of subordination is an adjunction relation, it is true that coordination is not subordination. Instead, it is a complementation relation (see Section 2.2.5 for our comment on challenge (b) of Dik (1968)), which is not exclusive to coordination. If, however, the definition of subordination is the relation between a projecting element and a non-projecting element, then adjuncts, complements, and specifiers are all subordinate to their sisters. I have argued that the two conjuncts are in Spec-Complement relation, so both conjuncts are subordinate to the conjunction. In this sense, the asserted contrast between subordination and coordination disappears. Again, the Spec-Complement relation is not exclusive to coordination. Furthermore, as I will show in the next section, conjuncts are not always semantically distinct from modifiers. In short, contrasting coordination to other syntactic relations is confusing because it implies that it has a special structural status when it actually does not.

2.4 The possible modifier function of conjuncts

I have argued against the adjunct status of conjuncts syntactically. Though my focus in this book is not on semantics, in this section I briefly state my understanding of the semantic relation between adjuncts and conjuncts.

Consider first asymmetrical coordination, discussed in Section 2.3.4. In (2.46a) below, the second conjunct expresses a purpose, like a purpose adverbial, and in (2.46b), the first conjunct expresses a "despite" meaning, again like an adverbial (for more data like these in both English and other languages, see Goldsmith 1985; Lakoff 1986; Kehler 2002; Blakemore and Carston 2005; Amfo 2007):

(2.46) a. The screw which$_i$ I've got to [try] and [find $_i$] holds the frammis to the
myolator.   (Ross 1967)
  b. What kind of music can you listen to $_-$ and still get your work done?

It has been claimed in the literature that the apparent coordinators here are
not real, since *and* in (2.46a) can be replaced with the word *to* and *and* in
(2.46b) can be replaced with the adverb *yet* (Schachter 1977: 100; Zoerner
1995: 80; Postal 1998). However, this replacement approach is ad hoc. No
syntactic principle can tell us why the *and* in (2.46a) cannot be replaced by
yet and why the *and* in (2.46b) cannot be replaced by *to*. I have argued in
Section 2.3.4 that data like (2.46) are true coordination data. The "illogical"
relationship between modifiers and conjuncts is seen not only in asymmetrical
coordination constructions, but also in data like the following.[9]

(2.47) a. I need something like a book.   (Lang 1984: 25)
  b. I need a book or something.

(2.48) a. Tom left before Jane arrived.   (McCawley 1988a: 262)
  b. Tom left and then Jane arrived.

(2.49) a. Harry called up Bill, though he didn't want to.   (Bever *et al.* 1989: 335)
  b. Though Harry called up Bill, he didn't want to.
  c. Harry called up Bill, but he didn't want to.

In (2.47), the two examples are synonymous. In (2.47a), *like a book* is
syntactically a modifier of *something*, whereas in (2.47b), *something* and *a
book* are two conjuncts. The two examples in (2.48) are also synonymous,
although (2.48b) is a coordinate construction, whereas (2.48a) is not. In (2.49),
either of the two non-coordinate constructions in (2.49a) and (2.49b) can be
expressed by the coordinate construction in (2.49c) (also see Haspelmath 2007:
(74)).

Moreover, a wh-argument and a wh-adverb may also be remerged with a
coordinator to form a coordinate complex, as seen in data like (2.50) (see
Zhang 2007b for a syntactic analysis of such constructions):

(2.50)   What and when does John (normally) eat?

---

9 It has also been claimed in the literature that aspectual *come/go* constructions such as (ia) are
derived from coordinate constructions such as (ib) below. However, Shopen (1971) argues against
this derivation relation (see Jaeggli and Hyams 1993: 319).

(i) a.   They go visit the dentist every year.
    b.   They go and visit the dentist every year.

In all of these cases, the semantic differences between conjuncts and adverbials are blurred. The fact that conjuncts can semantically serve as modifiers suggests that there is no sharp semantic contrast between conjuncts on the one hand, and certain adverbials and attributives on the other. We thus should not expect any construction-specific semantics to correlate with any (assumed) construction-specific syntactic configuration in our analysis of coordination complexes. This has been correctly pointed out by Dik (1968: 2):

> There is no guarantee that there is a one-to-one relation between linguistic structures on the one hand, and logical or psychological organization on the other: items which are logically or psychologically "coordinated" may be linguistically expressed in subordinative constructions, and vice versa. Consequently, the explanation of the linguistic facts in terms of logical or psychological phenomena almost automatically leads to a division of linguistically similar items and to a grouping together of linguistically diverse ones, on the basis of extra-linguistic considerations.

Ideas similar to Dik's can be found in Levine (2001: 160), Carston (2002, Chapter 3) and Amfo (2007: 682), among other places. I likewise conclude that although conjuncts are syntactically different from adjuncts, they may function semantically like adjuncts (modifiers). Note that this conclusion is in contrast to Munn's (1993: 63) claim that conjuncts are syntactically adjuncts but are semantically different from adjuncts.[10]

2.5 The issue of so-called bar-level sharing

Borsley (1994: 233) claims that there are two types of sharing between conjuncts and their hosting complexes: "a coordinate structure must not only share categorial features with its conjuncts but must also share their bar-level." I will leave the issue of categorial sharing to Chapter 3. In this section, I address the issue of so-called bar-level sharing.

The issue of constituent-level in coordinate complexes might seem to be purely theoretical, but it does have empirical significance.

Pesetsky (1982: 440) states that conjuncts have the same bar-level as their mother: "the constituent formed by the coordination of occurrences of X^n, where n is some number of bars, is itself X^n." Since the mother and daughters

---

10 Not only the meaning of a conjunct can be encoded by an adjunct, the meaning of a predicate can also be expressed by an adjunct:

(i) a.　　Oddly, Bill eats grass.
　　b.　　It is odd that Bill eats grass.

share the same bar-level in his analysis, the aunt of a conjunct (i.e. the sister of the coordinate complex) should count as a sister of the conjunct for all grammatical purposes. I illustrate this hypothesis in (2.51).

(2.51)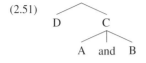

The aunt-as-sister theory:

Since daughter A and mother C have the same bar-level, and since C and D are sisters, the aunt–niece relation between D and A counts as a sister relation.

Although Pesetsky claims that "nothing important seems to follow from this stipulation" (p. 440), some other authors do think the bar-level of conjuncts is an important issue, and the claims made about this issue have been linked to the analyses of the configuration of coordinate complexes.

A generally adopted assumption is that only phrases may appear as specifiers and complements (e.g. Stowell 1981; Chomsky 1994). In a coordinate complex, if the coordinator is the head, conjuncts must, accordingly, be phrasal, if they are specifiers and complements. This is clearly seen in Kayne (1994). Borsley (1994) argues that since conjuncts do not need to be phrasal, the hypothesis that coordinate complexes have a complementation configuration is not convincing. In this section I address Borsley's challenge by considering word and word-part conjuncts, which are smaller than phrases. I will show that the non-projecting elements, specifically, specifiers or complements, do not in fact need to be phrases. Once this theoretical issue is clarified, then, Borsley's challenge to the complementation hypothesis is diffused.

Let us first review Kayne's (1994) hypothesis that conjuncts must be phrases. Kayne (1994) claims that apparent word-level coordination involves con-joined phrases to which a deletion process has applied (see also Wilder 1997: 63). Consider, however, examples like the following, which have been noted since Abbott (1976), and are also discussed in Jackendoff (1977: 192). The readings of the a-sentences are in contrast to those of the corresponding b-sentences.

(2.52) a. Hobbs whistled and hummed a total of 16 tunes.
     b. Hobbs whistled a total of 16 tunes and hummed a total of 16 tunes.

(2.53) a. Hobbs whistled and hummed the same tune.
     b. Hobbs whistled the same tune and hummed the same tune.

(2.54) a. Hobbs criticized and insulted many people.
     b. Hobbs criticized many people and insulted many people.

In (2.52a), for instance, there are 16 tunes involved, whereas in (2.52b), there are 32 tunes involved. Obviously it is impossible for (2.52a) to be derived from

(2.52b) by deletion, since deletion must obey the recoverability condition on interpretation (Chomsky 1965; 1968). Based on such data, Borsley (2005: Section 4) correctly points out that Kayne's deletion analysis of word coordination is problematic. One has to admit that verbs can be conjuncts. Takano (2004) uses similar arguments to show that verb conjuncts exist in both English and Japanese. Bresnan and Thráinsson (1990) also argue for the existence of verb coordination in Icelandic, independent of verb phrase coordination and ellipsis constructions.

However, in Kayne's (1994) theoretical framework as in ours, conjuncts are Specifiers and Complements. Following the assumptions that Specifiers and Complements must be phrasal, Borsley (2005) then uses the existence of word-level conjuncts to argue against the Specifier and Complement status of conjuncts.

My response to this argument is to distinguish constituent levels from projectivity. If we adopt Chomsky's (1994) bare phrase structure theory, Specifiers and Complements are simply non-projecting elements in a binary branching representation; their sisters project, whereas they do not. The crucial property shared by Specifiers and Complements is their non-projectability, rather than their constituent level. We thus need to distinguish two types of dichotomy: word vs. element larger than a word, and projecting vs. non-projecting. The former is a morphological classification, whereas the latter is a purely syntactic classification. The status defined by the former is stable in syntax, whereas the status defined by the latter depends on the merger.

Accordingly, despite the fact that they are words rather than phrases, verb conjuncts do not project within the coordinate complex, and thus they are still regarded as non-head elements. On the other hand, the coordinate complex formed by the verbs can be regarded as a head, if it selects a complement and projects a VP. I list four possibilities in (2.55), and some illustrating examples in (2.56).

(2.55)

	Words or smaller elements	Elements larger than a word
Projecting element	e.g. coordinators in coordinate complexes, such as *and* in (2.56b/c)	e.g. coordinate verb complexes, such as *whistled and hummed* in (2.56b)
Non-projecting element	e.g. word conjuncts, such as *whistled* in (2.56b)	e.g. phrasal conjuncts, such as *a Tibetan folk song* in (2.56c)

(2.56) a. Hobbs [$_{VP}$ whistled [a total of 16 tunes]].
     b. Hobbs [$_{VP}$ [$_V$ whistled and hummed] a total of 16 tunes].
     c. Hobbs [$_{VP}$ whistled [$_{DP}$ *Jingle Bells* and a Tibetan folk song]].

In (2.56a), the verb *whistled* is a head, since it selects the DP [*a total of 16 tunes*], and projects the VP. In (2.56b), however, although it is a word, the verb *whistled* alone is not a head in the coordinate complex [*whistled and hummed*], since it does not project. Moreover, the whole complex, headed by the coordinator, is also a head, since it selects the DP [*a total of 16 tunes*], and projects the VP, although it is larger than a word. In (2.56c), the coordinator projects a DP. Accordingly, the coordinator is a head in the coordinate DP complex. The projected DP is not a projecting element when it is merged with the verb *whistled*. Instead, the DP is selected by the verb, and the verb projects a VP. Thus the verb is the head of the VP in this example.

In this approach, the notion of bar-level should be given up, and the relativity perspective of Chomsky's (1994) bare-phrase structure must be adopted. Whether an element is a head or not depends on whether it projects when it merges with another element. The notions head and projection are crucial to structure building of all levels, while the notion maximal projection (i.e. phrase) is not (Williams 1989: 282). In this sense, I second Koopman and Szabolcsi's (2000) statements: "We are not assuming that the material that counts as a word for the purpose of phonology is dominated by any particular kind of syntactic label" (p. 223 fn. 8) and "Words do not correspond to syntactic atoms or heads" (p. 39).[11] If the notion of bar-level is not justified, the background for Pesetsky's (1982) theory that aunts count as sisters in coordination disappears, and so does Borsley's (1994) challenge to the complementation structure of coordination.

I have clarified that the phrase level of an element is not related to the syntactic status of head or Spec/Complement. In fact, the issue of phrase level itself is far from clear. The fuzziness can also be seen in so-called co-compounds (Wälchli 2003, see also Heycock and Zamparelli 2003: 451, fn.5), such as *bow and arrow, brother and sister, night and day*. In such compounds, bare nouns are conjoined by a conjunction, expressing a close lexico-semantic relationship between them. Wälchli (2003: abstract) claims that "co-compounds in most languages are intermediate between words and phrases."

An issue related to the above discussion is the syntactic significance of coordination of word-parts. Word-parts are not phrases but they can be

---

11 In Cowper and Hall (2000: 26), their approach to word-level element coordination is ascribed to Marantz's (1997) assumption that the same principles of composition govern phrasal, non-phrasal, and morphological structures. Their approach is compatible with mine.

conjuncts. Such elements are again simply non-projecting elements in the relevant coordinate complexes.

(2.57) a. to study psycho- and socio-linguistics
   b. postmen and -women
   c. inteligente y profunda-mente [Spanish]
    'intelligent and profoundly'
   d. glücklicher-oder unglücklicherweise [German]
    'fortunately or unfortunately'

Coordinate complexes of word-parts might be considered to be Right Node Raising (RNR) constructions, regardless of how the constructions are derived: by movement (applying Postal 1998), special merger (Wilder 2008), deletion (see Booij 1985; Munn 1993: 8), or incremental merger (applying Phillips 2003). Under such an approach, each conjunct in data like (2.57) is supposed to be a word. If so, my above analysis of the word conjuncts applies here and thus there is nothing new to say. However, Artstein (2005) argues that the coordination is indeed at the word-part level, rather than at the word level or higher. His conclusion suggests that the claim that bound forms are not coordinatable is wrong (see textbooks such as Haspelmath 2002: 151 for such a claim). His analysis seems to be intuitively natural, although he does not mention the issue of projectivity at all.

Not only can conjuncts be part of a word, but so can entire coordinate complexes. In the following Chamorro example, the incorporated object is a coordinate complex (Chung and Ladusaw 2003: 87):

(2.58) Kao man-gäi-[fotgun kandit yan kahun ais] siha?
   Q AGR-have-stove electricity and box ice they
   'Do they have an electric stove and a refrigerator?'

One also finds coordination of a word and a prefix (Huddleston and Pullum 2002: 1325):

(2.59) Please list all publications of which you were the sole or co-author.

I conclude that neither the existence of non-phrasal conjuncts nor the existence of word-internal coordinate complexes poses any real challenge to hypothesizing a complementation structure for coordinate complexes. Instead, such facts may help us to get a deeper understanding of the relation between the structure and sizes of syntactic elements.

In this section, I have examined an aspect of the projectivity issue of coordinate complexes. I have showed that the bare phrase structure hypothesis, which abandons the bar-levels of syntactic elements, provides us with a simple analysis of word conjunct complexes. I therefore am able to maintain the conclusion reached in Section 2.3: coordinate complexes have a complementation structure.

2.6   Chapter summary

The structure of coordinate complexes is not different from that of other syntactic complexes. I have argued that a coordinate complex has a binary-branching structure, and between the two conjuncts, one is internal and the other is external to the coordinator. I also argued that the relation between external and internal conjuncts is a Spec–Comp relation. The structure of coordination is complementation, and coordinators are lexicalizations of the head of this complementation structure. This is different from any adjunction analysis such as Munn (1992). Moreover, the asymmetrical syntactic relation between conjuncts is compatible with their possible asymmetrical relation in semantics. Furthermore, I clarified that conjuncts, which are non-projecting elements in coordinate complexes, can be of any constituency level (word-fragment, word, phrase), and this freedom in conjunct size does not affect the complementation structure of coordinate complexes.

My analysis shows that coordination does not introduce any new configuration into the computational system. This is the first major conclusion of this book:

NO SPECIAL CONFIGURATION EXISTS IN COORDINATION.

The theoretical implication of this conclusion is that unlike complementation and adjunction, the notion "coordination" is not primitive in syntactic computation.

II No special syntactic category

3　The categorial makeup
of coordinate complexes

3.1　Introduction

One clear fact about coordinate constructions is that the category of the whole complex is identical to at least one of the conjuncts. The goal of this chapter is to determine the syntactic computation behind this categorial feature unification.

I follow the traditional assumption that major parts of speech are composed of categorial features, and the categorial features of a nominal are $[+N, -V]$, the categorial features of a verb are $[-N, +V]$, the categorial features of an adjective are $[+N, +V]$, and so on.

In the theoretical syntax literature on coordination, it has long been proposed that coordinators are head elements (De Groot 1949: 112, 222–223; Pesetsky 1982; Thiersch 1985; Munn 1987; 1992; 1993; Woolford 1987; Collins 1988a; 1988b; Kolb and Thiersch 1991; Anandan 1993: 38; Kayne 1994; Johannessen 1998; Zoerner 1995; see also Dik's 1968: 53 review of De Groot's proposal and Progovac's 1998a; 1998b review of later proposals). As we know, the categorial features of a complex element are projected from the head of the complex. However, unlike other head elements, coordinators such as *and* do not have any categorial features. Thus the recognition that coordinators are head elements does not account for the fact that the category of the whole coordinate complex is identical to at least one of the conjuncts.

From the perspective of the structure of coordinate constructions, coordinate complexes have a complementation structure in which one conjunct is in the complement position (called the internal conjunct in Chapter 2) and the other conjunct(s) is/are in the Specifier position(s) (called the external conjunct in Chapter 2). By itself, however, such a structure does not account for the categorial unification, since it does not force either the Spec of X or the complement of X to share categorial features with the projected XP. As pointed out by Borsley (1994: 227), claiming that a coordinate complex has a complementation structure implies nothing about the categorial features of either coordinate complexes or conjuncts. We thus need an account for the generalization that "the categorial makeup of coordinate structures must reflect that of the conjuncts" (Borsley 1994: 226).

One common solution is to propose a new type of maximal projection, &P (or CoP, ConjP) (e.g. Munn 1987; Zoerner 1995; Johannessen 1998; and even textbooks such as Fromkin *et al.* 2007: 149). Can this &P be justified syntactically? For instance, is its distribution in contrast to that of other well-recognized syntactic categories? I will present negative answers to these questions. Instead, I will clarify that every coordinate complex is a regular N, or V, or A, or P element.

Every coordinate complex must be equipped with categorial features, in order to take part in syntactic computation ("All grammatical operations in natural languages are category-based"; Radford 1997: 29). If a coordinator is the head of a coordinate complex (Chapter 2), and if the coordinator does not have intrinsic categorial features, the categorial features exhibited in the coordinate complex as a whole must come from the conjuncts. This kind of feature transference has been independently motivated. I will propose that the categorial features of a coordinate complex come from just one of the conjuncts.

On the other hand, no element in a syntactic structure may have two sets of categorial features. If a coordinator has its own intrinsic categorial features, no transference of categorial features from a conjunct to the whole complex occurs.

In Section 3.2, I demonstrate that in some languages, certain coordinators have specific categorial requirements on conjuncts, in contrast to coordinators in languages such as English, which can conjoin elements of almost any category. In Section 3.3, I demonstrate that in the coordinate complexes headed by the latter type of coordinators, the external conjuncts determine the category of the whole coordinate complexes. In Section 3.4, I argue against the construction-specific syntactic category &P. In Section 3.5, I argue against the Clause Conjunct Hypothesis (e.g. Gleitman 1965; Tai 1969). Building on the arguments in this and the previous chapter, I analyze the structure of coordinate complexes that are composed of three conjuncts and one coordinator in Section 3.6. Section 3.7 is a brief summary of this chapter.

3.2   The categories of coordinators and conjuncts

In this section, I address the categorial relation between coordinators and conjuncts. I will show that cross-linguistically, coordinators may or may not c-select conjuncts.

3.2.1   Coordinators without c-selection restrictions

The goal of this subsection is to examine the categorial relationship between conjuncts and *and*-like coordinators in languages like English.

In English, conjuncts linked by *and* can be nearly any category and can be both phrasal and word-level elements (the following examples are mostly taken from Wilder 1999 and Cowper and Hall 2000), as well as word-parts (see Chapter 2).

(3.1)	Phrases:		
	a.	NP	We still need the [bat and ball].
	b.	NP	my [friend and colleague] (Heycock and Zamparelli 2005: 204)
	c.	DP	[John and Mary] are coming.
	d.	φP (Pron)	[your and her] letters; [yours and hers]
	e.	PP	[In London and in Berlin], it is still cold.
	f.	AP	the [red and blue] flag
	g.	VP	Mary has [[left] and [gone to England]]
	h.	IP	I don't know if [[Mary left] and [Peter returned]]
	i.	CP	[[What do you gain] and [what do you lose]]?
(3.2)	Words:		
	a.	N	He is both the [father and employer] of my friend.
	b.	Num	[[Two] and [three]] is five. (Dik 1968: 273)
	c.	P	The events took place [in and around] Toronto.
	d.	A	... both [[glad] and [sad]] about this ...
	e.	V	Judith [[washed] and [dried]] the towels.
	f.	I	We both [[can] and [will]] visit her.
	g.	I	Bill [[was] and [is]] the best tennis player in the club.
	h.	C	[[Can] and [will]] you do this?
	i.	C	[[If] and [when]] she arrives, the party will begin.

Like English, many other European languages also permit conjuncts to be words and phrases of almost any category (e.g. German *und* 'and,' discussed in Welsche 1995: 64–65, 193; and Russian *i* 'and,' discussed in McNally 1993: 349). Outside the Indo-European family, one finds the same pattern with the coordinators *ja* in Finnish, *és* in Hungarian, *da* in Georgian, *at* in Tagalog, and so on (see Payne 1985: 28).

Meanwhile, it is also obvious that in all languages, any given coordinate complex belongs to one of the well-recognized syntactic categories such as N or V. If coordinators alone do not decide the category of a coordinate complex, as shown by the above facts, what does? I answer this question in Section 3.3, but first we need more background.

3.2.2   *Coordinators with c-selection restrictions*

We have seen that the English coordinator *and* coordinates conjuncts of various categories. However, as pointed out by Payne (1985: 5), such a pattern "is by no means universal." For instance, coordinators in Japanese are sensitive to the categories of the conjuncts. This sensitivity was noted by Yamada and Igarashi (1967). Like many early generative syntacticians (Gleitman 1965; Tai 1969), they tried to derive all types of coordinate complexes from sentential or proposition coordinate complexes, via deletion. In the "Remaining Problems" part of their article (p. 154), they raise the question of how this Clausal Conjunct Hypothesis explains the fact that coordinators vary according to the categories of conjuncts. However, this "remaining problem" of theirs still remains today as a challenge to the syntactic analysis of coordination, since the issue of category is one of the fundamental issues of syntax (Radford 1997: 29). However, the fact that coordinators, cross-linguistically, can be sensitive to the categories of conjuncts has syntactic implications that have not been explored in any framework.

Sensitivity to the categories of conjuncts is seen in both overt coordinators and null coordinators, as I now show.

A.   Overt coordinators that require conjuncts to be of specific categories
In many languages, different coordinators are used to coordinate conjuncts of different categories. In Mandarin Chinese, for instance, the coordinators *gen, tong, yu,* and *ji* coordinate nominals only (Chen *et al.* 1982: 238), whereas the coordinators *erqie* and *you* cannot coordinate nominals. The contrast is shown in (3.3). Moreover, the coordinator *yushi* 'and thus' coordinates clauses only (see Chapter 2).

(3.3) a.   Dai Jiaoshou xihuan he   pijiu {gen/*you} lü-cha.
            Dai Professor like   drink beer and/and   green-tea
            'Prof. Dai likes to drink beer and green-tea.'

       b.   Dai Jiaoshou shanliang {you/*gen} youmo.
            Dai Professor kind   and/and   humorous
            'Prof. Dai is kind and humorous.'

Furthermore, the disjunction *yaome* 'or' cannot coordinate nominals, whereas the disjunction *huozhe* 'or' can. The contrast is shown in (3.4).

(3.4) a.   Lao Li {yaome/huozhe} zai du   xiaoshuo, {yaome/huozhe}
            Lao Li or/or   PRG read novel   or/or

            zai du   baozhi.
            PRG read newspaper
            'Lao Li is reading a novel or is reading a newspaper.'

b. Lao Li zai du   xiaoshuo {*yaome/huozhe} baozhi.
   Lao Li PRG read novel   or/or   newspaper
   'Lao Li is reading a novel or a newspaper.'

In the following table, we can see how the category compatibility between coordinators and conjuncts is exhibited in various languages.

(3.5)   Some patterns of category compatibility between coordinators and conjuncts

Language	Coordinator	Conjuncts	Main references
Fujian	*kei*	nominals	Payne (1985: 5)
	ka	non-nominal elements	
Japanese	*to*	nominals	
	si	finite clauses	Kuno (1973)
	te	non-finite verbs, Adjs	
Korean	*(k)wa*	nominals	Martin and Lee (1986: 51)
	ko	clauses	
Maasai	*oo*	non-clausal elements	Caponigro (2003)
	n	clauses	
Malagasy	*sy*	VPs	Keenan (1976: 274)
	ary	clauses	
Sissala	*ká*	clauses	Blass (1989),
	a	VPs	Johannessen (1998: 85)
	rí (or *arí*)	non-verbal elements	
Somali	*iyo*	nominals	
	oo	VPs	Berchem (1991: 324–327)
	na	clauses	
Turkish	*la*	nominals	Haspelmath (2006: (58))
	ıp	VPs	
Yapese	*ngea*	nominals	Jensen (1977: 311–312)
(Austronesian)	*ma*	clauses	

Coordinators are sensitive not only to the distinctions between major categories such as nominals and verbal elements, but also to finer syntactic classifications. For instance, in several languages, coordinators that conjoin pronouns, which are DPs or φPs in the analysis of Déchaine and Wiltschko (2002), are different from the coordinators that conjoin other types of nominals (Stassen 2000: 49, fn. 2). Moreover, in Gungbe, *bò* coordinates two IPs where the subject of the first IP necessarily controls that of the second (Aboh 2009: Section 2.1.1). Furthermore, *haishi* 'or' in Chinese serves to coordinate elements related to a regardless-condition or interrogative operator, whereas *huozhe* 'or' coordinates elements elsewhere (cf. Li and Thompson 1981: 654); the Finnish contrast between *vai* and *tai* is completely analogous (see Haspelmath 2007:

(69)). Similarly, the disjunction *oo* 'or' in Kanada can connect interrogative clauses but not declarative clauses (Amritavalli 2003: 3). However, I will concentrate on the conjunct–coordinator interactions with respect to the major syntactic categories, since interactions with respect to finer syntactic categories do not raise any additional issues.

In this subsection, I have demonstrated that the choice of overt coordinators can be sensitive to the categories of conjuncts.

B.   Null coordinators that require conjuncts to be of specific categories
Not only overt but also null coordinators can impose categorial requirements on conjuncts. For example, in Cayuga, a Northern Iroquoian language spoken in Ontario, the coordinator *hni'* conjoins nominals, as in (3.6a), whereas a null coordinator conjoins verbs and clauses, as in (3.6b) (Mithun 1988: 342; also see Johannessen 1998: 85).

(3.6) a.   Ne:' tsho: ne' [onehe' sahe'tá' hni'] okwayethwe hne:'   (Cayuga)
           it   only the corn   beans   also we.planted CONTR
           'No, we only planted corn and beans.'

      b.   Tho   tsho: nhe:yóht ake'tré' atká:ta'
           there only so.it.is I.drove it.stopped
           'I was just driving along and it stopped.'

Similarly, the Chadic language Háusá uses *dà* to conjoin DPs, whereas it does not use any overt coordinator to conjoin verbal phrases or clauses (data from Gazdar *et al*. 1985: 179 fn. 1 and Hartmann 2000: 22):

(3.7) a.   Dà níí dà kái dà shíí, múú àbòòká nèè.   (Háusá)
           and I   and you and he   we   friends are
           'I, you, and he, we are friends.'

      b.   Múúsá káá   shá gíyàà (*dà) káá gásà kíífíí.
           Musa INFL$_{PERF/3SG.MASC}$ drink beer   and INFL roast fish
           'Musa drank beer and roasted fish.'

Zoerner (1995: 37) presents the following list (parataxis is another term for null coordinator):

(3.8)   Barasano: *kede* for coordinating NPs, parataxis elsewhere
           Chemehuevi: *wai* for NPs, parataxis elsewhere
           Tera: *nde* for NPs, parataxis elsewhere

Another example is Japanese, where a null coordinator cannot coordinate conjuncts if the first one has tense-marking. In (3.9a), where the first conjunct has a past-tense marker -*ta*, the coordinator *sosite* is obligatory (Takano 2004: 172 fn. 4; see Payne 1985: 27 for parallel data in other languages):

(3.9) a. John-ga   sono ronbun-o kopiisi-ta *(sosite) fairusi-ta.   (Japanese)
John-NOM that paper-ACC copy-PST and   file-PST

b. John-ga   sono ronbun-o kopiisi (sosite) fairusi-ta.
John-NOM that paper-ACC copy   and   file-PST
Both: 'John copied and filed that paper.'

Japanese also disallows the use of a null coordinator to conjoin an AP with a relative clause. In (3.10a), the two modifiers of the nominal are both APs, and the conjunctive *-te* is optional. In (3.10b), however, one modifier is an AP and the other is a clause, and *-te* is obligatory (Saiki 1985: 371, 372).[1]

(3.10) a. akaku (-te) atsui hon   (Japanese)
red   -TE thick book
'the red and thick book'

b. minikuku *(-te) Takashi-o   nagutta otoko
ugly   -TE Takashi-ACC hit   man
'a man who is ugly and who hit Takashi'

The contrasts between (3.9a) and (3.9b) and between (3.10a) and (3.10b) indicate that the distributions of null coordinators do not always correspond to whether the conjuncts are nominals or not. This fact does not support Zoerner's (1995) claim that the distributions are related to Case. Therefore his conclusion that coordinators head a Case-related functional projection is not convincing (see Bošković 2006 for a discussion of the Case-licensing of conjuncts).

The two aspects listed in this subsection clearly indicate that coordinators, like other types of syntactic head elements, can have restrictions on c-selection.

3.2.3 *Representing the categorial dependency of coordinators on conjuncts*

We have seen that coordinators such as *and* may occur in coordinate complexes of any category. This fact means that such coordinators do not have any intrinsic categorial features.

I have also presented cross-linguistic data showing that different coordinators may have different categorial requirements on conjuncts. The fact that coordinators can have such properties has generally been ignored. I mentioned in Section 3.2.2 that it is a remaining problem in Yamada and Igarashi (1967). In Sag *et al.* (1985: 133) and Gazdar *et al.* (1985: 179), this fact is mentioned only in footnotes, and in Dik (1968) and Johannessen (1998), though this aspect of coordination is discussed, it is not taken into consideration in their

---

1 According to Kuno (1973), *-te* is a gerundive marker. Saiki (1985: 371) calls *-te* coordination morpheme. I will simply gloss the suffix *TE*.

syntactic analyses. If a coordinator has any special requirement for the category of a conjunct, the relation between the coordinator and the conjunct must be that between a head and its selected complement, since only head elements exhibit c-selection restrictions on their sisters. We thus cannot adopt either Goodall's (1987: 32) hypothesis that coordinators are inserted at PF when the structure of a coordinate complex is linearized, nor Moltmann's (1992a: 52) hypothesis that coordinators adjoin to conjuncts. The c-selection restriction between coordinators and internal conjuncts presented here thus provides an additional argument for the claim made in Chapter 2 that coordinators are head elements.

3.3   The categorial makeup of coordinate complexes

Having examined the categorial relation between the components in a coordinate complex, we now look at the categorial relation between these components and the whole coordinate complex.

3.3.1   *Coordinate complexes headed by* and-*like coordinators*
A.   The categorial decisiveness of external conjuncts
This section presents English data showing that the categorial features of external conjuncts must be compatible with the c-selection of the heads that merge with the coordinate complexes, whereas the categorical features of internal conjuncts do not need to be.

Clausal conjuncts and prepositions   The compatibility between the category of external conjuncts with the whole coordinate complex is seen in the complement of prepositions. (3.11b) shows that the preposition *on* may not take tensed clauses as complements. However, if the complement of a preposition is a coordinate complex, the internal conjunct can be a tensed clause. In (3.11a) the internal conjunct is a tensed clause and the external one is a DP. (3.11c) shows that if we switch the order of the two conjuncts in (3.11a), the result is not acceptable. The contrast indicates that it is the external conjunct that satisfies the c-selection of the preposition. The examples in (3.12) show the same point.

(3.11) a. You can depend on <u>my assistance</u> and <u>that he will be on time</u>.
         b. *You can depend on <u>that he will be on time</u>.
         c. *You can depend on <u>that he will be on time</u> and <u>my assistance</u>.

(3.12) a. We talked about Mr. Golson's many qualifications and <u>that he had worked at the White House</u>.

    b. *We talked about <u>that he had worked at the White House</u>.

    c. *We talked about <u>that he had worked at the White House</u> and his many qualifications.

The data in (3.11) and (3.12), first introduced by Sag *et al.* (1985: 165), have previously been used in the literature to argue for the asymmetry between two conjuncts (Munn 1996: 2; Johannessen 1998: 14).

Notice that not all prepositions allow the second conjunct of their object to be a clause. The preposition *despite*, for instance, does not (Bayer 1996: 585):

(3.13) *Despite LaToya's intransigence and that all the musicians quit, Michael signed the contract.

Here we focus on the existence of the asymmetrical syntactic pattern exhibited in data like (3.11a) and (3.12a), and its theoretical implications, rather than possible constraints on the pattern implied by data like (3.13) (one may find such constraints discussed in Whitman 2004). The crucial point here is that such sloppiness in c-selection is never allowed for external conjuncts, as shown in the (c) sentences above, where the external conjuncts cannot be clausal. External conjuncts thus must satisfy the category requirements that are imposed on the whole coordinate complex.

Moreover, the acceptability contrast between data like (3.11a) and (3.11c) cannot be semantic or pragmatic (contra Whitman 2004), since as Sag *et al.* (1985: 166–167) noticed, the contrast disappears if the coordinate complexes are not objects of prepositions. For instance, in a subject position, as in (3.14), and in the position of the object of a verb, as in (3.15), the combination of a clause and a nominal is fine:

(3.14) [[That our perspectives had changed over the years] and [the issue we had worked on as students]] were the topics of discussion.   [CP&DP]

(3.15) a. I didn't remember until it was too late [[John's inability to get along with Pat], and [that he had no background in logic]].   [DP&CP]

    b. I didn't remember until it was too late [[that John had no background in logic] and [his inability to get along with Pat]].   [CP&DP]

As we know, both clauses and nominals can be subjects, and both can be the object of *remember*. Thus regardless of whether the external conjunct is a clause or a nominal, they always satisfy the categorial requirement on the coordinate complexes by the contexts in (3.14) and (3.15). The acceptability contrast between (3.11c) and (3.12c) on the one hand, and (3.14) and (3.15b) on the other hand, is explained if it is the external conjunct that must satisfy the category requirements imposed on the coordinate complex.

Such a simple explanation cannot be achieved if we fail to see the asymmetry between external and internal conjuncts. In order to account for the contrast between (3.11a)/(3.12a) and (3.11b)/(3.12b), Sag *et al.* (1985: 166) formulate a rule (their rule (127)) which "guarantees that in general the objects of prepositions are 'ordinary' NPs, rather than sentential ones. But if a prepositional object is coordinated," the rule "will permit a sentential NP to appear as a conjunct." As for the contrast between the acceptable (3.14) and the unacceptable (3.11c)/(3.12c), another rule (their rule (132)) is formulated, which "says that sentential NPs always follow their non-subject sisters." Furthermore, as they note in a footnote, ellipsis is also needed to account for (3.15b). None of these ad hoc rules is needed in our approach.

In the discussion of (3.11) and (3.12), I view them from a categorial perspective. Alternatively, Goodall (1987: 46–49) views them from a Case-assignment perspective. Specifically, it is generally assumed that prepositions assign Case, and tensed clauses may not receive Case. If tensed clauses occur as the complements of prepositions, as in (3.11c) and (3.12c), the result is not acceptable, since the prepositions assign Case, but the Case may not be received by the clause. He must therefore stipulate that in (3.11a) and (3.12a), the first conjunct, which is a nominal, receives the Case assigned by the preposition, and then the tensed clause does not receive Case from the preposition. I address this stipulation at the end of Section 3.3.1B.

PP conjuncts and transitive verbs　Another type of example showing the categorial decisiveness of external conjuncts in English is illustrated below ((3.18d) is from Chris Wilder p.c. and the rest are from Grosu 1985):

(3.16)　a.　John devoured [$_{DP}$ only pork] and [$_{PP}$ only at home].
　　　　b.　?*John devoured [$_{PP}$ only at home] and [$_{DP}$ only pork].

(3.17)　a.　He read [$_{DP}$ only *The Times*] and [$_{PP}$ only on Sundays].
　　　　b.　?*He read [$_{PP}$ only on Sundays] and [$_{DP}$ only *The Times*].

(3.18)　a.　John writes only funny letters and only to funny people.
　　　　b.　John eats the most unlikely things and at the most unlikely hours.
　　　　c.　John has stolen more watches and from more unsuspecting victims than anybody else ever will.
　　　　d.　I eat [neither meat nor at restaurants].

In the acceptable sentence (3.16a), the first conjunct *only pork* is a nominal, satisfying the c-selection restrictions of the verb *eat*, whereas the second conjunct *only at home* is a PP, not satisfying the c-selection restrictions of the verb. If the two conjuncts switch their order, as in (3.16b), the sentence becomes unacceptable. Similarly, in each of the other examples above, the two conjuncts are of different categories, and the first conjunct must satisfy the c-selection restrictions of the verb that selects the whole coordinate complex (note that the focus marker *only*, or *neither... nor,* which also encodes a focus meaning (Hendriks 2002, among others), is necessary in such examples; see Chapter 7 for my account).

The discussion of the data in (3.11) through (3.18) shows that in English, the internal conjuncts do not always exhibit the expected category, although the external ones always do.

Pollard and Sag (1994: 203) propose a Coordination Principle, which states that the category of each conjunct is subsumed by (is an extension of) that of the whole coordinate complex. They claim that this principle "guarantees that whenever a syntactic environment imposes some condition on a phrase in a given position X, that condition is respected by every conjunct of a coordinate structure in position X." Data like (3.19b) and (3.19d) have been assumed to be ruled out by this principle. Specifically, the conjunct *happy* in (3.19b) does not satisfy the condition on the complement of the verb *remembered*. Similarly, neither of the two conjuncts in (3.19d), *am walking to the store* and *that I left*, satisfies the conditions on the element to the right of *Jessie believes Tracy*.

(3.19) a. Pat remembered the appointment and that it was important to be on time.
  b. *Pat remembered happy and that it was important to be on time.
  c. *Pat remembered happy.
  d. *Jessie believes Tracy [am walking to the store and that I left].
  e. *Jessie believes Tracy [am walking to the store].

The unacceptability of (3.19b), according to our analysis, comes from the fact that the external conjunct, *happy*, is not c-selected by the verb *remember*, as shown in (3.19c). Similarly, the unacceptability of (3.19d), in our analysis, comes from the fact that the external conjunct, *am walking to the store*, is not c-selected by the relevant head of the small clause, as shown in (3.19e). Therefore what Pollard and Sag try to account for is already covered without the Coordination Principle.

Sag *et al.* (1985), Bayer (1996), and Whitman (2002) claim that in the coordination of unlike categories, category contrasts between conjuncts are neutralized. Like the approach taken in Pollard and Sag (1994), this neutralization approach does not consider that the categories of the first and second conjuncts have different syntactic effects. In our approach, no categorial features of conjuncts are neutralized. Instead, in *and*-complexes the categorial features of the external conjunct are decisive, whereas those of the internal conjunct are syntactically invisible.

One might want to link this asymmetry in syntactic category effects to some asymmetry of conjuncts in agreement. In the literature, it has been noted that in certain cases the first conjunct (the external conjunct, in our terms) may determine the agreement pattern of the whole coordinate complex (Munn 1993; Aoun *et al.* 1994; 1999; Johannessen 1996; 1998; among others). Considering the asymmetry of conjuncts in agreement, Borsley (1994: 242) states: "To generate the correct structures, a linear precedence rule is necessary to ensure that an unmarked conjunct precedes a marked conjunct, and some principle is necessary to ensure the correct relation between the conjuncts and the coordinate structure." However, as I noted in Section 2.3.1, agreement is affected by multiple factors, not all of which are syntactic. In particular, external conjuncts do not actually play the decisive role in agreement patterns. Moreover, it is not clear how agreement properties, even if they were consistent, could decide category issues.

I have presented evidence for the decisiveness of external conjuncts in determining the category of coordinate complexes in English. This does not imply that coordination can be legally combined anything with anything else; sentences like *John read books and in the park* are not acceptable. Nevertheless, with certain kinds of semantic parallelism, such as the focus parallelism signaled by the reoccurrence of *only* in *John eats only pork and only at home* (Grosu 1985: 232), a nominal can be conjoined with a PP (further discussion of the relevant semantic constraints on coordination is given in Section 7.3.2B).

We conclude that in English, external conjuncts must satisfy the category requirements that are imposed on the whole coordinate complexes.

B.   The movement of categorial features from Specs to Heads

So far in our discussion of *and*-like coordinators, we have presented two facts. First, the conjuncts linked by *and* can be of nearly any category, as can the coordinate complexes headed by *and* (Section 3.2.1). Second, the categories of such complexes are the same as their external conjuncts (Section 3.3.1). The chameleon-like nature of coordinate complexes headed by *and*-like coordinators is analyzed in different ways in the literature. Rothstein (1991a: 108) suggests that although coordinators are heads, they do not project category features. She claims "[t]he constituent they project has the same categorial status as the complements, and satisfies subcategorisation frames accordingly"

(p. 103). Heycock and Zamparelli (2002: 14) also state: "we assume that CoordP allows the transit of the categorial features of its conjuncts (in the trivial sense that a coordination of DPs behaves as a DP, of VPs, as a VP and so forth); that *and* is a head of CoordP." Similarly, Yuasa and Sadock (2002: 89) claim that "A coordinate constituent is one of two or more sister nodes whose categorial information percolates to the mother node." Moreover, as we introduced before (see Section 3.3.1A), Pollard and Sag (1994: 203) propose a Coordination Principle, which states that "In a coordinate structure, the CATEGORY and NONLOCAL value of each conjunct daughter is subsumed by (is an extension of) that of the mother." However, none of these approaches covers the second fact, i.e., only external conjuncts must have the same categorial features as the coordinate complexes.

In Chapter 2, we reached the conclusion that coordinate complexes have a complementation structure where the external conjunct and internal conjunct are the Spec and Complement of the coordinator, respectively. Accordingly, the two facts listed above can be captured by the syntactic structure in (3.20):

(3.20)

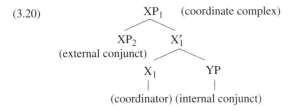

Since coordinators such as *and* may occur in coordinate complexes of any category, such coordinators do not have any intrinsic categorial features. In (3.20), the projection headed by a coordinator shares the category with the external conjunct. The observed category-sharing between external conjuncts and the coordinate complexes means that if an external conjunct is DP, the coordinate complex must itself be DP, and the head of this latter DP is lexicalized by a coordinator. In (3.20) the two daughters of XP_1 (XP_2 and X_1') are identical in category; thus two elements of the same category are merged. We call this structure the Upstairs-Twin-Structure. The Upstairs-Twin-Structure is also seen in possessive DPs, e.g., *John's child*, where the possessor DP (*John*) is the Specifier of the hosting DP (see Landau 1999: 10, 13 for a recent defense of this structure).

We now consider how the sharing of category between external conjuncts and the coordinate complexes is syntactically implemented in (3.20).

A generally accepted assumption is that "Every word has some categorial feature" (Collins 2002a: 43). In the previous sections, we have shown that coordinators such as English *and* do not seem to have any intrinsic categorial feature, and that their external conjuncts and coordinate complexes share categorial features. Since the heads of such complexes are realized by coordinators, it must be that the categorial features of the external conjuncts are transferred to the coordinators and then are projected to the whole complexes. Accordingly, even though it is always *and* that shows up at the head position in (3.21), the head of the coordinate complex is D in (3.21a), P in (3.21b), A in (3.21c), and V in (3.21d).

(3.21) a. DP   [[John] and [Mary]] are coming.
       b. PP   [[In London] and [in Berlin]], it is still cold.
       c. AP   the [[red] and [blue]] flag
       d. VP   Mary has [[left] and [gone to England]]

If a coordinator inherently has no categorial features (necessary for the syntactic computation of the projected coordinate complex), it needs to get them from somewhere. I propose that an *and*-like coordinator receives its categorial features from the external conjunct. This is implemented as feature percolation from external conjuncts to coordinators. After the transference, the categorial features of the coordinators are projected to the coordinate complex.

Our claim that coordinators have no intrinsic categorial features and are thus able to merge with conjuncts of various categories is parallel to the proposal in Distributed Morphology that roots do not have categorial features, enabling them to merge with functional morphemes of any categories (see Embick and Noyer 2007; among others).

The proposed feature dependency of XP on the Spec of X is independently seen in wh- and negation feature percolation. For instance, the negation feature is percolated from Spec in (3.22a) and (3.22b), and the wh-feature is percolated from Spec in (3.22c) (Grimshaw 1991; Webelhuth 1992; Koopman and Szabolcsi 2000: 41):

(3.22) a. Nobody's car would I borrow.   [NEG feature percolation]
       b. No one's mother had baked anything.   [NEG feature percolation]
       c. Whose book did you read?   [WH feature percolation]

If the negation in (3.22a) is sentential negation, which is able to trigger the subject-modal inversion, the [NEG] feature must move out of the word *nobody*, which is the Spec element of the possessive DP. Similarly, if the negation in (3.22b) is the licensor of the negative polarity item *any*, the [NEG] feature must move out of the word *no one*, which is the Spec element of the possessive DP, in order to c-command the word *any*. Likewise, in (3.22c), in order to check the [WH] feature of C, the relevant feature must move out of the word *whose*, which is the Spec element of the possessive DP. In addition to these features, Winter (2001: 177 fn. 29) mentions that some semantic features of a possessive DP can be decided by the Specifier (possessor) in certain cases (for more discussion of feature percolation, see Cole *et al.* 1993; López 2001).

The hypothesis that there is a syntactic relation between external conjuncts and *and*-like coordinators with respect to categorial features links together the two facts introduced in this subsection: first, conjuncts linked by *and*, as well as coordinate complexes headed by *and*, can be of nearly any category, and second, the categories of such complexes are the same as their external conjuncts. In contrast to this categorial feature approach, Goodall's (1987: 49) Case-assignment approach to the data introduced in Section 3.3.1 does not make such a link. Goodall (1987: 49) admits:

> Although this analysis gives us an answer to our original question about (98) [= (3.11a) and (3.12a) here – NZ], it also raises several new questions we had not previously considered. The most fundamental of these is why it is that Case-assignment can be blocked in coordination. Similarly, we would want to know how this affects the operation of the Case Filter and the θ-criterion. I do not believe that the model of coordination I am developing here shed any new light on these questions, so I will simply note that they form an interesting area of investigation that is worth pursuing.

3.3.2   *Categorial features of coordinators that have c-selection restrictions*
In this subsection, I show that Chinese coordinators such as *he, gen*, and *erqie* not only have c-selection restrictions, but also have certain intrinsic categorial features.

It is generally assumed that the c-selection of x must be satisfied by the complement of x, rather than by the Spec of x. Moreover, c-selection must be satisfied only once. Thus, it is impossible for all conjuncts to be subject to the same c-selection.

We have now learned that two conjuncts may have different categorial features. If a coordinator has c-selection restrictions, the category of its complement, i.e., the internal conjunct, is fixed. However, the category of its specifier, i.e., the external argument, is not determined by any element. If a coordinator has no intrinsic categorial feature, it may get any categorial features from the external conjunct, and those features will decide the category of the whole coordinate complex.

(3.23) a. Wo renwei {*yi   ge tiancai / Baoyu yexinbobo}
          I   think   one CL genius   Baoyu ambitious
          'I think {*a genius / that Baoyu is ambitious}.'

      b. *Wo renwei [Baoyu yexinbobo] gen [yi   ge tiancai]
          I   think   Baoyu ambitious   and   one CL genius

The example in (3.23a) indicates that the verb *renwei* 'think' selects a clause exclusively and disallows a nominal complement. The coordinator *gen* c-selects a nominal exclusively and disallows a clause (see (3.3)). In (3.23b), the c-selection of *gen* is satisfied. If *gen* had no intrinsic categorial features, the non-nominal categorial feature of the first conjunct [*Baoyu yexin bobo*] would be percolated to *gen* and then be projected to the whole coordinate complex, satisfying the c-selection of *renwei*. However, (3.23b) is not acceptable.

Coordinate complexes headed by *he/gen* may be merged only with elements that select nominals. Verbs such as *renshi* 'know' and *jiao* 'teach' select a nominal exclusively and disallow a clausal complement, as shown in (3.24a). The coordinate headed by *he/gen* may occur as the complement of *renshi*, as shown in (3.24b).

(3.24) a. Wo renshi {yi   ge xiaoshuojia / *Baoyu   yexinbobo}
          I   know   one CL novelist   Baoyu ambitious
          'I know {a novelist / that Baoyu is ambitious}.'

      b. Wo renshi [yi   ge xiaoshuojia gen yi   ge yinyuejia].
          I   know   one CL novelist   and one CL musician
          'I know a novelist and a musician.'

The above discussion shows that *he/gen* has intrinsic nominal features.

The following examples show that the distributions of coordinate complexes headed by *erqie* 'and' show just the opposite pattern:

(3.25) a. Wo renshi [yi   ge xiaoshuojia {he/   gen/* erqie} yi   ge yinyuejia].
          I   know   one CL novelist   and/ and/ and   one CL musician
          'I know a novelist and a musician.'

      b. Wo renwei [Baoyu   yexinbobo {erqie/* he/* gen} ta hen youqian].
          I   think   Baoyou ambitious   and /   and/ and   he very rich
          'I think that Baoyu is ambitious and that he is very rich.'

Such data show that coordinate complexes headed by *erqie* are not nominals, and *erqie* must have intrinsic verbal categorial features.

The intrinsic categorial features of *he/gen* and *erqie* can also be seen in (3.26).

(3.26) a. Baoyu xiande {gaoda/youqizhi/*qizhi}.
  Baoyu seem   tall/stylish/style
  'Baoyu seems to be {tall/stylish/*style}.'

  b. Baoyu xiande [gaoda erqie youqizhi].   [AP & AP]
  Baoyu seem   tall   and   stylish
  'Baoyu seems to be tall and stylish.'

  c. *Baoyu xiande [jiankang-qingkuang he   qizhi].   [NP & NP]
   Baoyu seem   health-condition   and   style

  d. Baoyu guanxin   [jiankang-qingkuang he   qizhi].   [NP & NP]
  Baoyu care.about health-condition   and   style
  'Baoyu cares about health condition and style.'

The example in (3.26a) shows that the verb *xiande* 'seem, look like' c-selects adjectives *gaoda* 'tall' and *youqizhi* 'stylish' but not the nominal *qizhi* 'style.' The coordinate complex headed by *erqie* in (3.26b) satisfies the c-selection of the verb, indicating that *erqie* does not have nominal features. The coordinate complex headed by *he* in (3.26c) does not satisfy the c-selection of the verb, although *jiankang-qingkuang he qizhi* 'health condition and style' is a well-formed coordinate complex itself, as seen in (3.26d). (3.26c) thus indicates that *he* does not have adjectival features.

3.3.3   Categorial unification in Spec-Head and Head-Compl relations

We have argued that coordinate complexes headed by *and* have the Upstairs-Twin-Structure in (3.20), repeated here as (3.27a). Another possible structure that can be built by the computional system is the Downstairs-Twin-Structure in (3.27b). In the latter structure, the category of a complex is identical to that of the complement. For example, in Larson's (1988) VP-shell structure, the head and its complement are identical in category. Similarly, McCloskey (1999) proposes a structure where C selects another CP, to represent the double *that* constructions in Standard English (e.g. *He thinks that if you are in a bilingual classroom that you will not be encouraged to learn English*). (3.27a) and (3.27b) are different in that the former represents uniformity of category in the immediate constituents of the top (or final) merger level of the syntactic complex, whereas the latter exhibits uniformity of category in the immediate constituents of the next lower (or earlier) merger level of the complex. A third type of structure that can be built by the computational system is the well-recognized (3.27c).

(3.27) a.   XP$_1$ b.   XP$_1$ c.   XP

     XP$_2$ X$'_1$ *cat-sharing*   YP X$'_1$ YP X$'$

       X$_1$ YP   X$_1$ XP$_2$ *cat-sharing*   X ZP

The Upstairs-Twin-Structure   The Downstairs-Twin-Structure
e.g. possessive DP   e.g. Larson's VP-shell,
                           McCloskey's double CP structure

This research thus shows that there is no construction-specific syntactic category in coordination. The top projection in (3.27a), i.e., XP$_1$, is not an &P, or any other new type of functional category. It is simply the same as whatever the external conjunct (XP$_2$) is. Some empirical problems of &P will be presented in Section 3.4.

3.4   Against &P

According to our approach, the term coordinator is a convenient name for a group of forms that realize the heads of coordinate complexes. Such words do not have a (complete) set of categorical features intrinsically. By contrast, some have argued for a special coordination-specific category like &P (or CoP for Coordination Phrase, or BP for Boolean Phrase) in the literature (Munn 1987; Zoerner 1995; Johannessen 1998; de Vries 2005; among others). Although the notion of &P has been repeatedly criticized (Wilder 1999; Sag 2000: 8; and Borsley 1994; 2005), the criticisms have been ineffective since the crucial issue of the categorial makeup of coordinate complexes was not solved. The results described in the previous sections now enable us to provide a more conclusive argument against &P.

The c-selection restriction presented in this chapter, along with the interactions between coordinators and internal conjuncts presented in the last chapter (Section 2.3.3), provide substantial support for the claim that coordinators are head elements, consistent with claims long advocated in the literature (see De Groot 1949: 112, 222–223; Pesetsky 1982; Thiersch 1985; Munn 1987; 1992; 1993; Woolford 1987; Collins 1988a; 1988b; Kolb and Thiersch 1991; Anandan 1993: 38; Kayne 1994; Johannessen 1996; 1998; Zoerner 1995). However, the claim that coordinators are head elements is different from the claim that coordinators form an independent functional category. In this section, we argue against the category of &P.[2]

---

2 Camacho (1997) provides an alternative way of avoiding &P. In consideration of the free categorical environment of *and*, Camacho (1997) assumes that *and* in the sentence *Tom and Mary saw the movie* is simply in T (or I), with the following constituency:

3.4.1 The distributions of coordinate complexes are covered by simplexes

It has been claimed that &P is the category of coordinate complexes, and coordinators such as *and* and *or* are functional categories, independent of other categories such as N, V, and A. In this subsection, I show that the distributions of coordinate complexes are covered by simplexes, and that the categorial contrasts of various coordinate complexes are covered by those of simplexes. Therefore, coordinate complexes cannot be an independent category.

A.   The syntactic positions of coordinate complexes are covered by those of simplexes

No syntactic position is found to be taken by coordinate complexes exclusively. For example, verbs such as *compare* select plural nominals, and the selected element can be either a coordinate complex or a simplex plural nominal. Since the classification of syntactic elements into syntactic categories is decided by the syntactic distributions of the elements, the identification of any new category must be based on the existence of a new distribution. Coordinate complexes do not pass this test.

In fact, the distributions of coordinate complexes are not only covered by, but are also more restricted than, simplex elements. The restriction is seen in aspects like the following.

First, plurals can be subjects of quantity-denoting predicates and occur with quantity-related modifiers such as *a total of* or its Chinese counterpart *yigong* 'in total', whereas coordinate complexes cannot ((3.28) is cited from Dougherty 1970b: 854).

(3.28) a. The men were {numerous/plentiful/interspersed}.
       b. *Jack, Bill, and Tom were {numerous/plentiful/interspersed}.

(3.29) a. a total of two persons
       b. *a total of John and Tom

(3.30) a. yigong liang ge   ren
          total   two   CL   person
          "a total of two persons"

       b. *yigong Baoyu gen Daiyu
          total   Baoyu and Daiyu

(i)   [TP Tom [T' and [TP Mary [T [VP saw the movie]]]]

However, Camacho realizes that in (i), the coordinated elements *Tom and Mary* do not form a constituent, which as pointed out by Progovac (1998b: 5), counts against this analysis. In our approach, it is also possible for *and* to be in T in certain contexts, but only if the external conjunct is a T-element, as in *John [was and is] the best tennis player in the club*, or if the external conjunct is a TP, as in *I don't know if [Mary left and Peter returned]*.

Second, plurals can occur in the partitive construction *one of* __, whereas coordinate complexes cannot. The following data are cited from Büring (2002: 7):

(3.31) a. one of {us/the detectives}
    b. *one of {you and me/Schimansky and Tanner}

Third, plurals can occur in the partitive construction *half of* __, whereas coordinate complexes cannot. The following data are cited from Dougherty (1970b: 855).

(3.32) a. Half of the quartet wanted to quit.
    b. *Half of Mary, Sue, Jane, and Sally wanted to quit.

All of these examples show that if an element can be merged with a coordinate nominal complex, it can also be merged with a plural simplex, but not vice versa. The distributions of coordinate complexes are more restricted and thus fully covered by those of simplexes. The coverage relation means that such complexes do not represent a separate syntactic category in the computational system.

B.   The category contrasts of coordinate complexes are covered by
      those of simplexes

If coordinate complexes could neutralize the category contrasts of other elements, the following four coordinate complexes would form a natural class in merging with verbs, but they do not.

(3.33) a. [DP & DP]
    b. [VP & VP]
    c. [CP & CP]
    d. [AP & AP]

A well-established fact about c-selection is that it is local. The complex of (3.33a) can be selected by a transitive verb because transitive verbs c-select for DPs and because, in our approach, the whole complex is a DP. By contrast, if a coordinator projected an &P with its own categorial features, a transitive verb could not merge with the complex of (3.33a). If we try to solve the problem by positing that a transitive verb c-selects &P as well as DP, the verb should also be able to merge with the complexes of (3.33b), (3.33c), and (3.33d), since they are all &Ps. However, no such verbs have been found.

Since coordinate complexes do not show a distribution different from those of the currently recognized categories, nor do they "bleach" contrasts in the currently recognized categories, they cannot represent an independent category. Therefore, the assumed category &P does not exist in syntax.

3.4.2   *Neither closed classes nor case inflection argue for &P*

Here we examine two proposed arguments for the projection of &P: the closed-class nature of coordinators and case inflection patterns of conjuncts.

A.   Coordinators form a closed class

It has been claimed that because coordinators form a closed class and are unstressed elements, they therefore can head an independent projection, &P (Johannessen 1998). However, not all closed-class and unstressed elements head independent projections. For instance, demonstratives, pronouns, and Chinese locatives do not need stress, and they are all closed-class elements. Nevertheless, they are hosted by DPs or NPs; there is no DemP, PronP, or LocP. Similarly, pronouns have been argued to be proforms of DPs, φPs, and NPs (Déchaine and Wiltschko 2002). Therefore, stress and class size cannot be used as arguments for the existence of &P.

B.   Coordinators and Case

It has been claimed that coordinators are Case-assignors, and thus &P is a Case-related functional category (e.g. Zoerner 1995). For instance, in (3.34), the external conjunct *me* is accusative, which is not expected to be true of the whole coordinate complex in the subject position. The same point holds for the internal conjunct *me* in (3.35) and both conjuncts in (3.36).[3]

(3.34)   Me and Robin left.

(3.35) a. Robin and me left.
         b. Huck and me ain't cry-babies.   (Mark Twain, *Tom Sawyer*, Chapter 16)

(3.36) a. Me and them left.
         b. Him and me drinks nought but water.   (Chapman 1995: 37)

The existence of such data does not mean that the coordinator *and* has any intrinsic feature related to Case. We need to clarify that abstract Case encodes a mutual checking (or licensing) relation between a nominal and a functional head. For instance, the Nominative Case of a nominal and the Case feature of T

---

3 See Progovac (1998a) for an overview of the diversity of case-marking of conjuncts both within and across languages, and Progovac (1998b) for a review of some approaches to this issue in the literature.

check each other, and the Accusative Case of a nominal and the Case feature of v (or AgrO, Tr) check each other.[4] Non-nominal conjuncts do not have Case features. If coordinators must have a Case-relation with conjuncts, the derivation of coordinate non-nominal complexes will crash, since the Case-feature of the coordinators cannot be checked. Zoerner (1995: 45 fn. 2) notices this dilemma, but declares that the use of a coordinator in non-nominal coordinate complexes "reflects the $\&^0$'s use as a discourse marker," rather than a Case-assignor. Since he does not explain what this "discourse marker" status of coordinators means, this response does not help support the claimed Case-assignor status of coordinators.

One also needs to distinguish morphological case from abstract Case (see McFadden 2004 and Legate 2008 for recent discussions), which we understand to be a formal licensing relationship between a nominal and a functional head. Although I am not making any claim regarding the morphological cases of pronominal conjuncts (see Schütze 2001: Section 5.2 for a default case approach; also Bošković 2006), I claim that the coordinator *and* does not have any intrinsic feature related to Case. Accordingly, the issue of Case cannot be used as an argument for &P.

3.4.3   *Retrospection*

Based on the facts and arguments in this section, I conclude that coordinators neither bleach the category features of the relevant coordinate complexes, nor create any special category. Thus both of the following two assumptions are problematic: that there is a category-neutral &P, and that &P is categorically contrastive to other categories, such as N and V.

One needs to distinguish between two issues: whether coordinators can function as head elements, and whether they should be classified as an independent functional category. One example to illustrate the difference is the word *do* in English *do*-support. The word *do* can be a realization of T (or some other functional projection, see Laka 1994), but it does not head an independent *Do*P, in contrast to other functional and lexical categories. Similarly, we claim that coordinators are realizations of lexical or functional elements, but they do not constitute an independent syntactic category.

Grootveld (1994: 31) claims that coordinators head a functional projection that is categorially non-distinct from the head's complement, assuming all conjuncts are such complements. Zoerner (1995: 19) claims that "An &P lacks

---

4 In Chomsky (2000), Case features of nominals are checked or erased by the phi-features of functional categories under matching. This technical change does not affect the statement here. Both types of features are still uninterpretable, and still must be checked or erased mutually.

inherent features such as [±V] or [±N], which would limit the number of sites in which it could licitly surface; rather, it assumes the feature specification of its conjuncts." In Johannessen (1998), although CoP is claimed to be an independent category, "CoP get[s] its major category feature from one conjunct" (p. 112, also pp. 164, 168, 169). We can see that in these analyses, it makes no empirical difference if one gives up the label of CoP or &P and uses the category of a certain conjunct instead.

The &P proposal has been repeatedly criticized in the literature. Abney (1991: 225) correctly points out that coordinators such as *and* do not show any specific selectional properties. Based on the fact that coordinate complexes have no fixed position and the so-called &P is never selected for, Wilder (1999: Section 2) states that "analyzing the coordination constituent as a projection of & is problematic." Similar comments have been made by Sag (2000: 8) and Borsley (2005).

Traditionally, coordinators such as *and* have been regarded as "empty words." In Hockett (1958: 153), coordinators "serve not directly as carriers of meaning, but only as markers of the structural relationships between other forms." In Moltmann (1992a: 32), "'coordinator' does not denote a syntactic function." Blümel (1914: 52) even declares "Strictly speaking . . . such words should be excluded from dictionaries" (see Lang 1984: 67 for a review). Following Chomsky's (2007: 11) idea that a lexical item may have an edge-feature, which permits it to be merged with another syntactic element, we assume that it is the edge-features of coordinators that permit them to be merged with conjuncts. It is plausible to suppose that coordinators have other features as well. For instance, when a conjunction is merged with two individual-denoting conjuncts, it may project a plural feature, even when each of the conjunct is singular (see Section 5.2.3B for further discussion of the issue); a disjunction such as *or* projects a disjunctive feature, and adversative coordinators such as *but* projects an adversative feature. However, *and* does not have intrinsic categorial features, and it gets the features from the external conjuncts.

It is well recognized that not every part of speech corresponds to an independent syntactic category. Pronouns, demonstratives, articles, and expletives are all grouped into D-elements. Conjunction is also a part of speech, but this does not mean that it must be an independent syntactic category.

3.5 Against the Clausal Conjunct Hypothesis

The fact that conjuncts can be any category and any category-level (see Section 2.5) is in conflict with Gleitman's (1965) and Tai's (1969) Clausal Conjunct Hypothesis (CCH), which states that all conjuncts are clausal and that apparent non-clausal conjuncts are the result of reduction. Since the CCH is still alive (George 1980; Goodall 1987; Hoekstra 1994: 296; Johannessen 1998; Aoun *et al.* 1994; Aoun and Benmamoun 1999; Camacho 2003; and Schein forthcoming), in this subsection we provide further arguments against it.

The CCH requires two crucial operations. The first one is deletion, called Tranformation of Coordination-Reduction, which is used to derive phrasal coordination constructions. According to the CCH, (3.37a) is derived from (3.37b).

(3.37) a. Louise and George rode bicycles.
        b. Louise ~~rode bicycles~~ and George rode bicycles.

The second operation, as mentioned by Tai (1969: 144) and Goodall (1987: 18), is regrouping, which combines, for instance, *Tom* and *Jane* in (3.38) at a certain step of the derivation, so that the verb is changed from the singular form *eats*, as in the assumed source sentence (3.38b), into the plural form *eat* in (3.38a):

(3.38) a. Tom and Jane eat bread and crackers respectively.
        b. Tom eat*s* bread and Jane eat*s* crackers.

Lakoff and Peters (1966) argue against the CCH, observing that the CCH cannot, for instance, account for the contrast between (3.39a) and (3.39b):

(3.39) a. John and Mary are erudite.
           (Reading = John is erudite and Mary is erudite.)
        b. John and Mary are alike.
           (Reading ≠ *John is alike and Mary is alike.)

Lakoff and Peters note that if all coordinate complexes are derived from clausal coordinate complexes, the source of (3.39b) must be an ungrammatical one. Accordingly, the CCH must be wrong. Instead, they analyze (3.39a) as clausal coordination and (3.39b) as phrasal coordination. Tai (1969) defends the CCH, claiming that in data like (3.39b) the transformation of Coordination-Reduction is obligatory. Conceptually speaking, the CCH makes the syntactic derivation more complicated, since it requires both ungrammatical underlying forms and a rule to make them grammatical. In any analysis without the CCH, including ours, the coordination in (3.39a) is distributive and the one in (3.39b) is collective. Both are DP coordinate complexes, and no clausal coordination is involved.

The CCH has been extensively discussed in Dik (1968), Lang (1984: 86), Goodall (1987: 18), McCawley (1968; 1988a: 277), Munn (1993), Wilder

(1994; 1997; 1999: 9), among many other places. There are still some recent advocates of the CCH, as listed above, but McCawley (1968; see Dougherty 1970a: 532), Dougherty (1970b: 857), Wilder (1999: 13) and Eggert (2000) present arguments against the CCH. Parallel to these works, Schwarzschild (2001) also casts doubts on the CCH (t-only-conjunction in his terms) from a semantic point of view.

However, although no clausal coordination is involved in data like (3.39), and thus no conjunct reduction, I admit that some apparent nominal coordinate complexes are indeed the result of reduction. The following example from Collins (1988a; 1988b) truly looks like the result of RNR of two clausal conjuncts:

(3.40)   Perhaps John, maybe Mary, and certainly Bill went to the store.

In (3.40), each conjunct is modified by an adverb. The adverbs modify predicates, including nominal predicates, as in (3.41), and appositive nominals, which are also predicates, as in (3.42). But they cannot modify individual-denoting nominals, as shown in (3.43) (Munn 1993: 160; Schein forthcoming):

(3.41) a. John is perhaps a doctor.
        b. It was perhaps John that I met.

(3.42) a. I met someone, possibly a priest, yesterday.
        b. Someone, possibly Bill, came into the room.

(3.43) a. *I met [possibly a priest] yesterday.
        b. *[Possibly someone] came into the room.

It thus seems that data like (3.40) have a clausal coordination source, semantically and syntactically (via RNR) (see Schein forthcoming). One new argument for the reduction analysis of such examples is that if a conjunction cannot conjoin clauses, like *he* in Chinese, it cannot occur with any modal adverb in the parallel coordinate complex:

(3.44) a. [Baoyu he   (*yexu) Daiyu] qu-le   Shanghai.
           Baoyu and perhaps Daiyu go-PRF Shanghai
           'Baoyu and Daiyu have gone to Shanghai.'

        b. (Yexu)   [Baoyu, Daiyu, he Yuanyang] dou qu-le   Shanghai.
           Perhaps Baoyu   Daiyu and Yuanyang all go-PRF Shanghai
           '(Perhaps) Baoyu, Daiyu, and Yuanyang all have gone to Shanghai.'

        c. *Yexu   Baoyu,   dagai   Daiyu, he   kending Yuanyang dou
           Perhaps Baoyu   probably Daiyu and certainly Yuanyang all

           qu-le   Shanghai.
           go-PRF Shanghai

In (3.44a), the modal adverb *yexu* 'perhaps' cannot occur between the two conjuncts of the subject linked by *he*. This constraint suggests that real nominal coordinate complexes exclude such adverbs, which in turn suggests that in examples like (3.40), there is a clausal rather than nominal coordinate complex. In (3.44b), the adverb occurs outside the coordinate complex, and thus it has no interaction with the coordinate complex headed by *he*. In (3.44c), the modal adverb *dagai* 'probably' and *kending* 'certainly' both occur inside the subject coordinate complex headed by *he*, and as in (3.44a), this is not acceptable. The interactions between the adverbs and the coordinate complexes headed by *he* show that the occurrence of such adverbs in examples like (3.40) may indicate that the coordination is a clausal one (see Section 5.2.3C for some other cases of reduction of clausal conjuncts).

However, not all conjuncts are derived from clauses. No matter how appealing the CCH might be from a certain semantic point of view (e.g. Schein, forthcoming), it cannot capture certain syntactic facts.[5]

First of all, in many languages, clausal and non-clausal coordination may use different coordinators (see Section 3.2.2). In Mandarin Chinese, for instance, *ji* and *gen* coordinate nominals only, and never coordinate clauses (Chen *et al.* 1982: 238), nor do the Japanese conjunction *-to* and the Shanghainese conjunction *teq-*. In contrast, Chinese *erqie* can coordinate verbal phrases, including clauses, but it cannot coordinate any nominals. Moreover, the conjunction *yushi* 'and thus' coordinates only clauses (Chen *et al.* 1982: 515). If all conjuncts are, or are derived from, clausal conjuncts, it is hard to explain the syntactic distributions of these conjunctions.

Second, the CCH developed from the study of the distributive type of coordination, such as (3.37a). According to the CCH, data like (3.37a) are the result of a reduction of clausal conjuncts. In Chinese, however, the conjunction *ji* can occur only in the distributive coordination of DPs (see Chapter 5) and is not able to conjoin clauses. This is inconsistent with the CCH, which would wrongly predict that all *ji*-coordinate complexes were derived from syntactically illegal representations where *ji* conjoined clauses.

Third, if sentences like (3.45a) were derived from two clausal conjuncts, and if the predicate *in the bathroom* and the predicate *in the living room* were in the two clauses respectively, it would be impossible to identify the exact form of

---

5 Arguments against the CCH can also be seen in Vicente's (to appear) study of *but*. He shows that corrective *but*, as in (i), always requires clausal coordination, followed by PF deletion, whereas contrastive *but*, as in (ii), may conjoin elements of other categories.

(i)   Helen didn't eat one apple but three bananas.
(ii)   Helen ate one apple but three bananas.

the subject for each of the predicates ((3.45a) is from Heycock and Zamparelli 2002 and (3.45b) is from Krifka 1990: 168).

(3.45) a. The children are in the bathroom and in the living room.
       b. The planes flew above and below the clouds.

Certainly *the children* cannot be the subject of either predicate in (3.45a). Only some of the children are in the bathroom while others are in the living room, and the sentence does not tell us how many are in each group. *The children* thus does not have a syntactic position in the assumed two source clauses. If we give up the CCH, however, the syntactic representation of (3.45) is clear. The subject here is a simplex DP in its plural morphology. The predicate is a coordinate PP complex. The subject is base-generated higher than the coordinate PP complex. The copular *are*, which is required for non-verbal primary predication in English, agrees with the plural subject. There is only one clause. No clause-reduction occurs. (3.45b) presents the same challenge to the CCH.

Finally, as pointed out by Schmerling (1975: 220–221, cited by Sag *et al.* 1985: 151), AC constructions are not synonymous to the assumed unreduced form. The AC in (3.46a) encodes a single event whereas (3.46b) may encode two events.

(3.46) a. I went to the store and bought some whiskey.
       b. I went to the store and I bought some whiskey.

AC data are not distributive (see Section 5.2.2). Data like (3.46a) are not compatible with the CCH.

I conclude that the CCH cannot be syntactically right, in the generally accepted syntactic framework.[6,7]

3.6 The structure of coordinate complexes composed of more than two conjuncts

In this section, I present an analysis of the syntax of coordinate complexes that are composed of three or more conjuncts and a single coordinator. Following Winter (2006: 3), I call such complexes multiple coordinate complexes. I will not discuss complexes that are composed of three or more conjuncts and two or more coordinators, called repeated coordinate complexes in Winter (2006: 5).

---

6 In advocating the CCH, Schein (forthcoming) assumes that all theta roles are propositional. This is not a generally accepted assumption.

7 Partee (2005: Section 2.2) states that the CCH also caused problems for the ordering of various transformational rules proposed in the early seventies.

Repeated coordinate complexes are ambiguous and allow sub-grouping into the basic types that we are covering. The differences between multiple and repeated coordinate complexes presented by both Borsley (2005) and Winter (2006) falsify Payne (1985: 19), Goodall (1987: 32, 33), and Moltmann's (1992b: 54) claim that the repetition of coordinators has no syntactic or semantic effect.

Gazdar *et al.* (1985: 170) state that "no language can have, say, a three-place coordinator morpheme. If there were one in English, pronounced *triand*, we would find *Kim, Sandy, triand Lee* grammatical, but not **Kim triand Sandy* or **Kim, Sandy, Lee, triand Tracy*. We know of nothing like this in any attested language." Similarly, Zwart (1995: 12) says "I know of no language where multiple coordination is actually obligatory." The common implication of these quotes is that unlike binary coordination, three-place coordination is not a primary type of coordination.

Like binary complexes, multiple coordinate complexes allow both distributive and collective readings. For instance, (3.47a) is collective, (3.47b) is distributive, and (3.47c) is ambiguous between the two readings.

(3.47) a. John, Bill, and Tom collided.   (Dougherty 1970b: 855 (39b))
      b. John, Bill, and Tom knew the answer.
      c. Hobbs, Rhodes and Barnes lifted the rock.   (Borsley 2005)

One similarity between multiple coordinate complexes and the binary complexes discussed so far is that extraction from one or more conjuncts is possible. Examples like (3.48) are found in Lakoff (1986):

(3.48)   What did he go to the store, buy, load in his car, drive home and unload?

The extractability indicates that none of the conjuncts of multiple coordinate complexes is an adjunct. Thus we need to consider the following three analyses: the flat multiple-branching structure (Ross 1967: 88–92; Jackendoff 1977: 51, among many others) as in (3.49b), the multiple Spec structure as in (3.49c), and a layered complementation Downstairs-Twin-Structure, as in (3.49d) (see the &P-shell structure in Kayne 1994: 57; Zoerner 1995; and Johannessen 1998: 144).

(3.49) a. John Mary and Bill
      b.

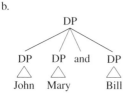

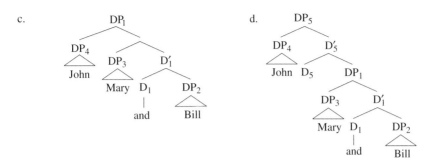

In this section, I argue against the flat structure analysis in (3.49b), and adopt Borsley's (2005) arguments against (3.49d). Consequently, (3.49c) is the only choice. The configuration in (3.49c) is also seen in other constructions cross-linguistically, and thus again does not create a coordination-specific configuration.

3.6.1   The coordinator must be grouped with an edge conjunct

My first argument against the flat structure is that the solitary coordinator in a multiple coordinate complex must be grouped with an edge conjunct. Dik (1968: 41, 58) makes the generalization that "if only one coordinator is present, its place is determined, generally, by the last member of the series," and "an almost universal rule puts the coordinator before or after the last member of the series."

(3.50) a. apples, oranges, and bananas
  b. *apples, and oranges, bananas
  c. *and apples, oranges, bananas
  d. I'd like it to be (*or) black, (or) white, or grey.
  e. Mary was fun to tease, easy to please, and known to have fleas.

(3.51) a. Yu, rou, gen shucai   dou yao chi.   (Chinese)
        fish meat and vegetable all   must eat
        'One must eat fish, meat and vegetables.'

  b. *Yu, gen rou,   shucai   dou yao   chi.
       fish and meat vegetable all   must eat

  c. *gen yu, rou,   shucai   dou yao   chi.
        and fish meat vegetable all   must eat

(3.52)   (I)   Marija, (i)   Milan, i   Petar studiraju lingvistiku.   (Serbo-Croatian)
            and   Mary   and Milan and Peter study   linguistics
            'Mary, Milan, and Peter are students of linguistics.'

   In (3.50a), which is cited from Dougherty (1970b: 853 (20)), the coordinator
and precedes the last conjunct. In (3.50b) and (3.50c), however, it does not,
and the two sentences are not acceptable. The same contrast is seen in other
examples in (3.50) and (3.51). The Serbo-Croatian example in (3.52) shows
that the first two occurrences of the coordinator *i* is optional, in the presence of
the last one. All of these data confirm that the last conjunct hosts the coordinator
in these languages.

3.6.2   *The category decisiveness of non-final conjuncts in English*
My second argument against the flat structure is that in English, all of the
non-final conjuncts determine the category of the whole coordinate complex. We saw in Section 3.3.1 that only the category of the final conjunct
is allowed to be different from the category of the whole coordinate complex
in English. Now we present the fact that this is also true in multiple coordinate
complexes.

(3.53) a. You can depend on my assistance, John's cooking skill, and that Mary will
            be on time.
        b. *You can depend on my assistance, that Mary will be on time, and John's
            cooking skill.
        c. *You can depend on that Mary will be on time, my assistance, and John's
            cooking skill.

   In (3.53a), the whole coordinate complex is selected by the preposition
on. In the complex, the first and second conjuncts are both DPs, which are
compatible with the c-selection of the preposition, whereas the last conjunct
is a clause, which is not compatible with the c-selection of the preposition.
However, the sentence is acceptable. If we change the order of the three conjuncts, as seen in (3.53b) and (3.53c), the resulting sentences become unacceptable. Therefore, in English, just as with two-conjunct complexes, the category of the non-final conjuncts determines the category of multiple coordinate
complexes.
   This and the previous subsection show the uniform behavior of all of the
non-final conjuncts in contrast to the final conjunct. The contrast falsifies the
multiple branching structure of (3.49b).

3.6.3   Borsley's arguments against the layered complementation in English
Borsley (2005) presents three arguments against the layered complementation
structure of multiple coordinate complexes in English, i.e. (3.49d). All of his
generalizations indicate that no two conjuncts form a maximal projection independent of the third conjunct. But grouping the last two conjuncts is represented
in (3.49c).

A.   The *both* argument
Generally, the word *both* can occur to the left of X in a non-collective coordinate
construction [X *and* Y]. If any two conjuncts of [A, B *and* C] could form a
constituent independent of the third conjunct, we would therefore expect the
strings [*both* A, B *and* C] and [A, *both* B *and* C] to be acceptable. However,
neither is acceptable:

(3.54) a. *Both John, Mary and Bill are asleep.   (Lasersohn 1995: 151)
       b. *The chicken was both cold, sour and expensive.   (Schwarzschild
          1996: 143)

(3.55) a. *John, both Mary and Bill are asleep.
       b. *The chicken was cold, both sour and expensive.

   In Lasersohn (1995: 151), the unacceptability of (3.54a) is captured by the
claim that among the three conjuncts, "no two of them form a coordinate
structure to the exclusion of the third." This is exactly the right description.

B.   The gapping argument
Generally, if two clauses are conjoined and have parallel structures and identical
verbs, the verb in the second clause may undergo gapping. Borsley cites the following example from McCawley (1988a: 269) to show that this generalization
does not hold of B and C in [A, B and C].

(3.56)   *Tom ate a hamburger, Alice drank a martini, and Jane a beer.

   If [A, B and C] had a structure of [A & [B&C]], we would expect that
gapping can apply to C alone, taking the verb of B as the antecedent. Such a
gapping should be possible within the cycle of [B & C], independently of A,
which occurs outside the cycle. However, the above sentence is not acceptable,
posing a problem for the [A & [B&C]] analysis.[8]

---

8 Note that if the verbs in three conjuncts are identical, the last one can be gapped (Heycock and
  Zamparelli 2000: (13b)):

C.   The distributivity argument

In addition to the above two syntactic arguments, Borsley (2005) presents a further semantic argument. Generally, [X and Y] may have a collective reading if the context allows. This is also true for multiple coordinate complexes. Thus (3.57) means either that each of the three persons lifted the rock independently, a distributive reading, or that they lifted the rock together, a collective reading.

(3.57)   Hobbs, Rhodes and Barnes lifted the rock.   (= (3.47c))

Note that if [H, R *and* B] had the structure [H & [R&B]], we would expect Rhodes and Barnes to form a group in lifting the rock, leaving Hobbs to do so independently. However, this sentence does not allow such a reading. Thus the constituency of [H & [R&B]] is unlikely.

Similar observations are made in Dougherty (1970b: 858 (61)–(63), 860 (83)) and Winter (2001: 65 (99); 2006: 6).[9]

The lack of a group meaning for any conjunct pair within multiple-conjunct complexes indicates that the multiple Spec structure in (3.49c) is right. In this structure, the top Specifier cannot be stranded, nor can the two Specs form a constituent, excluding the complement.

The same distributivity effect can also be seen in sentences with the distributive adverb *respectively*. Borsley describes the reading contrast between the following two sentences:

(3.58) a. The two girls were seen by Rhodes and Barnes, respectively.
        b. The two girls were seen by Hobbs, Rhodes and Barnes, respectively.

If [A, B *and* C] had the structure [A & [B&C]], we would expect the "matrix" Specifier-Complement relation between A and [B and C] to be in construal with the adverb *respectively*, as it is in (3.58a). If so, the coordination of [B *and* C] in

(i)   John wrote the first chapter, Mary wrote the second chapter, and Bill ~~wrote~~ the conclusion.

This fact might show the contrast between final and non-final conjuncts, but it does not show that the last two conjuncts may form a maximal projection.

9 Note that if *the rock* in (3.57) is changed into the bare plural *rocks*, as in (i), a new reading becomes possible: H and R lifted a rock (together) and R and B lifted another rock (together). This is possible if R lifted a rock with one hand with H, and lifted another rock with the other hand with B. See Winter (2001: 256) for discussion.

(i)   Hobbs, Rhodes and Barnes lifted rocks.

Since this is still a symmetrical collective reading, the complexity is not incompatible with the observation reported in the text.

(3.58b) could be collective. The intended meaning would be that one of the girls was seen by Hobbs alone, and the other girl was seen by Rhodes and Barnes together. However, Borsley points out that (3.58b) is semantically anomalous. The fact that [*Rhodes and Barnes*] does not allow a collective reading here again casts doubt on the assumed layered complementation structure in (3.49d). In a multiple Spec structure, no single Spec may take part in computation independently, and the cluster that excludes the outer Spec may not take part in any computation either. For more semantic arguments in support of Borsley's conclusion, see Winter (2006).

All of these syntactic and semantic arguments support the multiple Spec structure in (3.49c), as Borsley concludes at the end of his Section 3. Multiple Spec structure is independently supported by other constructions (e.g. Pesetsky 2000; Ura 2000; Collins 2002b), and poses no theoretical problems. "[T]o say that there are any number of specifiers is not an assumption, it's just to say you may continue to merge indefinitely: it merely states that language is a recursive system" (Chomsky 2002: 133). We thus once more reach the same conclusion as in Chapter 2:

> No SPECIAL CONFIGURATION EXISTS IN COORDINATION.

Multiple Spec structure is never required by any lexical item, and thus it is not obligatory. This accounts for Gazdar *et al.*'s (1985: 170) observation that no coordinator requires three or more conjuncts.

3.7   Chapter summary

We have presented cross-linguistic data to show that coordinators can c-select conjuncts. We have also shown that in coordinate complexes headed by *and*-like coordinators, the external conjunct determines the category of the whole coordinate complex. In order to account for this fact, we have proposed that the categorial feature is transferred from the external conjunct to the coordinator in a coordinate complex. Moreover, since coordinate complexes neither show a distribution other than that of the currently recognized categories, nor neutralize contrasts in the currently recognized categories, they cannot represent an independent category, thus arguing against the &P hypothesis. Furthermore, by showing that coordinate complexes can be any category, we have argued against the Clause Conjunct Hypothesis. Finally, based on the arguments in this and the previous chapter, we have argued that the structure of coordinate complexes composed of three conjuncts and one coordinator is a multiple Spec complementation structure.

The theoretical contribution made in this chapter is that unlike categories such as N and V, the notion "coordinator" is not primitive in syntactic computation. If coordinators do not have intrinsic categorial features, it is the conjuncts that provide the categorial features to them. We thus reach the second major conclusion of this book:

No special category exists in coordination.

III No special syntactic constraint

4 *The Conjunct Constraint and the lexical properties of coordinators*

4.1 Introduction

4.1.1 The CCi and CCe

The Coordinate Structure Constraint (CSC, Ross 1967: 89) states: "In a coordination structure, no conjunct may be moved, nor may any element contained in a conjunct be moved out of that conjunct." As emphasized by Postal (1998: 95), the CSC was intended as a linguistic universal. However, from a minimalist perspective it is implausible that the theory of syntax has, in addition to operations such as Merge and Remerge, which apply in the computational system in its constructive sense, construction-specific stipulations such as the CSC, which give special instructions where the normal operations cannot apply. Nevertheless, it seems that the CSC has remained relatively immune to reduction to other more general principles. The goal of this chapter is to reduce the CSC to other general principles.

The CSC contains two parts (Grosu 1972; 1973). The first part is that no conjunct may be moved, and the second part is that no element may be extracted from conjuncts. Following Grosu (1972), we call the first part the Conjunct Constraint (CC), and the second part the Element Constraint (EC). This chapter discusses the CC, and the next discusses the EC. CC effects are shown in (4.1) and (4.2).

(4.1) a. *John$_i$ seems to be [$_i$ and Mary] in the room.
   b. *Who$_i$ did John kiss [$_i$ and a girl]?
   c. *The speaker who$_i$ I watched [$_i$ and Bill] was vain.
   d. *[Go to the club]$_i$ John might [$_i$ and [have some fun]].
   e. *Can$_i$ you [$_i$ and will] stay at home?

(4.2) a. *Mary$_i$ seems to be [John and $_i$] in the room.
   b. *Who$_i$ did John kiss [a girl and $_i$]?
   c. *The speaker who$_i$ I watched [Bill and $_i$] was vain.
   d. *[Have some fun]$_i$ John might [[go to the club] and $_i$].
   e. *Will$_i$ you [can and $_i$] stay at home?

In each of the examples in (4.1), the first conjunct moves, and in each of the examples in (4.2), the second conjunct moves. The CC is violated in both groups of examples. The movement is an A-movement in (4.1/4.2a), interrogative wh-movement in (4.1/4.2b), relativization wh-movement in (4.1/4.2c), topicalization movement in (4.1/4.2d), and head movement in (4.1/4.2e).[1]

CC effects are also observed in languages other than English. In the following Norwegian examples, a conjunct of the coordinate object complex is raised in (4.3a), and a conjunct of the post-verbal coordinate subject complex is raised in (4.3b). Neither is acceptable (Johannessen 1998: 222). The unacceptability of raising the subject out of the Spanish coordinate complex in (4.4a) shows the same restriction (Zoerner 1995: 78 (25)).

(4.3) a. *Ola$_i$ så   jeg [Per og _$_i$].   (Norwegian)
      Ola saw I   Per and
      Intended: 'I saw Peter and Ola.'

   b. *Per$_i$ vasket   klaer   [Ola og _$_i$].
      Per washed clothes Ola and
      Intended: 'Ola and Peter washed clothes.'

(4.4) a. *Él$_i$ con   cuidado   [_$_i$ y ella] manejaron el   coche.   (Spanish)
      he with care   and she   drove   the car

   b. [Él y   ella] con   cuidado manejaron el   coche.
      he and she with care   drove   the car
      'He and she carefully drove the car.'

Postal (1998: 83) states: "The Conjunct Constraint is almost never questioned." Current research within the minimalist program has also kept silent about the CC.

I will argue that the CC should be split into the CCe, i.e., no external conjunct may move, and the CCi, i.e., no internal conjunct may move. The CCi means that no coordinators may be stranded. I therefore group coordinators with other types of elements that may not be stranded. As for the CCe, external conjuncts in complexes headed with coordinators like *and* cannot move because their categorial features have been transferred to the head, as argued

---

1 One needs to distinguish data like (4.1) from data like (i) and (ii), which are derived by PF deletion (Section 2.3.2).

   (i) John bought a book yesterday, and a newspaper.

   (ii) Welchen Knaben hat Hans geküsst und welches Mädchen?   [German]
       which   boy   has Hans kissed and which   girl

in Chapter 3. In short, it is the lexical/morphological properties of the specific type of coordinators that are responsible for the effects of the CC.

The organization of this chapter is as follows. I show the problems with current approaches to the CC in Section 4.1.2 and present my own analysis of the CCi and CCe in Section 4.1.3. Then in Section 4.2, I present the main argument for my new account of the CCi. My two arguments for the new account of the CCe are given in Sections 4.3 and 4.4. Section 4.5 is a brief summary.

4.1.2 *Previous approaches to the CC*

The CC has previously been analyzed as a unified syntactic constraint (Sag 1982; Pesetsky 1982; Pollard and Sag 1994; Zoerner 1995), semantic constraint (Johannessen 1998), phonological constraint (Merchant 2001), or as a consequence of the Parallelism Requirement (Napoli 1993).

A.   The CC as unified syntactic constraint

The A-over-A principle account   Sag (1982: 334) and Pesetsky (1982: 435) (see also Riemsdijk and Williams 1986: 20) claims that CC effects are accounted for by the so-called A-over-A principle. This approach claims that in (4.5), neither of the two lower NPs may be moved, since they are hosted by the upper NP.

(4.5)

$$
\begin{array}{c}
\text{NP} \\
\diagup \ \Big| \ \diagdown \\
\text{NP} \quad \text{and} \quad \text{NP}
\end{array}
$$

Let us examine the A-over-A principle itself. There are two versions of the principle. One version says that if a rule ambiguously refers to A in a structure of the form (4.6), the rule must apply to the higher, more inclusive, node A. This principle is claimed to prevent extraction of the NP *Africa* out of the NP *my trip to Africa* in which it is included in (4.7a) (Chomsky 1964; Ross 1967).

(4.6) $\ldots [_A \ldots [_A \ldots$

(4.7) a. I won't forget [$_{NP}$ my trip to [$_{NP}$ Africa]]
      b. *Africa, I won't forget my trip to.
      c. My trip to Africa, I won't forget.

Chomsky (1964) points out several potential counterexamples to the A-over-A principle:

(4.8) a.   Who would you approve of my seeing?
     b.   What are you uncertain about giving to John?
     c.   What would you be surprised by his reading?

In (4.8a), for instance, the nominal *who* moves out of the nominal *my seeing who*. Data like (4.9) also show that the principle is too strong. The extraction of the DP *that book* is possible, although it is contained in the DP *five reviews of that book*.

(4.9)   That book, they published [$_{DP}$ five reviews of _].   (Gazdar *et al.* 1985: 148)

Since this version of the A-over-A principle is empirically inadequate, I do not think its application to the CC can be justified. Some effects of the principle can be covered by other constraints. The acceptability of (4.8) and (4.9), for instance, can be captured by Kuno's (1987) topichood analysis of extraction, or by Davies and Dubinsky's (2003) semantic condition for extraction from nominals. Davies and Dubinsky claim that extraction from unambiguous process nominals, such as (4.8), is generally possible, and extraction from representational nouns, such as (4.9), is possible when the verb is a verb of creation or a verb of use (e.g. *write, edit, publish*), but not with a verb like *destroy*:

(4.10)   *Who did they destroy a book about?   (Davies and Dubinsky 2003: 3)

Another version of the principle says that if a rule ambiguously refers to A in a structure of the form of (4.6), the rule must apply to the IMMEDIATELY higher, more inclusive, node A. The following examples may show the principle (Sag 1982: 334):

(4.11) a.   Fido jumped [$_{PP}$ from [$_{PP}$ under [$_{DP}$ the table]]].
     b.   Fido ran [$_{PP}$ out [$_{PP}$ into [$_{DP}$ the meadow]]].

(4.12) a.   From under which table did Fido jump _?
     b.   Out into which meadow did Fido run _?

(4.13) a.   Which table did Fido jump from under _?
     b.   Which meadow did Fido run out into _?

(4.14) a.   *Under which table did Fido jump from _?
     b.   *Into which meadow did Fido run out _?

The two sentences in (4.11) are canonical forms. In (4.12a,b), the matrix PP has undergone a wh-movement. Since in (4.12) the wh-movement applies to the matrix PP rather than the embedded PP, the A-over-A principle is not violated. In (4.13a), the moved wh-phrase is a DP, rather than PP. Similarly, in (4.13b), the moved wh-phrase is a DP. The A-over-A principle does not apply to (4.13), since the trace of the wh-DP is not immediately dominated by another DP. Instead, it is immediately dominated by the PP headed by *under* or *into*. In (4.14a), however, the trace of the PP *under which table* is immediately dominated by another PP, which is headed by *from*. In this case, the A-over-A principle is violated. Similarly, in (4.14b), the trace of *into which meadow* is immediately dominated by another PP, which is headed by *out*, and again the A-over-A principle is violated. Sag claims that the unacceptability of the two sentences in (4.14) is captured by the A-over-A principle.

Like the former version, however, this alternative version of the A-over-A principle is also empirically inadequate. First, it cannot explain quantifier floating (Sportiche 1988). It is generally assumed, as shown in (4.15a), that the quantifier *all* is a D-element, takes a DP complement, and projects another DP. In quantifier floating constructions, the DP complement of *all* is raised out of the hosting DP (see Adger 2003: 263 for a summary; also see Fitzpatrick 2006 for more discussion of quantifier floating).

(4.15)   a.   b.

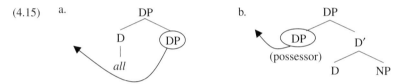

Second, the possibility of possessor DP raising out of possessive DP, as illustrated in (4.15b) (Szabolcsi 1983; 1994; Landau 1999; among others), indicates that the principle is too strong to rule in such acceptable movement of Spec elements.

Since the A-over-A principle is not a valid principle with respect to movement of either complements or Spec elements, it cannot be used to account for CC effects.

The trace subcategorization account   Pollard and Sag (1994: 201) claim that under virtually any assumptions about the nature of coordinate structures, it is the mother of the coordinate structure that is (strictly) subcategorized, not the individual conjuncts. Since a conjunct is never subcategorized for, it can never be realized as a trace, following their Trace Principle, which states that "Every trace must be subcategorized by a substantive head" (p. 172). However, the movement illustrated in (4.15b) is wrongly ruled out in this account, since it is the top DP rather than the possessor DP that is subcategorized by a head. Moreover, the account is not able to explain the contrast between *Can and will* *you stay at home* and *$^*Can_i$ you [t_i and will] stay at home*, a contrast that has nothing to do with subcategorization.

Sag (2000: 8) claims that the CC can be accounted for by the assumptions that wh-traces are not syntactic constituents and that conjuncts must be syntactic constituents. His claim might cover (4.1b) and (4.2b), but it cannot cover the other data in (4.1) and (4.2), where no wh-conjunct appears. Thus the CC seems to have nothing to do with the status of wh-traces.

The Minimal Link Condition account   Zoerner (1995: 75ff.) proposes that CC effects can be covered by the Minimal Link Condition, since he assumes that an attracting feature external to a coordinate complex never looks as low in the structure as the conjunct, but instead sees the feature on the &P node and stops its search there. This proposal is too strong. If coordinate complexes have a complementation structure, as he also argues, then conjuncts are Spec and Complement elements. Empirically, raising of Spec elements and Complement elements is possible in general, as seen in (4.15), so why would it be blocked specifically in coordinate complexes? Theoretically, the assumed &P does not c-command either conjunct, and thus the Minimal Link Condition is not relevant here.[2]

B.   A semantic approach

Johannessen (1998: 235) proposes a semantic account for the fact that the EC can be violated (see Grosu 1973, and my Section 2.3.4 and Chapter 5) while the CC cannot:

> When something is extracted a special relationship is triggered between two elements. However, when a whole conjunct is extracted, there are no longer two available elements between which such a relationship could exist, and extraction must be ruled out. Thus the semantic factors not only constrain extraction of parts of conjuncts, but constrain extraction of whole conjuncts – to such an extent that the latter is not possible.

However, according to this semantic approach, any movement at all will cause an element to be away from its merger position, where it is integrated into the structure semantically, and thus will give rise to the same semantic problem claimed by Johannessen to be caused by CSC violations. Consider possessor raising. If the possessor is moved away from the possessed nominal,

---

2 Goodall (1987) proposes an account for the CC in terms of Principle C of the binding theory. Obviously, his effort does not consider non-nominal conjuncts, and thus it still needs another account for such conjuncts. See Sag (2000: 6) for arguments against Goodall's proposal.

does that mean the semantic relation between the two is lost? Also, in data like *What kind of beer does John normally drink*, the verb *drink* s-selects the liquid-denoting *what kind of beer*. When the latter moves, does that mean the semantic selection is lost? Since this semantic approach is not plausible, it cannot be used to account for CC effects.

C. A phonological approach

Grosu (1981: 56) proposes a Null Conjunct Constraint (NCC), which states that conjuncts may not be phonologically null. Merchant (2001) claims that the CC can be covered by the NCC. In Merchant's approach, the CC is related to PF. Considering the cases of null external conjuncts (conjunct-drop) to be presented in Section 4.2, we do not think that the NCC is applicable to external conjuncts. Null internal conjuncts, however, are indeed not seen. Thus the NCC can explain CCi effects, as will be discussed in Section 4.2.

D. A Parallelism Requirement approach

Napoli (1993: 409) speculates that the CC might be the result of a Parallelism Requirement. However, in the presence of *and*, the CC cannot be the result of the Parallelism Requirement, since this constraint can be satisfied by moving both conjuncts, and yet the resulting coordinate complex is still unaccept-able. Here are some unacceptable examples of the Across-the-Board type of dependency:

(4.16) a. *Which books did Bob read [_ and _]?
      b. *I wonder who you saw [_ and _]?   (Gazdar *et al.* 1985: 178)
      c. *The Pre-Raphaelites, we found [_ and _].   (Sag 1982: 332)

Similarly, Russian allows multiple wh-movement, but wh-movement of both conjuncts is impossible:

(4.17)   *[kokogo mal'čika]$_i$ [kakuju devočku]$_j$ ty l'ubiš' [$_i$ i $_j$]?
       which boy   which girl   you love   and

In the above discussion, I have shown that none of the unified approaches to the CC, whether syntactic, semantic, phonological, or parallelism-based, reveals the true nature of the CC. Since no satisfactory account for the CC is available, I pursue my own account in the following sections.

4.1.3 A new account of the CC

In this section I give brief introductions to my accounts of the CCi and the CCe, as background for the fuller arguments in Sections 4.2–4.4.

A.   The CCi: certain head elements need an overt complement

CCi effects in the presence of *and* are well established, as seen in (4.2). As an explanation of them, I propose that internal conjuncts may not move in the presence of a coordinator because, like certain other head elements, coordinators may not have silent complements. Thus, internal conjuncts may not be silent, regardless of whether the silence is caused by movement or deletion.

The fact that certain head elements do not allow their complements to be silent is seen from observations like the following. For instance, the complementizer *that* cannot be stranded (data from Adger 2003: 290; see Abels 2003: 116 for parallel examples in French and Icelandic):

(4.18) a. Everyone claimed [that the poison was neutralized].
       b. ?[That the poison was neutralized] was claimed by everyone.
       c. *[The poison was neutralized] was claimed that by everyone.
       d. It was claimed by everyone [that the poison was neutralized].
       e. *It was claimed that by everyone [the poison was neutralized].

The complementizer *for* also cannot be stranded (Law 2002: 84, among others):

(4.19)   *[John to leave]$_i$ is impossible [$_{CP}$[for t$_i$]]

Although Chinese transitive verbs in general may be stranded, as seen in (4.20a), causative verbs or particles such as *shi, rang, jiao, ba* 'cause, make' may never be stranded, as shown in (4.20b).

(4.20) a. Baoyu xiwang shang daxue,   Daiyu ye   xiwang.
          Baoyu hope   go   university Daiyu also hope
          'Baoyu hopes to go to a university, so does Daiyu.'

       b. *Zhe jian shi   rang   wo hen nankan,   na   jian shi   ye   rang.
          this CL   matter make I   very embarrassed that CL   matter also make
          Intended: 'This matter embarrassed me, so did that matter.'

Similarly, articles such as *the* in English are never stranded, nor are degree elements such as *feichang* 'very' in Chinese, nor are prepositions in many languages including Chinese.[3]

---

3 Various analyses have been proposed to account for why complementizers may not be stranded (e.g. Webelhuth 1989; Saito and Murasugi 1999; Wurmbrand 2001; Abels 2003). It is not true that head elements may be stranded only when the Spec position is filled (Lobeck 1990). Preposition stranding is possible in English, but not in languages such as Chinese, regardless of whether the Spec of P is filled.

It is thus possible that coordinators have the same property. They neither license movement of their complements, nor allow their complements to be deleted at PF. I will argue for this proposed account of the CCi in Section 4.2.

B.   The CCe: categorical features are carriers of overt movement
Regarding the CCe, I claim that external conjuncts cannot move in the presence of *and* because the categorical features of the former have been transferred to the latter (see Chapter 3).

The theoretical background for this claim on the CCe is the following. Any element that undergoes overt movement must have categorical features. In Chomsky (1995: 265; see also Ochi 1999: 90), all overt movement chains are composed of two sub-chains: a chain of formal features that take part in the required checking (CH <FF>) and a chain of categorical features (CH <CAT>). The latter chain does not involve feature checking, but it is simply the carrier of the former chain. In Chomsky's terms, overt formal feature movement is always pied-piped with a categorical chain. This implies that in the absence of categorical features, no overt movement is possible. If the categorical features of the external conjunct have been transferred away, the conjunct cannot move anymore, since the carrier is gone.

One might respond that in the copy theory of movement, a lower copy remains after the movement, and thus if categorical features move from external conjuncts, they still remain as a lower copy, before any deletion. However, as argued in Zhang (2004a) and asserted in Chomsky (2008: fn. 16), movement does not create a new copy of the moved element. Instead, it is simply an operation of Remerge. From a derivational perspective, I assume that when x is remerged in a new syntactic position, it disappears in its old position, syntactically (I make no claim about the PF representations). For instance, in (4.21), the [NEG] feature disappears in the possessor nominal after it is transferred to the sentential level (see Section 3.3.1A). This deletion is attested by the fact that the sentence does not have a double negation reading.

(4.21)   Nobody's car would I borrow.   [NEG feature percolation]

I claim that movement itself can be defined as Remerge at the new position and unmerge at the old position syntactically. Therefore, there is no syntactic (as opposed to PF) operation of deletion or unmerge that is independent of movement.

I will present two arguments for this analysis of the CCe in Sections 4.3 and 4.4.

4.2 The CCi and the asymmetry in conjunct drop

It is possible for one conjunct to be silent when its meaning is recoverable from the linguistic or discourse context. I call this silence of conjuncts a "conjunct-drop" effect. I claim that in the presence of an overt coordinator, the internal conjunct, which is the complement of the coordinator, may not be silent. Therefore internal conjuncts may not move, stranding the coordinator. The main argument for my new approach to the CCi is the asymmetry between external and internal conjuncts in conjunct drop.

4.2.1 Conjunct drop in right-branching coordinate complexes

In Chapter 2, we saw that coordinate complexes have a right-branching binary structure in languages such as English and Chinese. In such complexes, external conjuncts may be null, but internal conjuncts may not be. In (4.22), for instance, the speaker directly starts the sentence with the coordinator *and* (Hankamer and Sag 1976: 410).

(4.22) [Observing Ivan playing pretty good ragtime piano]
        And he doesn't have a left hand!

A coordinator used in such a way is called a discourse-initial or utterance-initial coordinator (Hankamer and Sag 1976: 410; see also Huttar 2003). Hankamer and Sag (1976: 411) state: "It seems that such cases involve essentially pragmatic omission of an understood left conjunct." Similarly, in (4.23), the last sentence starts with *and*, with the meaning of the first conjunct implied in the previous sentence (one can find Chinese data parallel to (4.22) and (4.23) in Shi 1986: Section 2.3; Shao and Rao 1985: 6 also discuss contextual or discourse conjuncts in Chinese).

(4.23) "It's time to put sentiment aside," announced *New York Times* columnist
        Nicholas Kristof one day last month. And who can disagree?   (Michael
        Kinsley, *The Washington Post,* Sept. 14, 2002)

By contrast, silent second (internal) conjuncts do not seem to be possible. Although we use the elided expression "And you?" we do not say "You and?" Moreover, the examples in (4.24b) and (4.25b) show that coordinator-final clusters are totally unacceptable when used alone. Note that the negation encoded by *not* scopes over the whole coordinate complex in each case, parallel to the corresponding a-sentences. The a-sentences are cited from Postal (1998: 87) and Lawler (1974: 370) (for a semantic description of the construction, see Goldsmith 1985: 141).

(4.24) a. Can linguists [study negation]? Not e and stay sane they can't.
       b. *Can linguists [stay sane]? Not <u>study negation and</u> e they can't.

(4.25) a. Can I [go outside without any clothes on]? Not e and stay healthy, you can't.
       b. *Can I [stay healthy]? Not <u>go outside without any clothes on and</u> e, you can't.

The contrast in acceptability between the a-sentences and the b-sentences in these examples indicates that the combination of the first conjunct and the coordinator cannot function independently of the second conjunct.

Similarly, as pointed out by Borsley (1994: 240), a parenthesis can be a combination of a coordinator and a following conjunct, as in (4.26a). It is obvious that a parenthesis may not be a combination of a coordinator and a preceding conjunct, as in (4.26b).

(4.26) a. The professor, <u>and he is an expert</u>, thinks the recession will continue.
       b. *The professor, <u>he thinks the recession will continue and</u>, is an expert.

Similar patterns are found in other languages which have right-branching coordinate complexes. In Irish, the external (i.e. first) conjunct may be a pro while the internal (i.e. second) conjunct can never be a pro (McCloskey and Hale 1984; McCloskey 1986). In Chinese, as we have seen in (4.20a), a transitive verb can end a clause, with the meaning of the implied object recoverable from the context. Regardless of how such sentences are derived (pro object, deletion of the object, or VP deletion after raising of the verb), the surface order of (4.20a) is verb-final. Unlike verbs, however, coordinators in Chinese cannot stand alone, that is, without an internal conjunct to their right.

The above facts from various languages all show that coordinators must be adjacent to their internal conjuncts.

4.2.2 *Conjunct drop in left-branching coordinate complexes*

In contrast to *and*-like coordinators, which require an overt final conjunct, in Japanese, the conjunctions *-shi* and *-to* and the disjunction *-toka* require an overt initial conjunct. The structure of coordinate complexes headed by these coordinators is left-branching (Munn 1987; Zoerner 1995: 11; also our 2.2.3), making the initial conjunct the complement of the coordinator, and thus the internal conjunct. Consistent with our analysis of the CCi, then, it is the final, or external, conjunct that need not be overt. Hinds (1986: 93) describes the relevant facts as follows. "For each of the types of coordination – *and, but*, and *or* – there is a sentence type in which the coordinator ends the utterance. While there may be a feeling of lack of closure, this feeling is not necessarily there at all times." He presents both types of examples. For the first type illustrated in (4.27), he uses three dots at the end to show the lack of closure:

(4.27) a. Kyoo-wa   atsui-shi, ...   (Hinds 1986: 86)
           today-TOP hot-and

           'It's hot today, and (moreover) ... '

       b. Kyooto-e-wa   ikanai-shi, ...
          Kyoto-to-TOP go.not-and
          '[I]'m not going to go to Kyoto, and (moreover) ... '

For the second type, Hinds notes that in (4.28a) (= his (318) on p. 93) "the first sentence ends in falling intonation. The second sentence is reproduced so the reader can see that it is not a continuation of the first sentence." (QT = quotative morpheme) Similarly, in (4.28b) (= his (319) on p. 93), "the coordinator *toka* appears with falling intonation in answer to a question."

(4.28) a. Nihon kaet-te   ojisan ii   tsut-tara unten suru kamoshirenai shi.
          Japan return-when uncle OK QT-say-if drive do   probably   and

          Nihon konde-ru kara   wakannai.
          Japan crowded since know-NEG
          'When [I] return to Japan if my uncle says it's OK [I]'ll probably drive, and. Japan's crowded, so [I] don't know.'

       b. Tatoeba ojiichan-ga   shi- shinda toki toka.
          e.g.   grandfather-NOM   died   time or
          'The time Grandfather died, or.'

The following data (Zoerner 1995: 33) further show that unlike English, Japanese does not allow the first conjunct to be contextual or implied in the discourse.

(4.29) a. A: Robin ate   fish.   B: And rice!
       b. A: Robin-wa   sakana-o tabeta. B: *to   gohan!
          Robin-TOP fish-ACC   ate   and rice

Since the *-to* and *-shi* coordinate complexes in Japanese are left-branching, final conjuncts are external conjuncts. As in the last subsection, all of the data in this subsection show that external conjuncts can be silent whereas internal ones cannot.

4.2.3   Clause-final coordinator-like elements

In the above two subsections, I have shown that coordinators require the presence of internal conjuncts. In this subsection I show that although certain coordinator-like elements can appear clause-finally in certain languages, they have different formal properties from regular coordinators. Thus their existence does not challenge the generalization that coordinators may not be stranded.

In German, the word *oder* 'or' can occur at the end of a root sentence, building a yes–no question. The *oder*-final sentences are always uttered with a rising intonation. Speakers of such sentences expect a confirmation. Thus the function of this *oder* is similar to that of *Isn't it?* in English (André Meinunger and Hans-Martin Gärtner, p.c.) or question markers in Chinese. In some dialects, the counterpart of *oder* in this usage does not share its form with any disjunction (André Meinunger, p.c.). The Norwegian sentence-final *eller* 'or' has the parallel function, as pointed out by an anonymous reviewer of *Studia Linguistica*.

Another case in which questions are introduced by a sentence-final coordinator-like element is the German expression *Na und? 'So what?'*

Similarly, *-oo* in Malayalam occurs either as a disjunctive, as in (4.30a), or as a sentence-final particle, as in (4.30b):

(4.30) a. John-oo Bill-oo Peter-oo   (Jayaseelan 2001: 64)
            John-or   Bill-or   Peter-or
            'John or Bill or Peter'

        b. John wannu-(w)oo?   (Jayaseelan 2001: 67)
            John came-or
            'Did John come?'

Paralel Sinhala and Japanese data can be found in Jayaseelan (2008: 3) and Hagstrom (1998). As correctly pointed out by Jayaseelan (2008: 3), the disjunctive-like element at the clause-edge position "cannot be a disjunctive connective, since it does not connect anything." Following Hagstrom (1998) and Jayaseelan (2001: 70), I treat the sentence-final coordinator-like elements in these languages as clause-typing particles base-generated in the C-domain. By contrast, regular coordinators do not introduce any clause-typing information. Therefore, I do not think data like (4.30) affect the generalization that coordinators require overt internal conjuncts.

In this section I argued that CCi effects are covered by a general surface constraint disallowing certain head elements from being stranded. In this approach, CCi effects are not caused by any construction-specific syntactic constraint, but instead they are syntax – phonological interface effects that also affect certain other types of head elements. The phonological side of the constraint rules out any representations in which the complement of the elements is a trace or is affected by deletion, while the sensitivity of the requirement to the part of speech of the head elements reveals a morphosyntactic side of CCi effects. For instance, the complementizer *that* does not allow a null complement, whereas prepositions such as *with* and *of* do (as in (4.9)). Consequently, we do not consider the CCi to be a purely syntactic constraint specific to coordinate constructions.

4.3   The CCe and the Chinese *de* constructions

We have seen that external conjuncts can be null in Section 4.2. Thus the CCe cannot be a phonological constraint. I have proposed instead that external conjuncts cannot move in the presence of *and*, because the categorial features of the former have been transferred to the latter.

My arguments for this new account of the CCe come from two sources. (A) When categorial transference occurs in other constructions, the categorial feature-providing elements may not move. In other words, CCe-like effects are attested independently of coordinate constructions. (B) If coordinators have their own intrinsic categorial features, the CCe may be violated, since external conjuncts do not transfer their categorial features away and thus are able to move by pied-piping on the categorial feature chain. In other words, CCe effects are predictably absent in certain types of coordinate constructions. I will present argument A in this section, and argument B in Section 4.4.

In Mandarin Chinese, *de* is a bound form (an enclitic, according to C. R. Huang 1989). It is phonologically weak (it has an intrinsic neutral tone, which means that the syllable is short and cannot bear any stress), and is attached to an element to its left. It occurs between a modifier and the modified element, as in (4.31a), or between a relational noun and its semantic licensor, as in (4.31b), or between a noun and its complement, as in (4.31c).

(4.31) a. [honghong] de   pingguo
     red   DE   apple
     'red apple(s)'

   b. [Lulu] de   linju
     Lulu DE   neighbor
     'Lulu's neighbor'

   c. [jintian dizhen]   de   yaoyan
     today earthquake DE   rumor
     'the rumor that there's an earthquake today'

In Li and Thompson (1981), *de* is called associative marker, since it occurs between two elements that have a certain semantic relationship.[4] The term associative marker is abstract enough to cover the various semantic relations between the two linked elements. The modified element in (4.31a), the relational noun in (4.31b), and the Head noun in (4.31c) are the semantic kernel of the complex nominal. I thus call them kernel elements. The non-kernel element of a *de* construction functions as a major constituent of the kernel element.[5] In the examples discussed in this section, the underlined part is the kernel element and the part in brackets is the non-kernel element.

In this section, I first distinguish two types of associative markers in Mandarin Chinese (both pronounced *de*), one that occurs in kernel-final constructions and one that occurs in kernel-initial constructions (Section 4.3.1). Then I present data to show that the *de* of the former type occurs with kernel elements of various categories (Section 4.3.2), argue that *de* heads the whole complex containing the kernel and non-kernel elements (Section 4.3.3), and finally report that in such constructions, kernel elements may not move (Section 4.3.4). If *de* is indeed the head of the whole complex, the fact that it occurs with kernel elements of different categories shows that it must get its categorial features from the kernel element. Therefore, the immobility of the kernel elements supports my claim that transferring the categorial features away from an element blocks it from moving (Section 4.1.3B).

4.3.1   *Two kinds of* de *constructions*

De may follow a modifier, as in (4.32a), forming a kernel-final construction. It may also precede a modifier, as in (4.32b), forming a kernel-initial construction.

---

4 I do not discuss other uses of *de*, such as in resultative constructions, in the *shi . . . de* 'be . . . DE' constructions, and in nominalization. I assume that the particle *de* in such constructions is different from the associative marker discussed here.

5 The notion of major constituent is borrowed from Hankamer (1973: 18). A major constituent is the modifier, complement, or subject of a certain element. Its existence has been attested at least in gapping constructions: the remnants of a gapping operation must be major constituents (Hankamer 1973: 18; Neijt 1979: 40, 111). Note that if both of the internal and the external argument of a nominal precede the nominal, in addition to *de*, the preposition *dui* 'to' occurs to the left of the internal argument (see Fu 1994: Chapter 4 and Saito *et al.* 2008: 257):

(i) Manzu   de   *(dui) Luoma de   huimie
    Barbarian DE   to   Rome   DE   destruction
    'the barbarians' destruction of Rome'

(4.32) a. Baoyu zai [hen kuai] de <u>langdu</u>.   (kernel-final)
       Baoyu PRG very fast   DE read.aloud
       'Baoyu is reading (something) aloud fast.'

    b. Baoyu <u>langdu</u>   de [hen kuai].   (kernel-initial)
       Baoyu read.aloud DE very fast
       'Baoyu read (something) aloud fast.'

These two constructions are different in at least two respects. First, in kernel-final constructions the phonological host of *de* may be a phrase, such as *hen kuai* 'very fast' in (4.32a), whereas in kernel-initial constructions it must be a head element, such as *langdu* 'read aloud' in (4.32b) (Tang 1990: 431). Data like the following show that *de* may not follow a phrase in kernel-initial constructions:

(4.33)   *Baoyu <u>langdu</u>   <u>na</u> pian wenzhang de [hen kuai].   (kernel-initial)
       Baoyu read.aloud that CL paper   DE very fast
       Intended: 'Baoyu read that paper aloud fast.'

Since the categorial levels of the phonological hosts of the *de*s in the two constructions are different, I claim that they are different kinds of bound forms, following Tang (1990: 431).

Second, the kernel element must be verbal in kernel-initial constructions, whereas it can be other categories in kernel-final constructions. We have seen the verbal kernel element *langdu* 'read aloud' in (4.32). The following examples show that the kernel element can be a noun in kernel-final constructions (also (4.31)), but not in kernel-initial constructions.[6]

(4.34) a. [hen shangxin] de <u>xuesheng</u>   (kernel-final)
       very sad   DE student
       'very sad students'

    b. *<u>xuesheng</u> de [hen shangxin]   (kernel-initial)
       student   DE very sad

We can see that *de* is similar to coordinators in that they both occur with two syntactic constituents.[7] Specifically, the *de* in kernel-final constructions is

---

6 In writing, many people use different characters to distinguish the associative marker that precedes a nominal kernel element (的), as in (4.31), (4.34a), from the one that precedes a verbal kernel element (地), as in (4.32a), and from the one that occurs in kernel-initial constructions (得), as in (4.32b). However, the standard grammar books (e.g. Chao 1968; Zhu 1984) do not make this distinction.

7 Unlike Rebuschi (2005) and Y. A. Li (2007), I do not claim that *de* and conjunctions are semantically similar. A complex composed of a conjunction and two singular conjuncts can

similar to the English coordinator *and* in that they both occur in complexes of different categories, whereas the *de* in kernel-initial constructions is similar to the Chinese coordinator *erqie*, as in (4.35), in that neither may occur in complexes of non-verbal categories.

(4.35)   Wo renshi [yi ge xiaoshuojia {he/*erqie} yi   ge yinyuejia].
        I   know   one CL novelist   and/and   one CL musician
        'I know a novelist and a musician.'

    In the following subsections I focus on the *and*-like *de* of kernel-final constructions.

4.3.2   The various categories of kernel-final constructions

De in kernel-final constructions in Mandarin Chinese exhibits two major properties.

    First, *de* may occur with non-kernel elements of various types.

(4.36) a. [lao] de <u>jiaoshou</u>
          old   DE professor
          'old professor(s)'

          b. [wu-li]   de <u>jiaoshou</u>
              room-in DE professor
              'the professor(s) in the room'

        c. [yiqian] de <u>jiaoshou</u>
          past   DE professor
          'professor(s) of the old days'

          d. [women] de <u>jiaoshou</u>
               1PL   DE professor
              'our professor(s)'

        e. [yan malu] de <u>shangdian</u>
          along street DE shop
          'the shops along the street'

          f. [dui   zongjiao] de <u>taidu</u>
              toward religion   DE attitude
              'the attitude towards religions'

        g. [zuotian lai] de <u>jiaoshou</u>
          yesterday come DE professor
          'the professor that came yesterday'

          h. [zuotian lai]   de Li Jiaoshou
              yesterday come DE Li professor
               'Professor Li, who came yesterday'

        i. [qita] de <u>jiaoshou</u>
          rest   DE professor
          'other professors'

          j. [suowei] de <u>jiaoshou</u>
            so-called DE professor
            'so-called professor(s)'

---

satisfy the plurality requirement of collective verbs or predicates, but a complex composed of *de* and two singular nominals may not, as seen in (i).

(i) Lulu hebing-le   {wenjian jia he   wenjia yi / *wenjian jia de wejian yi}.
    Lulu combine-PRF file   A   and file   B   file   A   DE file   B
    'Lulu combined {file A and file B / * file B of file A}.'

The non-kernel element is an adjective in (4.36a), a locative nominal in (4.36b), a temporal nominal in (4.36c), a personal pronoun in (4.36d), a prepositional phrase in (4.36e) and (4.36f), a relative clause in (4.36g), a non-restrictive relative clause in (4.36h), and a non-predicative adjective in (4.36i) and (4.36j). These various categories of the non-kernel elements have no impact on the category of the whole complexes. All of the examples in (4.36) are nominals.

In these examples, *de* plays no role in deciding the category of the complexes, either. Kitagawa and Ross (1982) use the following rule to capture this fact, analyzing *de* as a general modifying marker (Mod):

(4.37)   Mod Insertion: $[_{NP} \ldots XP\, N^{\alpha}] \rightarrow [_{NP} \ldots XP\, Mod\, N^{\alpha}]$, where Mod $= de$

Second, *de* may occur with kernel elements of various categories (Tang 1990: 421). We have seen that the kernel elements in (4.36) are nominal, whereas those in (4.32) above are not. More data are shown in (4.38), with the kernel elements underlined.

(4.38) a. Na   ge   [hen deyi]   de   <u>xiaohai</u> ling-le   jiang.   NP
           that CL   very proud   DE   kid   receive-PRF award
           'That proud kid received the award.'

       b. Na   ge   xiaohai   [hen deyi]   de   <u>ling-le</u>   <u>jiang</u>.   VP
           that CL   kid   very proud   DE   receive-PRF   award
           'That kid received the award very proudly.'

       c. Na   tian wanshang ta   [tebie]   de   <u>xingfen</u>.   AP
           that day   evening   he   especially   DE   excited
           'That evening, he was especially excited.'

       d. [Diu-le   qianbao]   de   <u>ta</u>   hen   zhaoji.   Pronoun
           lost-PRF wallet   DE   he   very   worried
           'He, who has lost his wallet, was very worried.'

       e. [Diu-le   qianbao]   de   <u>Baoyu</u>   hen   zhaoji.   Proper name
           lost-PRF wallet   DE   Baoyu   very   worried
           'Baoyu, who has lost his wallet, was very worried.'

The kernel element is the nominal *xiaohai* 'kid' in (4.38a), the eventive predicate (verbal) *ling-le jiang* 'received the award' in (4.38b), the stative predicate (adjectival) *xingfen* 'excited' in (4.38c), the pronoun *ta* 'he' in (4.38d), and the proper name *Baoyu* in (4.38e). *De* occurs in all of these kernel-final constructions.[8]

---

8 Proper names and pronouns can be modified by adjectives or relative clauses in Chinese, a
  language that has no articles. Like the adjective *charitable* in *the charitable Miss Murray*, the

In the two kernel-final examples in (4.39), the non-kernel element is the same, *hen kuaile* 'very happy.' However, the kernel element is the nominal *xuesheng* 'student' in (4.39a), but the verbal *qian-le zi* "signed the name" in (4.39b).

(4.39) a. Wo   kanjian-le   yi   ge   [hen kuaile]   de   xuesheng.
         I   see-PRF   one   CL   very happy   DE   student
         'I saw a very happy student.'

      b. Na   ge   xuesheng   [hen kuaile]   de   qian-le   zi.
         that CL   student   very happy   DE   sign-PRF   name
         'That student signed {his/her} name very happily.'

Considering a wide range of such data, Tang (1990: 424) states "all the occurrences of *de* in question have the same behavior in that they do not carry any specific semantic content but express a modifier/modifiee relation. It does not appear to be the case that these *des* are of different sorts." She proposes that *de* is a functional head in all of these constructions.

We have mentioned that the *de* in kernel-final constructions is similar to the English coordinator *and*. The two constituents linked by these elements can be any category. However, for *and*-coordinate constructions, it is the left (i.e. external) conjunct that determines the category of the whole complex, whereas for *de*-constructions, it is the right (i.e. kernel) element that determines the category of the whole complex.[9]

(4.40) a. [$_{XP}$ [$^{\text{ext.conjunct}}$ XP] *and* [$^{\text{int.conjunct}}$ YP]]   b. [$_{YP}$ [$^{\text{non-kernel}}$XP] *de* [^{kernel}YP]]

4.3.3   De *as the head of the whole complex*
The goal of this subsection is to show that like coordinators, *de* is the head of the whole complex. Many scholars have assumed that *de* is grouped with the modifier (non-kernel), and the combination of the modifier and *de* functions

---

modifiers of proper names and pronouns are always non-restrictive in Chinese (J.-W. Lin 2003). They can be either eventive, as in (4.35h), or stative, as in (i).

(i)   Bu   yuan   fa-pang   de   ni   yinggai   duo   yundong.
         not   want   get-fat   DE   you   should   more   exercise
         'You, who do not want to get fat, should do more exercise.'

9 Other elements of the same form may also be distinguished with respect to whether they have intrinsic categorial features. For instance, corrective *but* heads clausal coordinate complexes only, and contrastive *but* heads coordinate complexes of various categories (see footnote 5, Chapter 3). Also, the aspectual *come* and *go* are syntactically different from the lexical *come* and *go* (Jaeggli and Hyams 1993). In Aboh (2009), it is argued that in many serializing languages, the functional and lexical verbs have the same morphological form. Elements of the same form may also be distinguished with respect to whether they have other intrinsic formal features (see the two types of bound pronouns discussed by Kratzer (2009)).

as an adjunct of the kernel element, as shown in (4.41a). For these scholars, then, *de* is not the head of the whole complex, and thus there is no structural parallelism between (4.40a) and (4.40b) above. In this subsection, I argue against this assumption and argue for the structure in (4.41b) for kernel-final constructions. In this structure, *de* is the head, taking the non-kernel element (XP) as its specifier and the kernel element (YP_1) as its complement.

(4.41)

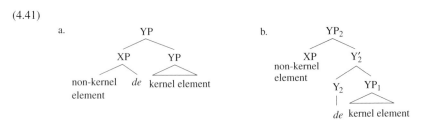

I assume that if the kernel element is relational (e.g. *taidu* 'attitude,' *linju* 'neighbor,' or body part terms such as *shou* 'hand'), it is possible that the non-kernel element is merged with the kernel element first, satisfying the selection of the latter (Castillo 2001; Ogawa 2001), and then is remerged as the Specifier of *de*.

As for kernel-initial constructions, which are always verbal, I speculate that they are derived from (4.41b) by the raising of the kernel element (YP_1) (cf. Karimi 2007 for Kurdish *Ezafe* constructions), when the head Y_2 is realized by another type of *de*, which is a suffix and takes a verb head as its morphological base (Shen and Ting 2008). In other words, it is the kernel element, not the non-kernel one, that is directly merged with *de*. I leave the issue of the exact computation of kernel-initial constructions for future research. In any case, the relation between *de* and the non-kernel element is not that between a head and its complement in either kernel-initial or kernel-final constructions.

In kernel-final constructions, the phonological adjacency between the non-kernel element and the enclitic *de* does not mean that they form a syntactic constituent, as pointed out by C. R. Huang (1989: 30).

As is well known, phonological phrases are not necessarily isomorphic to syntactic constituents. For instance, the syntactic constituency of (4.42a) is not reflected in the phonological grouping in (4.42b) (Jackendoff 1997: 26).

(4.42) a. [$_{DP}$ a [$_{NP}$ [$_{AP}$ big] house]]   b. [$_{\phi}$ [$_{\omega}$ a big] [$_{\omega}$ house]]

Another example is seen in the position of the Latin coordinator *-que*. This coordinator generally follows the first word of a conjunct, although it does not form a syntactic constituent with the word. Compare the two coordinators, *et* and *-que*, in (4.43).

(4.43) a. senatus et   populus romanus   [Latin]
           senate and people   Roman
           'the senate and the Roman people'

      b. senatus populus-que romanus
           senate people-and   Roman
           'the senate and the Roman people'

Thus phonological constituency does not mean syntactic constituency. *De* may undergo morphological merger with every major constituent of the whole complex at PF, regardless of the constituent's syntactic category, after the complex has been built in syntax (see Matushansky 2006 for the notion of morphological merger).

Despite these considerations, it has been sometimes assumed that *de* and the non-kernel element to its left do form a syntactic constituent, excluding the kernel element, as in (4.41a) (Cheng 1986; Tang 1990: 424; Ning 1993; Rubin 2002; 2003; Aoun and Li 2003; among many other places). In Cheng (1986); *de* is treated as a complementizer, taking the non-kernel element to its left as its complement, although it "places no restrictions on the category of its complement" (p. 319). In Tang (1990: 428), *de* is treated as a functional category taking the non-kernel element as its complement, and surfaces to the right of the element. In Rubin (2002; 2003), *de* is a Mod (for modification) element, where "Mod is a functional category forming a shell around the content of the modifier, XP" (Rubin 2002: 1) and ModP is an adjunct of the modified element (Rubin 2002; 2003):

(4.44)   (see Rubin 2002: 1)

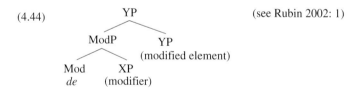

In contrast, in Zhang's (1999) n analysis, Simpson's (2003) D analysis, and den Dikken's (2006) Linker analysis of *de*, the complement of *de* is either the kernel element or the element that contains the kernel element. In other words, they do not group *de* with the non-kernel element, separate from the kernel element. This is also the basic characteristic of (4.41b).

The arguments for the constituent status of the combination of *de* with a non-kernel element, as represented in (4.44), are not convincing.

One argument given in Ning (1993) for a complementation relation between *de* and the non-kernel element is that when the non-kernel element linked by *de* is a clause, it must contain a gap, a requirement that can be treated as

a selectional property of a head on its complement. Contradicting this putative requirement, however, clauses to the left of *de* may actually be gapless
(Tang 1979: 243, 289; Aoun and Li 2003: 186; Chang 2006; Zhang 2008c).
Unlike English examples such as *the time when I left*, such constructions do
not have any syntactic position for a relative pronoun (there is no relative
pronoun in Chinese). An example was given earlier in (4.31c), and here is
another:

(4.45)   Wo jisuan-chu-le   [qiche xingshi] de <u>sudu</u>.
         I   calculate-out-PRF car   run   DE speed
         'I calculated the speed at which the car was running.'

Zhang (2008c) argues that the kernel element in (4.45) is a relational noun
and the relative-clause-like clause is the subject of the noun. Clausal subjects
contain no gap that is associated with their predicates (Rothstein 1991b: 145).
Therefore, nothing in data like (4.45) supports the constituency of a non-kernel
element and *de*.

Another argument for the assumed constituency of modifier plus *de* is that
every modifier can be followed by an instance of *de* (see Tang 1990), as in
(4.46a), and the combination may appear as a conjunct, as in (4.47b) (Aoun
and Li 2003: 150, 250 fn.12):

(4.46) a. jiaoshi-li   (de) zhengzai jianghua de xuesheng
          classroom-in DE   PROG   speak   DE student
          'the student who is speaking in the classroom'

      b. zhuyao (de) erqie women yijing   taolun-guo   de shiqing
         main   DE   and   we   already discuss-EXP DE matter
         'the main matters that we have discussed'

There are various possible ways to explain the multiple occurrences of *de* in
(4.46). First, similar multiple occurrences of a functional word with multiple
parallel elements appear in other constructions where the functional word is not
grouped with the elements syntactically. For instance, determiners may occur
with each modifier in Greek (Androutsopoulou 1994), Albanian, and Hebrew,
but they do not take the modifiers as their complement.

(4.47)   <u>to</u>   megalo <u>to</u>   kokkino <u>to</u>   vivlio   (Greek)
         the big   the red   the book
         'the big red book'

If both *de* in (4.46) and *to* in (4.47) are treated as the head of the entire
nominal complexes, their property of being "spread" to each modifier may be

represented in a similar way. This analysis of multiple occurrences of *de* has been proposed in Simpson (2003).

Second, based on the fact that only the final *de* is obligatory, we may claim that other occurrences of *de* are not syntactic in (4.46). Instead, they might simply demarcate major constituents of a complex (see footnote 5 of this chapter), and such demarcation is not a syntactic operation.

Specifically, in (4.46a), the optional *de* marks each Spec in a multiple Spec structure. As for (4.46b), the optional first *de* also behaves differently from the final obligatory *de*. The contrasts in form and reading between (4.48a) (= (4.46b)) and (4.48b) are telling. In (4.48a), the coordinator is *erqie*, the first *de* is optional, and the reading is that of modifier coordination. In (4.48b), however, the coordinator is *gen*, the first *de* is required, and the reading is that of nominal coordination.

(4.48) a. zhuyao (de) **erqie** women yijing   taolun-guo de shiqing   (= (4.46b))
           main   DE and   we   already discuss-EXP DE matter
           'the main matters that we have discussed'

     b. zhuyao *(de) **gen** women yijing   taolun-guo de shiqing
           main   DE and   we   already discuss-EXP DE matter
           'the main matters and the matters that we have discussed'

Recall that *erqie* may not conjoin nominals whereas *gen* conjoins nominals only (see (4.35)). Thus the conjuncts in (4.48a) are not nominal whereas those of (4.48b) are nominal. The structure of the first can be (4.49a), whereas that of the second can be (4.49b), in which a PF deletion occurs.

(4.49)

 *optional spreading*

     a.   [[_AP_ zhuyao] erqie [_CP_ women yijing taolun-guo]] de shiqing

     b.   [_DP_ zhuyao de ~~shiqing~~] gen [_DP_ women yijing taolun-guo de shiqing]

The mere availability of these alternative analyses indicates that the occurrence of *de* with each modifier in multiple-modifier constructions is not a convincing argument for the assumed constituency of *de* plus modifier (An ellipsis analysis of Greek multiple Det+Adj strings, as in (4.47), is proposed in Panagiotidis 2007: Section 4.4).

Not only are previous arguments for (4.41a) unconvincing, but there are also two additional crucial facts that support (4.41b) and falsify (4.41a), as I now show. They both show the following contrast: in kernel-final constructions, the relationship between *de* and the kernel element to its right is similar to that between a head and its complement, as represented in (4.41b), whereas in kernel-initial constructions, the relationship between *de* and the non-kernel element to its right is not like that between a head and its complement.

The first fact concerns the possible silence of the element to the right of *de*. In Chinese, ellipsis of a phrasal element is licensed by an overt head element that takes the phrase as its complement. In (4.50), the null object is licensed by the overt verb *mai-le* 'buy-PRF.' Similarly, in (4.51a), the VP ellipsis is licensed by the overt modal *hui* 'will.' In (4.51b), the VP ellipsis cannot be licensed by the adverb *ye* 'also,' which does not take the VP as its complement. In (4.51c), the VP ellipsis also cannot be licensed by the adverbial NP *jin-nian* 'this year.'[10]

(4.50)   Baoyu mai-le   xigua,   Daiyu ye   mai-le   ~~xigua~~.
          Baoyu buy-PRF watermelon Daiyu also buy-PRF watermelon
          'Baoyu bought a watermelon, so did Daiyu.'

(4.51) a. Baoyu hui   mai baoxian,   Daiyu ye   hui   ~~mai baoxian~~.
          Baoyu will   buy insurance Daiyu also will buy insurance
          'Baoyu will buy insurance, and Daiyu will also buy insurance.'

       b. *Baoyu hui   mai baoxian,   Daiyu ye   ~~hui mai baoxian~~.
          Baoyu will   buy insurance Daiyu also will buy insurance

       c. *Baoyu   qu-nian   mai-le   baoxian, Daiyu jin-nian   ~~ye~~
          Baoyu   last-year buy-PRF insurance Daiyu this-year also
          ~~mai-le   baoxian~~.
          buy-PRF insurance

The generalization to be drawn from the above data is that if XP is the complement of Y, the presence of Y licenses the silence of XP, whereas if XP is not the complement of Y, the presence of Y does not license the silence of XP.

In a kernel-final construction, the presence of *de* can license a null kernel element, as in so-called Headless modification constructions like (4.52a) and (4.53a). By contrast, if *de* is not overt, the kernel element cannot be null, as seen in (4.52b) and (4.53b).

(4.52) a. [Dai yanjing de ~~na~~   ~~ge~~ ~~ren~~]   lai-le.
          wear glasses DE that   CL person come-PRF
          'The person who wears glasses came.'

       b. *[Dai yanjing ~~de~~ ~~na~~   ~~ge~~ ~~ren~~]   lai-le.
          wear glasses DE that   CL person come-PRF

---

10 In kernel-final constructions, the non-kernel (left) elements may not be null, whereas the kernel (right) ones may be. *De* is thus different from *and* in coordinate complexes, which allows its specifier (the external conjunct) to be null (see Section 4.2.1). The difference follows from the fact that *de* is a bound form taking its preceding element as its phonological host, whereas *and* requires its complement (the internal conjunct) to occur to its right.

(4.53) a. Zheli bi   duodeshi, bie yong ni   baba xie   xin   de bi.
        here   pen many   not use   2SG dad   write letter DE pen
        'Here are many pens. Don't use the one with which your dad writes letters.'

      b. *Zheli bi   duodeshi, bie yong ni   baba xie   xin   ~~de bi.~~
         here   pen many   not use   2SG dad   write letter DE pen

If *de* and the non-kernel element to its left form a constituent, excluding the kernel element, it is not clear why the possibility of silence of the kernel element depends on the occurrence of *de*. If *de* and the kernel element have a head-complement relation, as I claim, the correlation is expected, since a similar correlation is also observed in other head-complement constructions, as in (4.50) and (4.51).

In kernel-initial constructions, however, *de* does not license a null modifier to its right, as seen in (4.54). This is compatible with my claim that *de* never takes a non-kernel element as its complement.

(4.54) a. *Baoyu xie   de hen zixi,   Daiyu ze   kan de ~~hen zixi.~~
         Baoyu write DE very careful Daiyu however read DE very careful
         Intended: 'Baoyu wrote (something) carefully, but Daiyu read (something) carefully.'

      b. *Baoyu zou   de hen man, Daiyu ze   pao de ~~hen man.~~
         Baoyu walk   DE very slow Daiyu however run DE very slow
         Intended: 'Baoyu walks slowly, but Daiyu runs slowly.'

Our second fact concerns the occurrence of the focus marker (FM) *shi* 'be.' *Shi* may occur in various positions, but not between a head and its complement. This is shown in (4.55) (the _ positions are all possible positions for *shi*).

(4.55) a. _ Baoyu _ zuotian _ mai-le   (*shi) na   ben shu.
         Baoyu   yesterday buy-PRF FM   that CL   book
         'Baoyu bought that book yesterday.'

      b. _ Cong (*shi) Taipei _ lai-le   (*shi) yi   wei kexuejia.
         from   FM   Taipei   come-PRF FM   one   CL   scientist
         'A scientist has come from Taipei.'

The examples in (4.56) show that *shi* may not occur between *de* and the kernel element to its right. This indicates that, as represented in (4.41b), the syntactic relationship between *de* and the kernel element is like that between a head and its complement.

(4.56) a. _ Na   jian hongse de (*shi) qunzi _ zai chuang dixia.
          that CL   red   DE FM   skirt   at   bed   under
          'That red skirt is under the bed.'

   b. _ Baoyu _ hen kuai   de (*shi) pao-zou-le.
      Baoyu   very quick DE FM   run-away-PRF
      'Baoyu ran away quickly.'

By contrast, in kernel-initial constructions, *shi* may occur between *de* and the non-kernel element to its right, as shown in (4.57). This indicates that *de* does not take a non-kernel element as its complement.

(4.57) a. Baoyu xie   de shi hen   zixi.
        Baoyu write DE FM very careful
        'Baoyu wrote indeed very carefully.'

     b. Daiyu ku de shi hen   shangxin.
        Daiyu cry DE FM very sad
        'Daiyu cried indeed very sadly.'

The focus marker *shi* has an interrogative version, *shi-bu-shi* 'be-not-be,' which introduces a yes-no question reading to the clause. The distribution pattern of *shi-bu-shi* in *de* constructions is exactly the same as *shi*:

(4.58) a. _ Na jian hongse de (*shi-bu-shi) qunzi _ zai chuang dixia?   (cf. (4.56a))
        that CL red   DE FM   skirt   at bed   under
        'Is that red skirt under the bed?'

     b. Baoyu xie   de shi-bu-shi hen zixi?   (cf. (4.58a))
        Baoyu write DE FM   very careful
        'Did Baoyu write very carefully?'

The above two arguments support our complementation structure in (4.41b), repeated in (4.59).

(4.59)

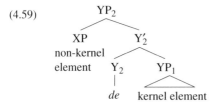

We elaborate the structure in (4.59) as follows. In this structure, the obligatory occurrence of XP can be accounted for by either or both of the following views. First, *de* as an enclitic needs some phonological material to its left. Second, *de* has an edge feature (i.e. an EPP-like feature; see Chomsky 2007 for the notion of edge feature), which requires the merger of XP at the Spec position. Therefore, although a non-kernel element can be a modifier of the kernel and modifiers are optional elements in general, in the presence of *de* the occurrence of the non-kernel element becomes obligatory.

The structure proposed in (4.59) is like Zhang's (1999) n analysis, Simpson's (2003) D analysis (also see Saito *et al*. 2008), and den Dikken's (2006) Linker analysis of *de* in not grouping *de* and the non-kernel element together. However, the current analysis differs from these in a derivational sense, since here *de* does not have any intrinsic categorial features, its D or n category is obtained from the kernel element, if the latter is a nominal, and *de* cannot be D or n, if the latter is not a nominal, as in (4.38b) and (4.38c). This analysis better captures the wide variety of *de* constructions. For example, in den Dikken (2006), *de* is analyzed as a Linker, which is introduced in the syntactic structure as a by-product of the application of Predicate Inversion, a movement operation by which a predicate raises across its subject into a higher position. However, *de* also occurs with non-predicative adjectives, such as *qita* 'rest' in (4.36i) and *suowei* 'so-called' in (4.36j). It is unlikely that the left position of non-predicative adjectives is derived by predicate inversion. My analysis thus gives a more accurate description of the facts than the Linker analysis.

The category of a *de* complex is always identical to that of the kernel element. As we know, the category of a complex should be projected from the head of the complex. If *de* takes the kernel element as its complement, it is the head of the complex. Since *de*, like the coordinator *and*, does not have categorial features, it has to get categorial features from the kernel element, so that the category of the projected complex can be specified. This implies that kernel elements provide *de* with categorial features.

4.3.4   *The chameleon-like nature of* de *keeps the kernel elements* in situ

In kernel-initial constructions, kernel elements must be verbal. Their position on the left might be derived by movement, but I leave this speculation for future research. What is important at this point in the argument is the cooccurrence of two properties of kernel-final constructions: kernel elements can be any category and they may not move.

In the following discussion, we set aside bare noun topic constructions like (4.60a), since it is hard to rule out the possibility that the sentence-initial topic is base-generated there and thus it is not moved from the gap position. Instead, the gap position may be taken by a null element, replacable by an overt noun as in (4.60b).

(4.60) a. Yinliao,   ta mai-le   san   bei   leng de _.
          beverage   he buy-PRF three cup   cold DE
          'As for a beverage, he bought three cups of a cold one / something cold.'

       b. Yinliao,   ta   mai-le   san   bei   leng de   niunai.
          beverage   he   buy-PRF three cup   cold DE   milk
          'As for a beverage, he bought three cups of cold milk.'

Instead, we focus on a set of elements that in constructions without a category-less linking element may be separated from their modifiers, but in the presence of such an element (e.g. as the kernel of a *de* construction) they may not move. This set consists of proper names and pronouns.

Note first that proper names and pronouns may move in general:

(4.61)   {Ta/Baoyu},   wo   zao jiu   renshi.
          he/Baoyu   I   early then   know
          '{He/Baoyu}, I got to know long time ago.'

Moreover, proper names and pronouns may be separated from their modifiers, such as non-restrictive relative clauses, cross-linguistically (de Vries 2002: 190):

(4.62)   Ik   heb   Joop gezien, die   twee zusters heeft.   [Dutch]
         I   have Joop seen   who   two   sisters has
         'I have seen Joop, who has two sisters.'

However, modified proper names and pronouns in Chinese (see footnote 8 of this chapter) require the presence of *de*, as shown in (4.63a) and (4.64a), and they may not move, as shown in (4.63b) and (4.64b):

(4.63) a. Diu-le   qianbao *(de) ta/Baoyu hen   zhaoji.
          lose-PRF   wallet   DE   he/Baoyu very worried
          'He/Baoyu, who lost his wallet, was very worried.'

       b. *Ta/Baoyu, diu-le   qianbao de _   hen   zhaoji.
          he/Baoyu   lose-PRF   wallet   DE   very worried

(4.64) a. Wo congbai boxue   *(de) Wang Jiaoshou.
          I   admire   knowledgeable   DE   Wang Prof.
          'I admire Prof. Wang, who is knowledgeable.'

       b. *Wang Jiaoshou, wo congbai boxue   de _.
          Wang   Prof.   I   admire   knowledgeable   DE

It is a puzzle that *de* licenses a null or elided kernel element (see (4.52a) and (4.53a)), but does not license the launching site of the movement of a kernel element. Generally, it has been noted that the sites of ellipsis are all and only those that meet the licensing conditions on the launching site of movement (Zagona 1988a; Chapter 4; 1988b; Lobeck 1987a;1987b). In other words, if a syntactic position is a possible ellipsis site, it is also a possible launching site of movement. The fact that *de* licenses ellipsis but not movement thus needs an explanation.

We correlate this fact of *de* constructions with the parallel fact observed in coordinate constructions. Recall that *and* also allows the external conjunct to be null (see Section 4.2), but does not allow movement of this same conjunct. Importantly, it is the external conjuncts that provide the categorial features to the whole coordinate complexes headed by *and*. We now see a parallel situation in the *de* constructions. I use the following diagram to show the similarity of the external conjunct of *and* (YP_1 in (4.65a)) and the kernel element of the *de* constructions (YP_1 in (4.65b)):

(4.65)   a.   b.

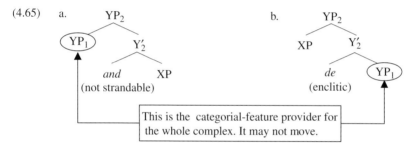

I concluded in the last subsection that the categorial features of a kernel element have been transferred to *de*. The immobility of the kernel element in *de* constructions supports the claim stated in Section 4.1.3B: Elements may not move if they do not have categorial features, which serve as carriers of overt movement.[11]

4.4   The CCe and the *he/gen* comitative constructions in Chinese

The CCe is obeyed in coordinate complexes headed by *and*-like coordinators, which have no intrinsic categorial features. In this section, however, I show that the CCe can be violated in coordinate complexes headed by coordinators that do have intrinsic categorial features. Recall that the conjunction *gen* in Chinese has intrinsic nominal categorial features (Section 3.3.2). We will see that the first conjunct of a *gen* coordinate construction may move, although this movement

---

11 For a discussion of why CC effects are not found in covert wh-movement, see Zhang (2009).

occurs under a certain semantic condition, namely when coordination is non-distributive.

4.4.1   Introduction: he/gen *constructions in Chinese*

The words *he* (*han* in some Mandarin varieties) and *gen* are usually translated as 'and' or 'with.' Constructions containing *he/gen* always have two nominals, DP1 and DP2, such as the underlined parts in the examples in (4.66) through (4.68).

(4.66) Baoyu {he/gen} Daiyu ge   mai-le   yi liang che.
        Baoyu HE/GEN Daiyu each buy-PRF one CL   car
        'Baoyu and Daiyu each bought a car.'

(4.67) a. Baoyu {he/gen} Daiyu he-mai-le   yi   liang che.
          Baoyu HE/GEN Daiyu co-buy-PRF one CL   car
          'Baoyu and Daiyu bought a car together.'

     b. Gongsi   hebing-le   disan bumen {he/gen} diliu bumen.
        company combine-PRF third branch HE/GEN   sixth branch
        'The company combines the third branch and the sixth branch.'

(4.68) Weile gei   Daiyu yixie xianjin, Baoyu {he/gen} Daiyu mai-le
        to   give Daiyu some cash   Baoyu HE/GEN   Daiyu buy-PRF

        yi   jia gangqin.
        one   CL   piano
        'In order to give Daiyu some cash, Baoyu bought a piano from Daiyu.'

Semantically, the construction represented by (4.66) is distributive. Distributive constructions are indicated by the occurrence of a distributive adverb, such as *ge* 'each,' *gezi* 'separately,' and *fenbie* 'respectively.' In (4.66), the individuals denoted by the two nominals *Baoyu* and *Daiyu* take part in car-buying events separately.

The construction represented by the two examples in (4.67) is non-distributive or comitative. Such constructions are indicated by the occurrence of a collective predicate, such as *xiangzhuang* 'collide' and *jiehun* 'marry,' by a collective marker, such as the verbal prefix *he-* 'co-,' or the adverb *yiqi* 'together,' or by a collective verb, such as *hebing* 'combine.'[12] In (4.66), *Baoyu* and *Daiyu* are both agents of their respective car-buying actions. In (4.67a), however, *Baoyu* and *Daiyu* together are the agent of a single car-buying action. Similarly, in (4.67b), *disan bumen* 'third branch' and *diliu bumen* 'sixth branch' together are the affected entity of the combining action.

---

12 See Teng (1970: 355) for a list of collective predicates in Chinese (he calls them "multiple-reference verbs").

DP1 and DP2 have the same thematic roles in both the distributive and comitative constructions. The construction represented by (4.68) is neither distributive nor comitative. In this sentence, *Baoyu* is the goal (also the agent) while *Daiyu* is the source of the piano-buying action, and thus their semantic roles are in contrast.

It is generally accepted that the string "DP1 *he/gen* DP2" is a nominal constituent in distributive examples like (4.66) and post-verbal comitative examples like (4.67b), and the word *he/gen* is a coordinator inside this constituent. Accordingly, the constituent is a coordinate nominal (see Zhu 1982: 176; among others). If *gen* occurs to the right of a collective transitive verb such as *hebing* 'combine,' *jiajie* 'graft,' *hunyao* 'mix,' and *bijiao* 'compare,' as in (4.67b), it cannot be a preposition. This is because in Chinese, no PP adjunct may occur to the right of a verb. Collective verbs require a plural internal argument. In (4.67b), neither of the two DPs to the right of the verb is plural. A plausible analysis of the example is thus that the two DPs and *gen* form a coordinate complex, which as a plural nominal satisfies the selection of the collective verb.

Now turn to examples like (4.68). It is not controversial that in such examples the string "DP1 *he/gen* DP2" is not a syntactic constituent. Instead, DP1 is the subject and "*he/gen* DP2" is an adjunct of the predicate, and the word *he/gen* is a preposition or verb.

What is unclear is the syntactic constituency of preverbal comitative examples like (4.67a), and thus the status of the *he/gen* there. In 4.4.2 I argue that in such constructions the string "DP1 *he/gen* DP2" is also a coordinate nominal. Then in Section 4.4.3 I present evidence showing the correlation between collectivity and the possibility of separating the conjunct and coordinator. The conclusion of this section is that the CCe can be violated in collective *he/gen* coordination.

Note that in comitative constructions, the coordinators *he* and *gen* have identical distributions. Thus in all of the comitative examples in this book, the two words are interchangeable.

4.4.2   *Coordinator properties of the comitative* he/gen

Early discussion of the close relationship between comitative and coordinate constructions can be found in Jespersen (1924: 90). Cross-linguistically, the linking words in comitative constructions are often homonymous with words that have other functions (Mithun 1988: 339, 349; among others). In Chinese, the diachronic evolution of coordinators was verb > preposition > coordinator (Liu and Peyraube 1994). In modern Chinese, the words *he* and *gen* may introduce a comitative nominal, as in (4.67a) and (4.67b), a source, as in (4.68), or a goal, as in (4.69), and they can also be verbs, as in (4.70).

(4.69)   Baoyu gen   xuesheng jiang-qi-le   guoqu de jingli.
          Baoyu GEN student   tell-INCH-PRF past   DE experience
          'Baoyu started to tell his past experiences to the students.'

(4.70)   Baoyu zong   gen-zhe   Daiyu.
          Baoyu always follow-PRG Daiyu
          'Baoyu always follows Daiyu.'

For the *he/gen* in comitative constructions, as in (4.67), I use the term com-*he/gen*, and for the *he/gen* that functions as a preposition, as in (4.69) and (4.68), I use the term prep-*he/gen*.

In this section, I present four arguments to show the coordinator status of *he* and *gen* in comitative constructions. The first two argue for the constituency of the string "DP1 com-*he/gen* DP2." This constituent status supports in turn the coordinator status of *he* and *gen* in preverbal comitative constructions. The other two argue against the adjunct status of the string "*he/gen* DP2" in the constructions. Among my arguments, only the third (the reversibility of the two DPs) has previously been mentioned in the literature (Zhu 1982: 176).

A.   The string "DP1 com-*he/gen* DP2" as a topic
My first argument for the constituency of the cluster "DP1 com-*he/gen* DP2" is that the string may occur in a topic position.

(4.71)   Baoyu gen   Daiyu, wo tingshuo yiqi   he-xie-le   yi
          Baoyu GEN   Daiyu I   hear   together co-write-PRF one
          bu   xiaoshuo.
          CL   novel
          'Baoyu and Daiyu, I heard that (they) co-wrote a novel.'

Since only syntactic constituents may occur in topic positions, I conclude that the cluster "DP1 com-*he/gen* DP2" must be a syntactic constituent.

B.   The string "DP1 com-*he/gen* DP2" as an antecedent
My second argument for the constituency of the cluster "DP1 com-*he/gen* DP2" is that the string may have an appositive, such as *liang ge ren* 'two CL person' in (4.72). Since only syntactic constituents may be antecedents of appositives, I conclude that the cluster "DP1 com-*he/gen* DP2" is a syntactic constituent.

(4.72)   Baoyu gen   Daiyu (liang ge ren)   yiqi   qu-le   Taipei.
          Baoyu GEN Daiyu two   CL person together go-PRF Taipei
          'Baoyu and Daiyu, the two persons, went to Taipei together.'

The above two arguments support my claim that "DP1 com-*he/gen* DP2" is a syntactic constituent (an additional argument will be given in Section 4.4.3.F). If so, the cluster "com-*he/gen* DP2" cannot be an adjunct of the predicate in this construction. One might, however, still wonder whether the complex-internal cluster *he/gen*-DP2 is a PP complement of DP1, like *dui Daiyu* in (4.73a), or a PP adjunct of DP1, like *yan malu* 'along the street' in (4.73b).

(4.73) a. dui   Daiyu   *(de)   guanxin
          to   Daiyu   DE   care
          'the care of Daiyu'

       b. yan   malu   *(de)   shangdian
          along   street DE   shop
          'the shops along the street'

However, even if we ignore semantics (in (4.67a), for instance, *gen Daiyu* is neither an argument nor a modifier of *Baoyu*), we still have two formal considerations that argue against this preposition analysis. First, in Chinese the complement and any adjunct of a nominal must occur to the left of the nominal. In [DP1 com-*he/gen* DP2], the cluster *he/gen*-DP2 is to the right of DP1. Second, if a PP modifies a nominal or functions as the complement of a nominal, the functional word *de* must be present (Lü *et al.* 1999: 19). In the constituent [DP1 com-*he/gen* DP2], however, *de* is absent. It is thus unlikely that com-*he/gen* DP2 is an argument or modifier of DP1.

C.   The reversibility of DP1 and DP2
The third argument for the coordinator status of com-*he/gen* is that the two DPs of the construction can exchange their positions, without affecting the basic meaning of the construction, whereas the two DPs in prep-*he/gen* constructions cannot do so (see Zhu 1982: 176). In (4.74) through (4.76), DP1 and DP2 can switch their positions without affecting the basic reading.

(4.74) a. Baoyu   he   Daiyu   dingqin-le.
          Baoyu   HE   Daiyu   engage-PRF
          'Baoyu and Daiyu are engaged.'

       b. Daiyu he Baoyu dingqin-le.

(4.75) a. Qing   he   yang   he-cheng   shui.
          hydrogen   HE   oxygen   combine-become   water
          'Hydrogen and oxygen make water.'

       b. Yang he qing he-cheng shui.

(4.76) a. Baoyu he Daiyu he-zhu-le   yi   zuo fangzi.
   Baoyu HE Daiyu co-rent-PRF one CL   house
   'Baoyu and Daiyu rented a house together.'

  b. Daiyu he Baoyu he-zhu-le yi zuo fangzi.

The reversibility in the above data is parallel to the reversibility of the following examples of distributive coordination.

(4.77) a. Baoyu he Daiyu ge   zhu-le   yi   zuo fangzi.
   Baoyu HE Daiyu each rent-PRF one CL   house
   'Baoyu and Daiyu each rented a house.'

  b. Daiyu he Baoyu ge zhu-le yi zuo fangzi.

In (4.78), however, the preposition *gen* introduces a source, and if the source nominal *Daiyu* is exchanged with the agent nominal *Baoyu*, the basic meaning is changed. The encoded transaction direction in (4.78a) is different from that of (4.78b).

(4.78) a. Weile hua-diao   yixie xianjin, Baoyu gen Daiyu mai-le   yi
   to   spend-off some cash   Baoyu GEN Daiyu buy-PRF one
   jia   gangqin.
   CL   piano
   'In order to spend some cash, Baoyu bought a piano from Daiyu.'

  b. Weile hua-diao   yixie xianjin, Daiyu gen Baoyu mai-le   yi
   to   spend-off some cash   Daiyu GEN Baoyu buy-PRF one
   jia   gangqin.
   CL   piano
   'In order to spend some cash, Daiyu bought a piano from Baoyu.'

Constituent reversibility is seen between conjuncts of a symmetrical coordination, but not between elements that have different theta roles. If the comitative constructions in (4.74) through (4.76) are coordinate constructions, rather than constructions with PP adjunctions, the constituent reversibility is accounted for.

Note that the reversibility of com-*he/gen* constructions is merely flexibility in merger. This flexibility implies that it makes no difference which nominal is merged with the com-*he/gen* first, but it does not mean that we have a syntactic operation that can exchange the positions of two elements.

D. The obligatory occurrence of DP2

Removal of a PP adverbial does not affect the acceptability of a sentence, as shown in (4.79a) and (4.79b).

(4.79) a. Baoyu gen Daiyu mai-le   yi   liang che.
   Baoyu GEN Daiyu buy-PRF one CL   car
   'Baoyu bought a car from Daiyu.'

    b. Baoyu mai-le yi liang che.
       Baoyu buy-PRF one CL   car
       'Baoyu bought a car.'

Like the collective transitive verbs in (4.67b), collective and relational predicates select plural arguments. In a preverbal comitative construction, if DP1 is singular, the presence of DP2 is obligatory. In examples like (4.67a), repeated here as (4.80a), if we remove DP2 together with *gen*, the sentence becomes unacceptable, as seen in (4.80b). The obligatory occurrence of DP2 together with *gen* indicates that they are not a PP adjunct.[13]

(4.80) a. Baoyu gen Daiyu he-mai-le   yi   liang che.   (= (4.67a))
          Baoyu GEN Daiyu co-buy-PRF one CL   car
          'Baoyu and Daiyu bought a car together.'
      b. *Baoyu he-mai-le   yi   liang che.
          Baoyu co-buy-PRF one CL   car

    Section summary

Recall that it is not controversial that post-verbal comitative *he* and *gen* are coordinators. Our analysis has now demonstrated that they are coordinators, not prepositions, in preverbal position as well. We are thus justified in glossing comitative *he* and *gen* as 'and' in the remainder of this book.

    If comitative constructions are coordinate constructions in Chinese, the *he/gen* and the two DPs associated with them form a complex nominal in their base positions. In this respect, comitative constructions behave the same as other coordinate constructions, and as we have already shown that *he* and *gen*, as coordinators, have intrinsic categorial features (3.3.2). Moreover, since the conjuncts of comitative coordination are semantically related in a single eventuality, the coordination here is collective coordination, in contrast to distributive coordination.

    The conclusion achieved in this subsection predicts that in the context of a comitative *he/gen* construction, if DP1 is not adjacent to *he/gen*, the surface position must be derived by movement. Since DP1 is an external conjunct, however, such movement would represent a violation of the CCe.

---

13 It is true that the English *with*-phrase is also obligatory with collective predicates taking a singular nominal as subject:

(i)   John is friends *(with Bill).

Zhang (2007a: 146) uses facts like these to argue that comitative *with* is actually not a preposition, and thus the behavior of English *with* does not support the PP adjunct analysis of the Chinese com-*he/gen* constructions.

In the next subsection, I will demonstrate that separation of DP1 from comitative *he/gen* does occur. Based on the existence of this separation and the nature of its licensing, I will claim that the CCe can be relativized in collective coordination.

4.4.3   *Violation of the CCe in non-distributive coordination*
In this subsection, I show that separation of the first conjunct from the rest of a coordinate complex is possible in collective coordination, in contrast to distributive coordination.

Since comitative complexes are coordinate complexes, their base positions should be the same as those of any other coordinate complexes, depending on the selecting elements. For example, if a comitative coordinate complex is the subject of a transitive predicate, it is base-generated at Spec of VP. In this subsection, I will show that the first conjunct can be raised from the base position of subjects, thus violating the CCe. The raising is observed in six distinct contexts, as shown in A through F below. In contrast to comitative coordinate constructions, raising is not possible when distributive coordinate constructions appear in these contexts. We can thus see a systematic contrast between the two types of coordinate constructions with respect to CCe effects.

A.   Raising verbs between first conjuncts and coordinators
The first indication that first conjuncts may move is seen in examples where raising verbs appear between first conjuncts and coordinators.

In comitative coordinate constructions   A CCe violation is seen in (4.81), where the first conjunct and the coordinator are separated by the epistemic *hui* 'might,' which is a raising verb (C. J. Huang 1988b; Lin and Tang 1996).

(4.81) a. Huoche hui   gen qiche xiangzhuang ma?
         train   might and bus   collide   Q
         'Might the train collide with the bus?'

It is generally assumed that if a subject precedes a raising verb, the word order is derived by raising the subject from a position that is c-commanded by the verb. If so, in (4.81), *huoche* 'train' is raised. In this case, the raising launches from a coordinate complex, violating the CCe.

The readings of (4.81) can also be expressed as in (4.82). In (4.82), the whole comitative coordinate complex occurs to the left of the modal. In this case, no conjunct moves alone, and thus the example is irrelevant to the status of the CCe.

(4.82)   Huoche gen qiche hui   xiangzhuang ma?
          train   and bus   might collide   Q
          'Might the train collide with the bus?'

There is a consistent reading difference between examples like (4.81) and their counterpart examples like (4.82) from the perspective of information structure: the two DPs in (4.81) are not symmetrical, whereas the two DPs in (4.82) are. Specifically, in the absence of any contrastive stress, the DP preceding the raising verb is foregrounded (emphasized), whereas the one following the raising verb is backgrounded (not emphasized). In (4.81), *huoche* 'train' is foregrounded and *qiche* 'bus' is backgrounded; however, in (4.82), there is no such difference between *huoche* and *qiche*. The reading difference can be captured by Seiler's (1974) generalization that comitative constructions leave the extent of participation of the backgrounded partner in the action underspecified, from mere "accompanying" to full-fledged "partnership." The foregrounded participant of a comitative construction has the property of "Principality" (Teng 1970: 332) in contrast to the other participant. This reading contrast consistently occurs in other comitative constructions in which the first conjunct is separated from the rest of the coordinate complex.

In distributive coordinate constructions   Unlike the case with comitative constructions, in distributive coordinate constructions first conjuncts cannot be separated from the coordinators by raising verbs. *Fenbie* in (4.83) indicates that the coordination is a distributive one. In (4.83) the epistemic *hui* 'will' cannot appear between the first conjunct *Lao Li* and the coordinator. Since no conjunct may be separated from the coordinator in distributive coordinate constructions, the CCe is obeyed.

(4.83) a. *Lao Li hui   gen Lao Wang fenbie   qu-le   Shanghai ma?
              Lao Li will   and Lao Wang separately go-PRF Shanghai Q

       b. Lao Li gen Lao Wang hui   fenbie   qu-le   Shanghai ma?
              Lao Li and Lao Wang will separately go-PRF Shanghai Q
              'Might Lao Li and Lao Wang have gone to Shanghai separately?'

B.   Adverbials between first conjuncts and coordinators
The second indication that first conjuncts may move is seen in examples where adverbials appear between first conjuncts and coordinators.

In comitative coordinate constructions   In comitative constructions, first conjuncts can be separated from coordinators by adverbials such as *yijing* 'already' or by temporal or locative adverbials. In (4.84b) the first conjunct and the coordinator are separated by the circumstantial *zai Riben* 'in Japan.' (4.84b) is nearly synonymous with (4.84a).

(4.84) a. [Akiu gen Baoyu] zai Riben jian-le   mian.
         Akiu and Baoyu   at   Japan meet-PRF face
         'Akiu and Baoyu met in Japan.'

       b. Akiu$_i$ zai Riben [_$_i$ gen Baoyu] jian-le   mian.
          Akiu   at   Japan   and Baoyu   meet-PRF face

The following example shows that no resumptive pronoun is allowed for (4.84b):

(4.85)   *Akiu$_i$ zai Riben [ta$_i$ gen Baoyu] jian-le   mian.
          Akiu   at   Japan he   and Baoyu   meet-PRF face

The ban on resumptive pronouns in examples like (4.84b) indicates that the sentence-initial nominal is not a gapless topic, and is thus not base-generated in its surface position. Instead, it is moved out of a post-circumstantial position.

Since the conjuncts and coordinator of a coordinate DP complex must be merged into a constituent which excludes any circumstantial, the occurrence of the circumstantial between the first conjunct and the coordinator in (4.84b) suggests that the conjunct has been moved. If so, the CCe is violated.

In distributive coordinate constructions   Unlike the case with comitative constructions, in distributive coordinate constructions first conjuncts cannot be separated from the coordinators by adverbials. The distributive adverb *gezi* in (4.86) indicates that the coordination is distributive. In such examples, the first conjunct and the coordinator must be adjacent, consistent with the CCe.

(4.86) a. *[Baoyu] zai Riben [gen Daiyu] gezi   baifang-le pengyou.
          Baoyu   at   Japan and   Daiyu   separately visit-PRF   friend

       b. [Baoyu gen Daiyu] zai Riben gezi   baifang-le pengyou.
          Baoyu   and Daiyu   at   Japan separately visit-PRF   friend
          'Baoyu and Daiyu visited their friends separately in Japan.'

C.   Negation words between first conjuncts and coordinators

The third indication that first conjuncts may move is seen in examples where negation words appear between first conjuncts and coordinators.

In comitative coordinate constructions   Like the coordinator *and* in English, coordinators in Chinese may not be negated. The coordinators *he* and *gen* are not negated by the negation word *bu* or *mei*. However, in comitative constructions it is possible for a negation word to occur between the first conjunct and the coordinator. In (4.87), the first conjunct *Baoyu* and the coordinator *gen* are separated by the negation word *mei*.

(4.87)   Baoyu mei gen Daiyu he-mai yi   liang che.
          Baoyu not and Daiyu co-buy one CL   car
          'Baoyu and Daiyu did not buy a car together.'

Since the conjuncts and coordinator of a coordinate DP complex must be merged into a constituent that excludes any negation word, the occurrence of the negation word between the first conjunct and the coordinator in (4.87) suggests that the conjunct has moved. If so, the CCe is violated.

In distributive coordinate constructions   It is impossible for a negation word to occur between the first conjunct and the coordinator in a distributive coordinate construction. The adverb *fenbie* in (4.88) indicates that the coordination is a distributive one. In (4.88a), the negation word *bu* may not occur between the first conjunct *Baoyu* and the coordinator *gen*. Thus these distributive coordinate construction examples are consistent with the CCe.

(4.88) a. *Baoyu mei gen Daiyu fenbie   mai yi   liang che.
           Baoyu not and Daiyu separately buy one CL   car

       b. Baoyu gen Daiyu mei fenbie   mai yi   liang che.
          Baoyu and Daiyu not separately buy one CL   car
          'Baoyu and Daiyu did not separately buy a car.'

D.   Relativization of first conjuncts
The fourth indication that first conjuncts may move is seen in examples where first conjuncts are relativized.

In comitative coordinate constructions   First conjuncts of coordinate complexes can be relativized in Chinese, a fact noted in Tai (1969: 122). The predicate *he-zu fangzi* 'co-rent house' in (4.89a) and *xiangzhuang* 'collide' in (4.89b) are both collective. They each have a coordinate complex subject, but the first conjunct of the complex is relativized.

(4.89) a. Gen Daiyu he-zu   fangzi de xuesheng hen qiong.
           and Daiyu co-rent house DE student   very poor
           'The student who co-rents a house with Daiyu is very poor.'

     b. Wo kanjian-le gen huoche xiangzhuang de qiche.
         I   see-PRF   and train   collide   DE bus
         'I saw the bus that collided with the train.'

Relativization is derived by either null operator movement (Chomsky 1977) or the movement of the antecedent directly (Vergnaud 1974; Kayne 1994). In either approach, some element is moved from the first conjunct position in examples like (4.89).

In distributive coordinate constructions   Unlike the case with comitative constructions, first conjuncts cannot be relativized in distributive constructions. The following two sentences are a minimal pair. In (4.90a), the collective adverb *yiqi* 'together' occurs, whereas in (4.90b), the distributive adverb *fenbie* 'separately' occurs. The relativization of the first conjunct of *gen* is fine in (4.90a), but not in (4.90b) (see Tai 1969: 134).

(4.90) a. Gen Daiyu yiqi   zu   fangzi de xuesheng hen qiong.
           and Daiyu together rent house DE student   very poor
           'The student who co-rents a house with Daiyu is very poor.'

     b. *Gen Daiyu fenbie   zu   fangzi de xuesheng hen qiong.
          and Daiyu separately rent house DE student   very poor

E.   A-not-A forms of coordinators
The fifth indication that first conjuncts may move is seen in the A-not-A forms of coordinators.

In comitative coordinate constructions   In Chinese, A-not-A questions are yes-no questions. They are formed by the reduplication of the initial syllable of a predicate (a verb or preposition) or by reduplication of a larger prosodic unit of the predicate phrase, and an appropriate negation word (*bu* 'not' or *mei* 'not') between the reduplicant and the base. For instance, in (4.91a), it is the first syllable of the verb *xihuan* 'like' that is reduplicated, whereas in (4.91b), it is the whole verb *xihuan* that is reduplicated. The two sentences in (4.91) are synonymous.

(4.91) a. Lao Li xi-bu-xihuan ni?
           Lao Li like-not-like   you

    b. Lao Li xihuan-bu-xihuan ni?
           Lao Li like-not-like   you
           'Does Lao Li like you?'

The position of an A-not-A element marks the division between a VP and the functional projections above VP, assuming that subjects move out of VP to SpecIP in Chinese (Huang 1993). It is always the left-peripheral element of VP that is in the A-not-A form. Usually the element is the verb or the first syllable of the verb, but it need not be. For instance, if a VP starts with a directional PP, it is the preposition of this PP that is in the A-not-A form, as seen in (4.92). An adverb cannot be in A-not-A form (e.g. *hai* "still" in this example), but I assume that this is a special property of adverbs that can be left for future study.

(4.92)   Zhe liang che hai   wang-bu-wang   nan   kai?
          this   CL   car   still toward-not-toward south drive
          'Is this car still going to move to the south?'

Since the A-not-A formation can be applied to the first syllable of the predicate, it is a syntax–phonology interface operation. Following the basic thesis of C. J. Huang (1988a), I assume that the [Q] feature of an A-not-A form is licensed by the relevant feature of a c-commanding functional head, presumably Infl (or C; the choice is unimportant here).

Since an A-not-A form can mark the left edge of a VP, elements to the left of the A-not-A form must either be base-generated outside of VP or have moved out of VP. The data in (4.93) show that there are two possible A-not-A constructions for a comitative subject. In the construction in (4.93a), the coordinator *gen* is in the A-not-A form, whereas the nominal to the left of the A-not-A word, *Baoyu,* is the surface subject. If a subject comitative complex is base-generated at SpecVP, (4.93a) shows that the first conjunct moves. The movement launches from the base-position of the subject (i.e. inside the SpecVP) and lands at SpecIP. In this case, the CCe is violated. In the other construction, the verb is in the A-not-A form, as seen in (4.93b). If the whole comitative complex DP occurs to the left of the A-not-A word, as in (4.93b), the whole complex DP is raised from SpecVP to SpecIP. In this case, no conjunct moves alone, and thus such an example is irrelevant to the status of the CCe.

(4.93) a. Baoyu gen-mei-gen Daiyu jiehun?
    Baoyu and-not-and Daiyu marry
    'Did Baoyu and Daiyu marry?'

  b. Baoyu gen Daiyu jie-mei-jiehun?
    Baoyu and Daiyu marry-not-marry
    'Did Baoyu and Daiyu marry?'

   In distributive coordinate constructions The coordinators of distributive coordinate constructions cannot appear in A-not-A form. In (4.94), the presence of the distributive adverb *fenbie* 'separately' indicates that the construction is a distributive coordinate construction. The intended meaning of (4.94a) is expressed by (4.94b). In (4.94b), it is the verb, rather than the coordinator, that is in the A-not-A form (as noted above, adverbs like *fenbie* and *gezi* cannot be in an A-not-A form).

(4.94) a. *Baoyu gen-mei-gen Daiyu fenbie jiehun?
    Baoyu and-not-and Daiyu separately marry

  b. Baoyu gen Daiyu fenbie jie-mei-jiehun?
    Baoyu and Daiyu separately marry-not-marry
    'Did Baoyu and Daiyu get married, separately?'

 In (4.94b), the whole coordinate complex precedes the A-not-A form. This means that the whole complex is outside of VP, and no conjunct is raised by itself out of the complex. (4.94a) shows that the coordinators of distributive coordinate constructions cannot be in the A-not-A form. This fact indicates that in distributive coordinate constructions no conjunct may be raised out of VP alone, consistent with the CCe.

F.   First conjunct-oriented resultatives
The sixth indication that first conjuncts may move is seen in the existence of first conjunct-oriented resultatives.

   In comitative coordinate constructions If a comitative coordinate complex occurs with a resultative, the sentence is always ambiguous. The secondary predicate can either predicate over the whole coordinate complex, or just over the first conjunct:[14]

14 It is generally recognized that resultatives in Chinese can be subject-oriented, without any reflexive support (Y. Li 1990; Zhang 2007c; among others).

(4.95) Baoyu gen Daiyu zhuang de toupoxueliu.
       Baoyu and Daiyu collide DE bleed
       'Baoyu and Daiyu collided so that Baoyu bled.'
       'Baoyu and Daiyu collided so that they both bled.'

The fact that the resultatives can take a single conjunct as subject would be unexpected if the relevant conjunct remained inside the hosting DP. According to Williams (1980), subjects must c-command their predicates, including secondary predicates. Thus in order to achieve the first reading for (4.95), the first conjunct has to move out of the coordinate complex to c-command the resultative. The empirical issue remains the same if one adopts a PRO approach to secondary predication (Hornstein and Lightfoot 1987; Bowers 1993; 2001). Specifically, if the subject of a secondary predicate is a local PRO, which c-commands the secondary predicate, the controller of the PRO still needs to be a constituent outside of the coordinate complex. In this PRO-approach, the first conjunct in (4.95) is the controller of the PRO subject of the secondary predicate. As the controller of the PRO, the first conjunct must be syntactically outside of the coordinate complex.

On the other hand, the fact that resultatives can take whole coordinate complexes as subjects, seen in the second reading for (4.95), indicates that the raising of the first conjunct is not obligatory. This *in situ* possibility is parallel to what we saw in the previous subsections. In all of these tests, there are always two possibilities for the first conjuncts: they can either be raised or remain inside the coordinate complexes.

Note that the ambiguity remains even if DP1 is separated from the string *gen*-DP2:

(4.96) Baoyu zuotian gen Daiyu zhuang de toupoxueliu.
       Baoyu yesterday and Daiyu collide MOD bleed
       'Baoyu and Daiyu collided so that Baoyu bled yesterday.'
       'Baoyu and Daiyu collided so that they both bled yesterday.'

The existence of whole-coordinate-complex-oriented resultatives, seen in the second reading of the above data, on the other hand, indicates that the resultative may also take the whole coordinate complex in its base-position as its subject. Since resultatives are generally analyzed as the complement of V, it is c-commanded by the base-position of the coordinate subject, which is at Spec of VP. Therefore, the predication relation is licensed.

The fact that resultatives can take whole coordinate complexes as subjects also supports our claim that the two DPs form a constituent. The above examples stand in contrast to the following. In the intended source reading of *gen*, the *gen*-DP cluster is a PP, and the resultative is exclusively secondary predicate of the DP to the left of *gen*, i.e., *Baoyu* in (4.97).

(4.97)   Zhe ben shu, Baoyu gen Daiyu jie   de dou   fan-le.
          this CL book Baoyu from Daiyu borrow DE already tired.of-PRF
          'This book, Baoyu$_i$ borrowed from Daiyu so that he$_i$ already got tired.of it.'
          Irrelevant reading: 'This book, Baoyu and Daiyu borrowed from others so
          that they both got tired of it.' (distributive coordinate construction, *gen*
          is a coordinator)

The lack of ambiguity in the reading of the prep-*gen* construction in (4.97) is expected from the fact that the cluster *Baoyu gen Daiyu* is not a constituent, and thus it cannot have a secondary predicate. Instead, only the DP to the left of *gen*, which is the subject of the primary predication, can have a secondary predicate.

In distributive coordinate constructions   In contrast to (4.95), the first conjuncts of distributive coordinate constructions can never have any secondary predicate. The following sentence is not ambiguous. Only the whole coordinate complex can be the subject (or controller of the subject) of the resultative. We thus see yet another contrast between comitative coordinate constructions and distributive coordinate constructions regarding single conjunct raising.

(4.98)   Baoyu he   Daiyu qi   de zhi   fadou.
          Baoyu and Daiyu angry DE continuously shiver
          'Baoyu and Daiyu were so angry that they shivered continuously.'

G.   Section summary
The six contrasts above between comitative and distributive coordinate constructions with respect to the mobility of first conjuncts show that CCe effects are sensitive to the semantic type of the coordination: the first conjunct can move in comitative coordination but not in distributive coordination.[15]

4.5   Chapter summary

In Chapter 3, I claimed that the categorial features of external conjuncts are transferred to the coordinator *and*. In this chapter, I concluded that this transference keeps external conjuncts *in situ*, since elements without category-features

---

15 One might wonder why external conjuncts may not be moved from a postverbal position, regardless of the semantic type of the coordination. It is possible that there is some sort of intervention effect for non-local movement like this, but I will leave this issue for future research.

may not move overtly. Our analysis explains the effects that the CCe has been intended to cover.

Our account for the CCe is supported by two facts. First, in Chinese *de* constructions, kernel elements provide categorial features for *de*, which has no intrinsic categorial features and is the head of the whole complex, and so they may not move. Second, in comitative coordinate constructions in Chinese, initial conjuncts do not provide categorial features for the coordinators, since the coordinators have their own intrinsic categorial features (Section 3.3.2), and so the conjuncts may move.

This account of the CCe can be falsified if we find coordination in which the external conjunct may move and yet the coordinator has no categorial features.

The CCi, however, simply manifests a morphological property of coordinators shared with many other types of elements, namely that they need to be adjacent to their complement. Neither deletion nor movement of their complement (the internal conjunct) is possible.

Putting these points together, the CC is not a unified construction-specific syntactic constraint. Instead, it is related to the lexical/morphological makeup of coordinators such as *and*. In syntactic theory, the CCe, as part of the CSC, has usually been treated as a constraint specific to the elements merged with coordinators. However, as shown in Chapter 2, coordinate constructions do not represent any special syntactic structure, and as shown in Chapter 3, coordinators do not represent any special category. Thus, coordination is not a primitive notion in syntax. Conjuncts, as regular Spec and Complement elements, may undergo syntactic movement in general. Apparent CC effects actually derive from idiosyncratic morphological properties of particular coordinators. In particular, English *and* is unspecified for categorial features, and the transference of categorial features to it from the external conjunct blocks this conjunct from moving. In the minimalist program, movement is driven by morphological considerations (Chomsky 1995: 262). My study here shows that the blocking of movement can also be related to morphological properties of specific syntactic elements, in addition to the generally recognized locality restrictions (Chomsky 1975: 105).[16]

16 Given our claim that the CC depends on the nature of the overt coordinator, it follows that conjuncts of a coordinate complex that does not have an overt coordinator (i.e. asyndetic coordination) may move. In Chapter 6, we will show how this prediction explains the derivations of certain constructions.

5 *The Element Constraint and the semantic relatedness of conjuncts*

5.1 Introduction

Recall that Ross's (1967) Coordinate Structure Constraint (CSC) has two parts, the Element Constraint (EC) and the Conjunct Constraint (CC) (Grosu 1973). The EC states that no element may be extracted from conjuncts, as seen in (5.1a), and the CC states that no conjunct may move, as seen in (5.1b).

(5.1) a. *What kind of herbs did you [[eat _] and [drink beer]]?   (EC violation)
     b. *Which boy did John kiss [_ and that girl]?   (CC violation)

In the last chapter, I distinguished between two kinds of CC effects: those caused by the morphological properties of *and*-like coordinators and those caused by the distributiveness of coordination. The CC is absolute in coordinate complexes headed by *and*-like coordinators, but can be violated in other types of coordinate complexes, in non-distributive coordination. In this chapter, I present a parallel correlation between violation of the EC and non-distributiveness. Thus both parts of the CSC are relativized in non-distributive coordination.

Specifically, I will discuss the evidence showing that the EC can be violated in so-called asymmetrical coordination (AC), but not in symmetrical coordination. The goal of this chapter is to show that the EC depends solely on semantics and thus is not a constraint on syntactic operations.

The chapter is organized as follows. In Section 5.2, I introduce the contrast between natural and accidental coordination, and identify AC, as well as collective coordination, as a type of natural coordination. In Section 5.3, I discuss violation of the EC in natural coordination in both English and Chinese. Finally, Section 5.4 is a brief summary of the chapter.

5.2 Asymmetrical coordination as a type of natural coordination

5.2.1 Natural coordination

Natural coordination is a semantic relation in which the entities expressed by the conjuncts of a coordinate complex are closely related to each other

(Haspelmath 2004; 2007; Wälchli 2005; Dalrymple and Nikolaeva 2006; see also Mithun 1988: 332f.). A close relation is indicated if any element in the context is semantically associated to the combined meaning of the conjuncts, rather than to the meaning of each isolated conjunct. In contrast, accidental coordination involves coordination of elements which do not have a close semantic relationship with each other. For instance, if a coordinate complex is associated with a relational adjective such as *compatible* or *similar*, the conjuncts are semantically related and the coordination is natural, whereas if a coordinate complex is associated with a non-relational adjective such as *smooth*, the conjuncts are not semantically related to each other and the coordination is accidental (see Dalrymple and Nikolaeva 2006: 825, 834).

Non-distributive coordination is natural coordination. Coordinate complexes that are arguments of collective predicates or collective verbs, such as *John and Mary* in (5.2), are non-distributive. In such coordinate complexes, neither conjunct may function as an independent argument of the predicate or verb (**John collided in the street*).

(5.2)   [John and Mary] collided in the street.

The dichotomy between accidental and natural coordination covers various dichotomies proposed in the literature: sentence conjunction vs. phrasal conjunction (Lakoff and Peters 1966), non-joint vs. joint coordination (McCawley 1968), non-Boolean conjunction vs. Boolean conjunction in semantics (Massey 1976; Link 1983; Hoeksema 1983; Krifka 1990; among others), *jia-er-bu-he* (adding-without-joining) and *jia-erqie-he* (adding-and-joining) (Lü 1979: Section 75), and [+/− Separate] coordination (Payne 1985: 17). All of these dichotomies depend on whether the conjuncts are semantically related to each other or are essentially unrelated.

According to Haspelmath (2004; 2007), Wälchli (2005), and Dalrymple and Nikolaeva (2006), the classification of natural and accidental coordination is decided by both linguistic and non-linguistic contexts. Lexical semantics, pragmatics, morphology, and syntactic forms all can play roles in distinguishing the two types of coordination.

The semantic distinction between the grouping in natural (or collective) coordination and the grouping in accidental (or distributive) coordination can also be seen in plural nominals. We have shown that conjuncts of natural coordination are related to each other and thus the whole coordinate complex shows semantic integrity; by contrast, conjuncts of accidental coordination are not related to each other and thus the whole coordinate complex does not show semantic integrity. The accidental coordination reading of (5.3a) is that John can draw the cart and Peter can also draw the cart, while its natural coordination reading is that they can draw the cart together. It has long been recognized that this contrast also exists in plural nominals. (5.3b) is ambiguous in the same way as (5.3a). In its natural grouping reading, it means that the men can draw the cart together, whereas in its accidental grouping reading, it means that each of the men can draw the cart individually.

(5.3) a.   John and Peter can draw the cart.   (Dik 1968: 87)
       b.   The men can draw the cart.

We can see the contrast between the two types of readings for plural nominals not only in predication, but also in modification. In the natural grouping reading of (5.4), the multiple individuals denoted by *stories* contradict each other, whereas in the accidental grouping reading, each of them is internally inconsistent.

(5.4)   Jack told inconsistent stories.   (Schwarzschild 2002: 16)

We highlight this parallelism between coordinate complexes and non-coordinate elements in order to emphasize the fact that the contrast between natural and accidental grouping does not depend on the construction being a coordinate construction.

The natural and accidental grouping readings of plural nominals may also co-exist in the same sentence (data like (5.5) are seen in Dowty 1987: 98 and Lasersohn 1995: Chapter 5, among others):

(5.5) a.   John and Mary are a happy couple and are well-adjusted individuals too.
       b.   John and Mary met at the bar and had a drink.
       c.   The students closed their notebooks, left the room, and then gathered in the hall after the class.

In (5.5a), *John and Mary* is a natural coordination with respect to the first conjunct *are a happy couple*, which is a collective predicate, but an accidental coordination with respect to the second conjunct *are well-adjusted individuals*, which is a distributive predicate. Similarly, in (5.5b) *John and Mary* is a natural coordination with respect to the first conjunct *met at the bar*, which is a collective predicate, but an accidental coordination with respect to the second conjunct *had a drink,* which is a distributive predicate. In (5.5c), the plural nominal *the students* encodes an accidental grouping with respect to the first and second conjunct, but a natural grouping with respect to the last conjunct *then gathered in the hall after the class.*

5.2.2 Asymmetrical coordination

Natural coordination can be either nominal or verbal (Dalrymple and Nikolaeva 2006: 830). In this subsection I identify so-called asymmetrical coordination as natural coordination of verbal elements. In examples like (5.6), the coordination is not asymmetrical, since the conjuncts do not have to be semantically related to each other, or encode a natural sequence of events. In (5.6a), for instance, *to play the piano* has no semantic relation with *to learn exotic languages*. In such accidental coordination examples, the conjuncts do not form an integrated semantic whole. Goldsmith (1985: 134) calls the use of *and* in accidental coordination "truth-conditional *and*."

(5.6) a. Our first contestant likes to play the piano and (to) learn exotic languages.
    b. He did some weeding and wrote a few pages of the paper.

Since Schmerling (1975), Goldsmith (1985) and Lakoff (1986), semantic types of coordination other than the "truth-conditional" type have been explored extensively in languages such as English (Culicover and Jackendoff 1997) and German (Höhle 1990, among others). Goldsmith calls the conjunction "temporal *and*" in examples like (5.7a), "causal *and*" in examples like (5.7b), "despite" or "nonetheless *and*" in examples like (5.7c). One might like to add the term "conditional *and*" to cover examples like (5.7d) (Bar-Lev and Palacas 1980; Culicover and Jackendoff 1997).

(5.7) a. Mary bought the newspaper after work and she read it on the train.
    b. The light went off and I couldn't see.
    c. How many courses can we expect our graduate students to teach and (still) finish a dissertation on time?
    d. You drink another can of beer and I'm leaving. (= If you drink one more can of beer, I'm leaving.)

Differences in the various uses of *and* in (5.7) are not syntactically significant, and such examples have been covered by the general term asymmetrical coordination (AC) or Fake Coordination in the literature. Like the accidental coordination constructions in (5.6), AC constructions may express plural eventualities. What is special is that AC always encodes a certain semantic relation between the conjuncts, in which the conjuncts form an integrated semantic whole. Analyzing data like (5.7), Culicover and Jackendoff (1997: 213 fn. 13) explicitly claim that "we understand the two events as being connected as parts of a larger event; they did not occur independently, on different 'occasions,' so to speak." In Huddleston and Pullum (2002: 1283), AC is identified as joint coordination, yet another term for natural coordination.

In asymmetrical or natural coordination, conjuncts are semantically related to each other in some dimensions; Goldsmith's terms simply name the dimensions. As pointed out by Dik (1968: 271), "the semantic aspect of *and* does not in itself specify the kind of combination any further, but can give rise to a multitude of different relations in the final interpretation." Generally, it is the linguistic (e.g. word order) and non-linguistic contexts that indicate the exact semantic relation between the conjuncts in AC. For instance, by itself, *and* does not indicate the differences in semantic relations between the conjuncts in the two examples in (5.8).

(5.8) a.   She died, and they buried her.
     b.   They buried her, and she died.

Nevertheless, the accidental vs. natural status of coordination can be signaled by certain expressions. For instance, *and similarly* and *and . . . too* encode accidental coordination, whereas *and therefore*, *and as a result*, and *and then* encode natural coordination or AC. Although conjuncts in natural coordination might function semantically like modifiers, they do not have an adjunction relation to another element syntactically. This has been argued for in Culicover and Jackendoff (1997) and Kehler (2002: 61). I thus assume, as argued in Section 2.4, that AC is true coordination (*contra* Schachter 1977: 100 and Postal 1998).[1]

5.2.3   Some formal contrasts between natural and accidental coordination
The contrast between natural and accidental coordination can be formally represented in various ways, beyond the well-recognized contrast between collective adverbs such as *together* and distributive adverbs such as *separately*.

A.   The coordinator *ji* in Chinese
Conjunctions can be exclusively distributive. The conjunction *ji* in Chinese is such a conjunction, as demonstrated by the following evidence.

First, coordinate complexes conjoined by the conjunction *ji,* unlike those conjoined by *he* and *gen*, cannot be the subject of collective predicates. In (5.9a), for instance, *shi pengyou* 'be friends' is a collective predicate, and so is *shi yi dui fu-qi* 'be husband and wife.' The subjects of the predicates can be conjoined by *he* or *gen*, but not *ji*. (5.9b) shows the same point.

---

1 Note that although most of the examples above contain VP conjuncts, some of them have TP conjuncts (going beyond the range of examples cited by Goldsmith 1985; Lakoff 1986; and Culicover and Jackendoff 1997). Therefore, Postal's (1998) claim that AC is restricted to VPs is not accurate.

(5.9) a. Baoyu {he/gen/*ji} Daiyu shi pengyou/yi dui fu-qi.
      Baoyu and/and/and Daiyu be friend /one pair husband-wife
      'Baoyu and Daiyu are {friends/a couple}.'

    b. Baoyu {he/gen/*ji} Daiyu zai huayuan jianmian-le.
      Baoyu and/and/and Daiyu at garden meet-PRF
      'Baoyu and Daiyu met in the garden.'

Second, collective verbs are incompatible with objects conjoined by *ji*. In (5.10), the verb *hunyao* "confuse" is collective, and the components of the object cannot be conjoined by *ji*.

(5.10)   Akiu hunyao-le lundian {he/gen/*ji} lunju.
          Akiu confuse-PRF claim and/and/and argument
          'Akiu confused the claims and the arguments.'

Third, unlike coordinate complexes conjoined by *he* and *gen*, those conjoined by *ji* are never ambiguous between distributivity and collectivity. (5.11a) can be ambiguous; although the default reading is collective (i.e. Baoyu has been engaged to Daiyu), (5.11a) can also have a distributive reading, where Baoyu is engaged to a person other than Daiyu, and Daiyu is engaged to a person other than Baoyu. (5.11b), however, must be distributive, because of the presence of the distributive adverb *fenbie* 'separately.' Like (5.11b), (5.11c) is also not ambiguous, having only a distributive meaning, even though no distributive adverb is present.

(5.11) a. Baoyu {he/gen} Daiyu dingqin-le.   (default: collective)
      Baoyu and/and Daiyu engage-PRF
      'Baoyu and Daiyu are engaged.'

    b. Baoyu {he/gen} Daiyu fenbie   dingqin-le.   (distributive)
      Baoyu and/and Daiyu separately engage-PRF
      'Baoyu and Daiyu are both engaged (separately).'

    c. Baoyu ji Daiyu dingqin-le.   (distributive)
      Baoyu and Daiyu engage-PRF
      'Baoyu and Daiyu are both engaged.'

In short, whereas *he* and *gen* can occur in either collective or distributive contexts, the conjunction *ji* occurs in distributive contexts only.

Since *ji* is a distributive conjunction, the external conjunct of a *ji*-coordinate construction may not be extracted. In (5.12a), the external conjunct *Akiu* is adjacent to the conjunction *gen*, while in (5.12b), the external conjunct *Akiu* and *gen* are separated by the circumstantial *zai Riben* 'in Japan' (see Section 4.4.3B). In the two examples in (5.12), the predicate is collective and thus the coordination is a natural one. In (5.13a) the external conjunct *Shizhang* 'mayor' is adjacent to the distributive conjunction *gen*, while in (5.13b), the external conjunct *Shizhang* and *ji* are separated by the circumstantial *zai Riben* 'in Japan.' However, unlike (5.12b), (5.13b) is not acceptable.

(5.12) a. [Akiu gen Baoyu] zai Riben jian-le   mian.   (= (4.85))
     Akiu   and Baoyu   at   Japan meet-PRF face

   b. Akiu$_i$ zai Riben [$_{-i}$ gen Baoyu] jian-le   mian.
     Akiu   at   Japan   and Baoyu   meet-PRF face
     Both: 'Akiu and Baoyu met in Japan.'

(5.13) a. [Shizhang ji   qi   furen] zai Riben canguan-le yi   ge youeryuan.
     Mayor   and his wife   at   Japan visit-PRF   one   CL kindergarten
     'The mayor and his wife visited a kindergarten in Japan.'

   b. *[Shizhang]$_i$ zai Riben [$_{-i}$ ji   qi   furen] canguan-le yi
     Mayor   at   Japan   and his wife   visit-PRF   one

   ge youeryuan.
   CL kindergarten

Exclusively distributive conjunctions are also found in other languages, such as *i* 'and' in Czech (Skrabalova 2005). In Udihe, the word *zuŋe* 'and' is used for accidental coordination and the word *mule* 'and, with' is used for natural coordination (Dalrymple and Nikolaeva 2006: 831). In Lenakel, the tight conjunction *m* is for natual coordination and the loose conjunction *məne* is for accidental coordination (Haspelmath 2004: 13).

B. Singular vs. plural agreement in English

One formal property of natural coordination in English is that it may trigger singular agreement on verbs, auxiliaries, or pronouns (Moltmann 1997: 233ff.; Huddleston and Pullum 2002: 1283).

As noted in earlier chapters, agreement in coordination is affected by multiple factors, including notional information, lexical plurality, and linear (surface) word order (Lorimor 2007; Steiner 2008). Here we focus on notional information. Consider the variation in number agreement seen in the following coordinate complexes (McNally 1993: 363; Moltmann 1997: 238; Sauerland 2003: (11)):

(5.14) a. Bread and butter is all we had to eat.
   b. The bread and wine is on the table.
   c. Bread and butter {are/*is} found in aisles 1 and 7, respectively.
   d. Strawberries and cream is on the menu.

(5.14c) contains the distributive adverb *respectively*, making the coordination accidental. Thus only the plural number agreement is possible, in contrast to

(5.14a), (5.14b), and (5.14d), where the singular number agreement is allowed. The coordination in these three examples can be regarded as natural coordination.

Another relevant set of examples is the following:

(5.15) a. Three and five {is/are/makes/make} eight.
     b. Three and five {are/*is} odd numbers.

(5.16) a. Three and five is even.
     b. Three and five {are/*is} odd.

In (5.15a), neither conjunct alone can be the subject of the predicate *eight*. The subject is therefore a natural coordination complex, which may take the singular form of the copula. In (5.15b), however, each of the conjuncts in the subject can be independently related to the predicate *odd numbers*, ruling out natural coordination. Therefore, the plural form of the copula is used. Similarly, the singular copula *is* is used in (5.16a) because *even* reflects the sum reading of the coordinate subject. In contrast, the singular copula *is* cannot be used in (5.16b) because *odd* is not the predicate of the sum reading of the coordinate subject but of its distributive reading.

In the literature on the syntax of coordination, the fact that coordinate complexes can trigger the singular number agreement in certain cases has been studied by many scholars (Dik 1968: 210; McCloskey 1991: 594; Aoun *et al.* 1994; Aoun and Benmamoun 1999; Munn 1993: Section 2.5.7; 1999; Johannessen 1996; 1998; among others). This quirky agreement is not restricted to coordination, but is also found in nominals with a PP modifier (e.g. *the gang on the motorcycles* and *the gang near the motocycles*; see Humphreys and Bock 2005) (I thank Wayne Cowart for bringing my attention to the work by Humphreys and Bock) and possessive nominals (den Dikken 2001: 22, 24). In (5.17b) and (5.18b), the plural possessor *participants* triggers plural agreement with the copula, regardless of its surface position. Similarly, *the doors* in (5.19b) triggers plural agreement, although it is not the head of the complex nominal.

(5.17) a. The participants' identity is to remain a secret.
     b. The participants' identity <u>are</u> to remain a secret.

(5.18) a. The identity of the participants is to remain a secret.
     b. The identity of the participants <u>are</u> to remain a secret.

(5.19) a. The key to all the doors is missing.
     b. The key to all the doors <u>are</u> missing.

I believe that McNally (1993: 363) is right in claiming that agreement resolution can depend on the denotation of the nominal complexes (see also Dougherty 1970b: 853 for an early discussion of the contrast between "semantic" and "syntactic" agreement). Specifically, agreement depends on the contrast between natural coordination and accidental coordination, where the former can trigger singular agreement while the latter cannot. Since this contrast is not defined (purely) syntactically, agreement cannot be used as a diagnostic in the syntactic analysis of coordination (see Section 2.3.1). This conclusion fits with the following generalization of McCloskey (1991: 565):

> The semantic condition governing such agreement seems to be that plural agreement is possible just in case the conjoined propositions are contradictory or incompatible, or, more generally, when they specify a plurality of distinct states of affairs or situation-types. When the coordinated clauses denote compatible propositions (that is, when they denote two or more propositions that jointly specify a single complex state of affairs or situation-type), then singular agreement is preferred or required.

McCloskey's generalization is confirmed by Moltmann's (1997: 238) observation that when both singular and plural agreement are possible, the latter is used when the meanings of the two conjuncts are somehow "unrelated." A similar idea is seen in Sauerland (2003: Section 2.1).

Data like (5.14) above involve mass noun conjuncts. Coordinate complexes composed of conjuncts of other semantic types can also trigger singular agreement (Hegarty 2003; Moltmann 1997: 235). One such example is (5.20) (McCloskey 1991: 565) (the Dutch counterpart of (5.20) shows the same acceptability contrast; Petra Hendriks, p.c.).

(5.20)   That UNO will be elected and that sanctions will be lifted {is/??are} now likely.

C.   Other morphological representations

In the Finnish example in (5.21a), no single conjunct may be modified by the relational adjective *yhteensopivat* 'compatible' and thus the coordination *yliopisto ja teatteri* 'university and theater' is natural coordination. In this language, natural coordinate complexes may be modified by plural adjectives, as in (5.21a), whereas accidental coordinate complexes may not be modified by plural adjectives, as shown in (5.21b). The intended meaning of (5.21b) is expressed by (5.21c), in which each conjunct is modified by a singular adjective (Dalrymple and Nikolaeva 2006: 826, 829).

(5.21) a. On vaikeaa suunnitella {yhteensopivat/*yhteensopiva} yliopisto
          is difficult design   compatible.PL/compatible.SG   university

          ja teatteri.
          and theater
          'It's difficult to design a compatible [university and theater].'

       b. *Tässä   kaupungissa on hyvät   yliopisto ja   teatteri.
            this.INES city.INES   is good.PL university and theater
            'There is a good [university and theater] in this city.'

       c. Tässä   kaupungissa on hyvä   yliopisto ja   hyvä   teatteri.
          this.INES city.INES   is good.SG university and good.SG theater
          'There is a good university and a good theater in this city.'

The contrast between natural and accidental coordination is also seen in the following case patterns in Korean (Yoon and Lee 2005). In (5.22a), which has a collective reading, the nominative case marker occurs only on the final conjunct, whereas in (5.22b), which has a distributive reading, the nominative case marker occurs on both conjuncts.

(5.22) a. John-kwa Mary-ka cip-ey   ka-ss-ta
          John-and Mary-NOM home-LOC go-PST-DECL
          'John and Mary went home together."

       b. John-i   kuliko Mary-ka cip-ey   ka-ss-ta
          John- NOM and   Mary-NOM home-LOC go-PST-DECL
          "John and Mary went home separately."

Similar case patterns are found in Hebrew. In this language, the accusative case marker *et* occurs only once, in front of the entire coordinate complex, if the complex has a collective reading, as in (5.23a). By contrast, it precedes each definite conjunct if the definite coordinate complex has a distributive reading, as in (5.23b). Accordingly, if we use a verb which forces a collective reading of the object, such as *hifrid* 'separated' (or *hifgish* 'caused to meet' or *ixed* 'united'), only one *et* shows up, as seen in (5.24) (Winter 2001).

(5.23) a. Dan ar'a et   Ruti ve   Sara.
          Dan saw ACC Ruti and Sara
          'Dan saw Ruti and Sara together.'

       b. Dan ar'a et   Ruti ve   et   Sara.
          Dan saw ACC Ruti and ACC Sara.
          'Dan saw Ruti and Dan saw Sara, separately.'

(5.24) a. Dan hifrid   et   Ruti ve   Sara.
          Dan separate ACC Ruti and Sara
          'Dan separated Ruti and Sara.'

       b. ??Dan hifrid et Ruti ve et Sara.

The genitive case marker *'s* in English coordinate complexes also occurs once if the reading is collective and on each conjunct if the reading is distributive. (5.25a) means that John and Harry departed together and (5.25b) means that they did so separately (McCawley 1968: 161):

(5.25) a. John and Harry's departure for Cleveland   [collective]
        b. John's and Harry's departure for Cleveland   [distributive]

Yoon and Lee (2005) argue that distributive examples like (5.22b) are derived from clausal coordinate constructions by reduction, and the case of each case-marked nominal is related to one case-assignor in the clause containing it. If so, the possibility of reduction is again licensed by distributivity. Their analysis may also be applicable to the Hebrew (accusative case) and English (genitive case) constructions described above.

D.   Other formal representations

The contrast between natural and accidental coordination is also reflected in accent, gapping, and some special constructions.

If the semantics of the conjuncts in a coordinate complex are in contrast, parallel elements in the conjuncts can bear contrastive accents. This is not the case for AC. For instance, (5.26a) has two readings. It can mean either that the events expressed by the two conjuncts are independent (distributive) or that the first event is the cause of the second event (collective). Hendriks (2004: 6) states that if all constituents but the finite verbs are pronounced with contrastive accent, as in (5.26b), the AC reading seems to disappear, or at least becomes highly marginal. In other words, distributive readings are compatible with contrastive accent but collective readings are not.

(5.26) a. Sue became upset and Nan became downright angry.   (AC possible)
        b. SUE became UPSET and NAN became DOWNRIGHT ANGRY.   (*AC)

Levin and Prince (1986) (also see Moltmann 1992a: 49; Hendriks 2004; Chaves 2007: 30) observe that gapping is hardly ever found in AC. Compare (5.26a) with its gapping counterpart in (5.27).

(5.27)   Sue became upset and Nan _ downright angry.   (*AC)

Unlike (5.26a), which has the two readings noted above, (5.27) has only the distributive reading. In other words, distributive but not collective readings are possible in gapping.

The contrast between distributivity and collectivity is also seen in so-called SGF-coordination (Subject Gap in Fronted/Finite Clause Coordination, Höhle

1990) in Germanic languages, as in (5.28). In this construction, the subject gap in the second conjunct is referentially related to the subject of the first conjunct; however, the subject of the first conjunct does not occur in the position parallel to that of the gap in the second conjunct. In (5.28), the subject *der Jäger* 'the hunter' follows the verb in the first conjunct, whereas the gap in the second conjunct precedes the verb, assuming both conjuncts are in a V2 order.

(5.28)   In   den Wald ging der Jäger und _ fing   einen Hasen.   [German]
          into the   forest went the hunter and   caught a   rabbit

The construction is felicitous only with an AC reading, such as cause – effect and contiguity readings (Frank 2002; Hendriks 2004: 15; see also Johnson 2002). This restriction means that the coordination in this construction is natural, not accidental.

In this section, I have summarized various formal ways to represent the contrast between natural and accidental coordination. The following sections link this contrast with the EC.

5.3   The EC violation in asymmetrical coordination

In AC, extraction from either of the two conjuncts is generally possible, indicating that there is no EC effect in natural coordination. Many such EC violations are reported and discussed in Ross (1967: Section 5.2.2), Grosu (1973), Schachter (1977: 299), Goldsmith (1985), and Lakoff (1986), Heycock and Kroch (1994: 272), Culicover and Jackendoff (1997: 201), Wilder (1999: 9), Levine (2001: 156–161), Cormack and Smith 2005). (5.29) lists some examples.

(5.29) a. This is the thief that [you just point out the loot] and then we arrest _ [on the spot].   (relativization)
       b. How much wine can you drink _ and still stay sober?   (wh-ques)
       c. Swiftly John will run _ and end up falling down.   (Adv-fronting)
          (Benjamin Shaer, p.c.; see Shaer 2003: 243)
       d. Off the boy went _, and told his friends the news.
       e. [This advice] the committee decided to follow _ and proceeded to set up a new subcommittee.   (nominal-topic)
       f. Kiss her, I didn't _, and will probably regret it.   (VP-topic)

In (5.29a), relativization occurs in the second conjunct. In (5.29b), the wh-phrase moves from the first conjunct. In (5.29c) and (5.29d), manner and direction adverbs, respectively, are fronted from the first conjunct. In (5.29e) and (5.29f), the nominal topic and VP topic are fronted, respectively. (5.30) shows that extraction is possible from either conjunct in AC (Lakoff 1986; Kehler 2002: 128):

(5.30) a. Which knee did Terry run in these shoes and hurt _?
       b. Which shoes did Terry run in _ and hurt her knee?

The examples in (5.29) and (5.30) show that the EC can be violated in AC. The following examples in (5.31) show that when the EC is violated, the coordination must be asymmetrical. The wh-element *what* moves from a single conjunct in (5.31b), but nothing moves out of a single conjunct in (5.31a). Carlson (1987: 539; see also Kehler 2002: 127, 139) observes that in (5.31b) there must be a natural consequential relation between the two eventualities, whereas (5.31a) allows a (less salient) reading in which the two eventualities are not related.[2]

(5.31) a. John went to the store and bought some ice cream.
       b. What did John go to the store and buy?

Cross-linguistically, the absence of EC effects in AC is reported in Johannessen (1998: Chapter 6) and Peterson and VanBik (2004: 345–347). Violation of the EC is also seen in Chinese. The conjunction *erqie* 'and' occurs in either accidental coordination or the consecutive type of natural coordination. If *erqie* is used in a consecutive sense, extraction from the first conjunct is possible, as seen in (5.32): one has to read something before writing any notes about it, so the two events have a consecutive relation. In (5.32a), the topic *na fen baozhi* 'that newspaper' is associated with the object gap of the first conjunct. In (5.32b), the relativized nominal *baozhi* 'newspaper' is associated with the object gap of the first conjunct.

---

2 Kehler (2002: 139) reports that the repetition of the subject *I* in (ii) is not compatible with the extraction from a single conjunct:

(i)   I went to the store and I bought some whiskey.
(ii)   This is the whiskey which I went to the store and (*I) bought.

Recall that (i) is ambiguous between a one-event reading and a two-event reading (see Section 3.5). Only the former is an AC reading. Under the latter reading, the EC cannot be violated, and thus (ii) is not acceptable if it shares the base-structure with (i), i.e., *I* is present in the second conjunct. However, why can't (ii) have an AC reading? I speculate that in such examples, the repetition of the subject encodes a focus reading (I thank James Myers for pointing out the information structure of such examples to me). Recall that both the accent in (5.26b) and the gapping in (5.27) express focus, and they do not have an AC reading. If EC violations are allowed only in AC and the presence of focus blocks the AC reading, the fact that *I* cannot appear in the second conjunct of (ii) is accounted for.

(5.32) a. Na   fen baozhi,   Baoyu kan-le   _, erqie hai   xie-le   biji.
             that CL   newspaper, Baoyu read-PRF   and   also write-PRF notes
             'That newspaper, Baoyu read it and wrote notes.'

       b. na   fen [Baoyu kan-le   _ erqie hai   xie-le   biji] de baozhi
             that CL   Baoyu read-PRF   and   also write-PRF note DE newspaper
             'the newspaper that Baoyu read and also wrote notes on it.'

As in English, if there is no semantic relation between the conjuncts (i.e. the speaker reports two unrelated eventualities), extraction from a single conjunct is impossible in Chinese. In (5.33b), the event of reading a newspaper is not related to the event of taking a bath, so the coordinate complex conjoined by *erqie* does not tolerate the object gap in the first conjunct, which is associated with the relativized nominal *baozhi* 'newspaper.'

(5.33) a. Akiu kan-le   na   fen baozhi,   erqie xi-le   zao.
             Akiu read-PRF that CL   newspaper and   wash-PRF bath
             'Akiu read that newspaper and took a bath.'

       b. *na   fen [Akiu kan-le   _ erqie xi-le   zao] de baozhi
             that CL   Akiu read-PRF   and   wash-PRF bath DE newspaper

Since there is no semantic connection between the conjuncts in (5.33), the coordination is accidental. The presence of the EC effect in (5.33b) and the absence of the effect in (5.32) result from the contrast between accidental and natural coordination.

The fact that natural coordination tolerates EC violations whereas accidental one does not is also observed in Quantifier Raising, a covert movement operation (May 1985). Data like the following are discussed in Ruys (1992) and de Vos (2005: 42):

(5.34) a. A policeman serenaded every widow.
           'Some policeman serenaded all the widows.'   [narrow scope]
           'For each of the widows, there was some policeman or other who serenaded her.'   [wide scope]

       b. A policeman went to town and (he) serenaded every widow as well.
           'Some policeman went to town and also serenaded all the widows.'
           [narrow scope]
           *'Some policeman or other went to town and for each
           of the widows, there was some policeman or other who serenaded
           her.'   [wide scope]

The quantifier *every* in (5.34a) can have either narrow scope, as in the first reading, or wide scope, as in the second reading. In the latter case, the quantifier presumably undergoes covert movement and lands in a position higher than *a policeman.* (5.34b) is a coordinate construction, and the expression *as well* indicates its accidental coordination reading. In this example, the wide scope reading of *every* disappears, suggesting that covert movement from the second conjunct is impossible. Importantly, de Vos notes that in the contiguous reading of (5.35), a natural coordination reading, both narrow and wide scope readings of *every* are available. In other words, it is possible for the assumed covert movement to launch from the second conjunct.

(5.35)   A policeman went and serenaded every widow.
          'Some policeman serenaded all the widows.'   [narrow scope]
          'For each of the widows, there was some policeman or other who
          serenaded her.'   [wide scope]

One might think that in examples like (5.29) above, the EC is not violated, but instead the apparent gaps in the conjuncts are actually null resumptive pronouns or conjunct-internal operator movement. The quantifier raising contrast in (5.34b) and (5.35), however, does not permit this kind of analysis. There is no possibility of either resumptive pronouns or operator movement in (5.35), but the EC still seems to be violable.[3]

In addition to the semantic condition of natural vs. accidental coordination, there is indeed a formal condition on certain EC violations: wh-adverbials cannot be extracted from single conjuncts (Culicover 1990; Postal 1998: 66):

(5.36) a. Which student did Nora go to the drugstore, come home, and talk to _
            for an hour?
        b. *How long did Nora go there, come home, and talk to that student _?

As is well known, compared to wh-arguments, wh-adverbials show special syntactic properties, and in particular they are usually less active. For instance, no *in situ* wh-adverbial can be licensed in English (C. J. Huang 1982), no wh-adverbial can undergo long-distance fronting in Chinese (Tsai 1994: 162), and no multiple wh-adverbial fronting occurs cross-linguistically (Rudin 1988). Therefore, the restriction of wh-adverbials implied by the above examples is not related to the coordinate construction per se, and thus cannot be used to argue for the EC as a formal syntactic constraint.

In short, in both overt and covert movement, when the EC is violated, the coordinated conjuncts are semantically related. The situation is just as Goldsmith (1985: 134) claims: "The Coordinate Structure Constraint fails here not because of some formal failing of English or the grammar, but, it seems,

---

3 See May (1985: 59), Ruys (1993), Fox (2000), Szabolcsi (2001: 619), V. Lin (2001; 2002), Potts (2002), and Kasai (2002) for more discussion on the relationship between QR and the CSC.

because of the meaning of the construction." Specifically, as we have shown, it is because of the semantic relatedness of the conjuncts found in natural coordination.

In other words, extraction out of conjuncts is blocked only in certain special cases (involving non-AC constructions and adverbials); there is no need to posit a constraint against such movement in general.[4,5]

5.4   Chapter summary

In this chapter, I discussed the semantic contrast between natural and accidental coordination, and identified both AC and collective coordination as natural

---

4 As shown in Chapter 4, the CC is not violable in *and*-complexes. Hence examples that combine violations of the EC with violations of the CC in *and*-complexes are always unacceptable, and shed no light on the EC itself. The following data are cited from Sag (1982: 332) and Gazdar *et al.* (1985: 178).

(i)   a.   *I wonder who you saw [_ and [a picture of _]].
      b.   *I wonder who you saw [[a picture of _] and _].

(ii) a.   *The Pre-Raphaelites, we found [_ and [books about _]].
      b.   *The Pre-Raphaelites, we found [[books about _]] and _].

5 Despite admitting that the traditional EC does not work in AC, Pesetsky (1982) presents an alternative syntactic approach to EC-like effects. A crucial assumption of Pesetsky (1982) is that in a symmetrical coordinate complex, the coordinator assigns a single theta role to a number of conjuncts simultaneously, whereas in an asymmetrical coordinate complex, the coordinator assigns different theta roles to the conjuncts. Pesetsky thus claims that the formal relations between conjuncts and coordinators are special in AC, permitting EC violations in AC to be licensed in the syntax. Unfortunately for this analysis, however, the theta-role approach to the relation between coordinators and conjuncts is not compatible with the generally accepted theta theory in at least the following ways.

By definition, in AC the semantic functions of the conjuncts are different (e.g. one conjunct could be a cause and the other a result). However, we do not see any semantic relation between conjuncts and coordinators. Thematic relations represent abstract semantic relations between verbs and nominals. For instance, in *John laughed*, *John* is an agent of the event denoted by *laughed*, whereas in *John fell*, *John* is a theme of the event denoted by *fell*. By contrast, coordinators and conjuncts do not show any such semantic relation. In AC, the defining semantic relation is expressed between the conjuncts, not between the conjuncts and the coordinator.

Moreover, with respect to the number of theta-role receivers, a theta-role approach to the EC does not explain why a single coordinator in symmetrical coordination may assign a theta role to a number of conjuncts simultaneously, whereas other theta-role assignors may only assign a theta role to a single nominal. Similarly, with respect to the number of assigned theta roles, a theta-role approach to the EC does not explain why a single coordinator in AC can assign multiple theta roles to a number of conjuncts, whereas other theta-role assignors can assign only one theta role to a nominal. The theta-role explanation for the absence of EC effects in AC is thus ad hoc at best. It simply stipulates certain special mechanisms to formulate the peculiarities of AC, without providing a general account for related phenomena.

coordination. I then examined violation of the EC in natural coordination in English and Chinese. Finally, I showed that Pesetsky's (1982) syntactic analysis of the EC has serious problems.

In Chapter 4, I investigated how the availability of external conjunct movement correlates with the non-distributiveness, showing that the CCe is relativized semantically. Parallel to this, in this chapter I showed how the availability of element movement out of conjuncts correlates with non-distributiveness as well, showing that the EC is also relativized semantically.

If, cross-linguistically, both the CC and the EC can be violated systematically in non-distributive coordination (i.e., natural coordination), the CSC cannot be a general syntactic constraint on movement.

In the summary in (5.37), *Yes* means the presence of the CSC effect, and *No* means the absence of the CSC effect.

(5.37)

	In natural coordination	*In accidental coordination*	*Explanation*
EC	No	Yes	RPR (see Chapter 7)
CCe	No, if the coordinator has intrinsic categorial features (e.g. Chinese *he/gen*)	Yes	RPR (see Chapter 7)
	Yes, if the coordinator has no intrinsic categorial features and the external conjunct alone satisfies the c-selection imposed on the whole coordinate complex (e.g. English *and*)		The categorial features of the external conjunct are transferred to the coordinator, which is the head of the whole complex; elements may not move if their categorial features have been removed (see Chapter 4)
CCi	Yes		Like many other types of head elements, coordinators may not be stranded (see Chapter 4)

6 Three puzzles solved by rejecting the CSC

6.1 Introduction

In the last two chapters, I argued that neither the CC nor the EC is a constraint on syntactic operations. The CSC is thus not part of the computational system. Getting rid of an ad hoc stipulation is desirable by itself, but rejecting this particular stipulation also allows us to improve our understanding of some hitherto puzzling facts about natural language. In this chapter, I show what we gain if we give up the CSC. Specifically, I examine three constructions that seem to be in conflict with certain basic syntactic laws observed elsewhere. The first construction seems to conflict with principles of selection, theta-role licensing, and syntax–semantics mapping, the second with principles governing the syntactic relation between elements and their shared modifier, and the third with principles governing the launching site of certain movement operations. Postal (1998) ends his book by stating that the third of these constructions raises such serious challenges for syntactic theory that they can only be avoided by denying that the construction actually exists. However, as I show in this chapter, if we give up the CSC, all three of the constructions can be derived in accordance with standard principles. Thus, abandoning the CSC may actually strengthen the explanatory power of syntactic theory.

Each of the three remaining sections in this chapter is devoted to one of these three constructions, which I will call Split Argument Constructions, Modifier-Sharing Constructions, and Interwoven Dependency Constructions.

6.2 Deriving Split Argument Constructions by giving up the CC

6.2.1 The Split Argument Construction (SAC)

The Split Argument Construction (SAC) refers to sentences like (6.1), in which preverbal and post-verbal arguments (underlined) share the same thematic relation with the verb, and which have a reading expressible as in (6.2), where a coordinate complex containing the two nominals functions as a single argument and theta-role bearer for the same verb. In English, the coordinate DP complex in the non-SAC counterpart occurs in a subject position, as in (6.2).

(6.1) a. <u>John</u> married <u>Jane</u>.
     b. <u>Italy</u> borders <u>France</u>.

(6.2) a. [<u>John</u> and <u>Jane</u>]   married.
     b. [<u>Italy</u> and <u>France</u>] border.

The example in (6.3) is a SAC in Chinese. In the corresponding non-SACs in (6.4), the coordinate complex occurs in a subject position in (6.4a), and in object position in (6.4b).[1]

(6.3)   <u>Tudou</u> yijing   shao-le   <u>niurou</u>.
         potato   already cook-PRF beef
         'The potatoes have already been cooked with the beef.'

(6.4) a. [Tudou gen niurou] shao-zai yiqi   le.
         potato and beef   cook-at together PRT
         'The potatoes and the beef have been cooked together.'

     b. Baoyu shao-le   [tudou gen niurou].
         Baoyu cook-PRF potato and beef
         'Baoyu cooked the potatoes and the beef.'   (either separately or together)

In English, in addition to *marry* and *border*, other collective verbs such as *date, divorce, hug, fight, meet* may also occur in SACs (Levin 1993: 36–37). Parallel examples can also be found in German:

(6.5) a. Die Prinzessin heiratet den Grafen.
         the princess   marries the earl
         'The princess marries the earl.'

     b. Die Prinzessin und der Graf heiraten (sich/einander).
         the princess and der earl marry   one.another
         'The princess and the earl marry (one another).'

---

1 My definition of SACs excludes constructions in which the preverbal nominal and the postverbal nominal do not appear as conjuncts in any alternative construction. Data like the following are not SACs, although the two DPs seem to have a similar thematic relation to the verb. Such examples might be derived by DP raising from complex DPs. However, this derivation has nothing to do with coordination and thus is not our concern here. I thank Jianming Lu, Yang Shen, and Bojiang Zhang for urging me to make this clarification.

   (i) a.   Na kuai rou   chao-le rou-si.   b. Juzi   yijing   bo-le   pi.
            that chunk meat fry-PRF meat-shred   orange already peel-PRF peel
            'That chunk of meat has been cut into   'The orange has been peeled.'
            shreds and fried.'

In the Chinese SACs such as (6.3), the preverbal and post-verbal nominals both seem to be patient(s) of the transitive verb. The verbs in such constructions can be either ordinary transitive verbs such as *shao* 'cook' in (6.1), *chao* 'fry,' *dun* 'stew,' or collective transitive verbs such as *lianxi* 'connect,' *ban* 'mix,' and *jiehe* 'combine.' The SACs in (6.6), in which collective verbs occur, alternate with the non-SACs in (6.7).

(6.6) a. <u>Lilun</u>   yinggai lianxi   <u>shiji</u>.
     theory should   connect reality
     'Theories should be linked to reality.'

    b. <u>Na</u> <u>ge</u> <u>jidan</u> zhenghao ban   <u>mifan</u>.
       that CL egg   perfectly mix rice
       'That egg can be perfectly mixed with the rice.'

(6.7) a. [Lilun gen shiji] lianxi   zai yiqi   le.
     theory and reality connect at   together PRT
     'The theory has been linked to reality.'

    b. <u>Na</u> <u>ge</u> <u>jidan</u> gen <u>mifan</u> ban zai yiqi   le.
       that CL egg   and rice   mix at   together PRT
       'That egg has been mixed with the rice.'

A constraint on SACs shared by English and Chinese is that such a construction encodes only a single eventuality. In other words, the verb or predicate may not be distributive. This can be seen from three sources of evidence. First, distributive adverbs such as *separately* and *both* may not occur in SACs.

(6.8) a. *John married Jane separately.   (cf. (6.1))

    b. *Zhe ge jidan zhenghao fenbie   pan fan.   (cf. (6.6))
       this CL egg   perfectly separately mix rice

Second, intrinsically distributive verbs or predicates may not occur in SACs:

(6.9) a. *John sneezed Mary.
     Intended: 'John and Mary sneezed.'

    b. *Jidan xi-le   doufu.
       egg   wash-PRF tofu
       Intended: 'Eggs and tofu have been washed (together).'

Third, the contrast in interpretation between (6.3) and (6.4b) shows that SACs exclude distributive readings.

Levin (1993: 36–37) calls the alternation between SACs and non-SACs in English the Understood Reciprocal Object Alternation. The two DPs in English

SACs must have a reciprocal relation. For instance, even if *John and Mary* in (6.10a) is interpreted as a couple that together receives a single gift, the reading of this sentence still may not be expressed by (6.10b), since the relation between the conjuncts in (6.10a) is not reciprocal. Note that the reciprocal relation is a specific type of non-distributive relation.

(6.10) a. Someone gave John and Mary a gift.
　　　 b. John gave Mary a gift.

　　SACs challenge basic principles of generative grammar governing s-selection of collective verbs, theta-role licensing theory, and the mapping between syntax and semantics.

　　First, a collective verb requires a plural nominal. Yet when such a verb is in a SAC, each of the two arguments may be singular; thus the selection of the verb is not satisfied in the usual way. It seems that the selection of the verb is not satisfied by any syntactic constituent in the surface representation.

　　Second, the verb in a SAC seems to assign two identical theta roles to two nominals. In no other construction is this possible. The problem is also seen from the perspective of the DPs. In a SAC the participant or thematic role of one nominal is the same as that of the other. However, in no other construction may two nominals receive identical theta roles from the same verb.

　　Third, if every SAC alternates with a construction in which the two DPs form a coordinate complex, why do the two DPs in the SAC itself appear so far apart? This separation represents an apparent mismatch between the positions of the DPs and their interpretation. If the DPs in the two constructions have different base positions, the alternation seems to violate Baker's (1988; 1997) Uniformity of Theta-Assignment Hypothesis (UTAH), which states that identical thematic relationships between items are represented by identical structural relationships between these items in their base positions.

　　Fourth, unlike the arguments of other transitive verbs, the subject and the object of a SAC may exchange their positions, without affecting the basic meaning of the construction:

(6.11) a. <u>Italy</u> borders <u>France</u>.
　　　 b. <u>France</u> borders <u>Italy</u>.

　　In this section, I will show that SACs can be derived by movement of the external conjunct out of a coordinate DP headed by a null D. Since this analysis requires denying that the CC is a genuine constraint on syntactic operations, giving up the CC makes it possible to get a better understanding of the syntax of SACs.

6.2.2   *The two DPs of a SAC form a coordinate complex*

I claim that the two DPs of a SAC form a coordinate DP in their base-positions. Arguments for this claim come from the four challenges listed in the previous subsection.

First, collective verbs such as *marry* and *fight* in English, and *ban* 'mix' and *lianxi* 'connect' in Chinese, require their selected argument to be plural. In a SAC, if neither of the two DPs is plural, neither alone can be the real argument of the verb. If the two singular DPs form a coordinate complex, which is plural, the collective verb is licensed in the construction.

Second, the theta-role licensing problem mentioned above does not occur if the two nominals of a SAC form a complex in their base positions, and the complex has a unique theta-role relation with the verb.

Third, the deviation from the mapping between syntactic positions and semantic interpretations does not occur either, if the two nominals of a SAC form a coordinate complex in their base positions. Then the two DPs in the alternating constructions, such as (6.1) vs. (6.2), have the same base positions.

Fourth, the alternation in (6.11) is also found in coordinate constructions. If the two nominals of a SAC form a coordinate complex in their base positions, either one may be merged with the coordinator first, just like conjuncts.[2]

Note that like ordinary preverbal arguments, the preverbal DP of a SAC is backgrounded, and like an ordinary postverbal argument, the postverbal DP of a SAC is foregrounded, if the construction is uttered without any contrastive stress. This difference in information structure is not relevant to the unification of the theta role of the two nominals.

6.2.3   *Deriving SACs by conjunct raising*

A.   DP Spec raising out of a complex DP

I have claimed that the two DPs of a SAC form a coordinate complex. Specifically, in a SAC, the first nominal (DP_1 in (6.12)) is base-generated as the Spec of the complex DP (DP_3 in (6.12)), and the second nominal (DP_2 in (6.12)) is

---

2 One might wonder whether comitative constructions like (ib) are derived from coordinate constructions like the SAC in (ic), since they pose the same four challenges. See Kayne (1994)
   and Zhang (2007a) for arguments that English comitative constructions are indeed derived from
   coordinate-like constructions.

  (i) a.   John and Jane met (each other) in the street.
      b.   John met with Jane in the street.   (comitative construction)
      c.   John met Jane in the street.   (SAC)

base-generated as the complement of the complex DP. The head of the complex DP is a null D (D_3 in (6.12)).

(6.12)

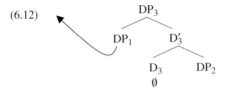

I propose that SACs are derived by the raising of the first conjunct of the base-generated coordinate nominal, as shown in (6.12). The mechanism of this movement is independently found in possessor-raising (see Szabolcsi 1983; 1994; Landau 1999, among others): in both cases, a DP Spec is raised out of a complex DP.

Recall that I argued in Chapter 4 that in *and*-complexes, external conjuncts may not move (the CCe effect) because their categorial features have been transferred to the coordinator *and*. Recall also that external conjuncts may move, however, if the head of a coordinate complex is not realized by *and*, but by a coordinator that has categorial features, such as the conjunctions *he* and *gen* in Chinese. Now in (6.12), the head of the complex DP_3 is a null D, which already has categorical features and so does not take any from DP_1. Therefore, as in *he/gen* constructions, the movement of DP_1 is computationally licensed here.

In Chapter 4 (Section 4.4.3) I also argued that single conjuncts may move only in non-distributive coordination. Since the verbs or predicates of SACs may not be distributive, the proposed conjunct raising in (6.12) is also compatible with this semantic condition on conjunct movement.

The raised DP_1 in SACs parallels nominals appearing with "floating quantifiers" like *all*, discussed by Sportiche (1988) and others. Like the position of *all*, the surface position of the complex DP, which contains DP_2 and the launching site of DP_1, demarcates an argument position.

Before I move to address the syntactic positions of the two DPs of a SAC in the next two subsections, I need to clarify that topicalization constructions such as (6.13a) and *ba* constructions such as (6.13b) are semantically similar to SACs. Although their existence does not challenge the analysis proposed here, I put such constructions aside since it is controversial whether the preverbal patient DP in them is derived by movement or not. If the DP is base-generated at the surface position, it might simply be co-indexed with a null conjunct that is conjoined with the postverbal DP.

(6.13) a. <u>Tudou</u>, ni   keyi dun   <u>niurou</u>.
            potato you can   stew beef
            'As for potatoes, you can stew them with beef.'

      b. Baoyu ba <u>tudou</u> shao-le   <u>niurou</u>.
         Baoyu BA potato cook-PRF beef
         'Baoyu cooked the potatoes and the beef together.'

B.   The syntactic position of the preverbal DP of a SAC

The preverbal DPs of SACs exhibit the syntactic properties of nominals that have undergone A or A-bar movement, supporting the conjunct raising hypothesis illustrated in (6.12).

In English, it is not controversial that the preverbal DP of a SAC is in the subject position, which is derived by A-movement. Like an ordinary subject, the DP triggers agreement with the auxiliary, as seen in (6.14a). Moreover, like an ordinary subject, the DP may precede a raising verb such as *seem*, as seen in (6.14b). Accordingly, the proposed movement in (6.12) is A-movement in English.

(6.14) a. John {has/*have} married Jane.
      b. John seems to have married Jane.

Of course, the first DP (or its null version, i.e., a null operator) of an English SAC may also undergo further syntactic operations, deriving various related constructions:

(6.15) a. It was John who married Jane.
      b. The man that married Jane was John.

I now discuss the syntactic positions of the preverbal nominals in Chinese SACs. Consider the non-argument position first. If the subject position of a SAC is filled by an agent, and no *ba* occurs, the preverbal patient DP, which is associated with the postverbal DP, is not in an argument position. The preverbal patient DP may be in a focus position, preceded by the focus marker *lian* 'even,' as shown by the underlined part in (6.16). This post-*lian* position of the focused DP is derived by A-bar movement (Shyu 1995).

(6.16)   Baoyu <u>lian zuihou yi   bao tudou</u> dou dun-le   niurou.
           Baoyu even last   one bag potato also stew-PRF beef
           'Baoyu stewed even the last bag of potatoes with beef.'

Moreover, SACs may also have a relative clause version. If relativization is derived by the A-bar movement of the modified element or a null operator co-indexed with the modified element, as generally assumed, such SACs are derived by the movement of single conjuncts.

(6.17) a. Baoyu xiang-qi-le   na   bao [RC dun-le   niurou] de tudou.
          Baoyu recall-INCH-PRF that bag   stew-PRF beef   DE potato
          'Baoyu recalled the bag of potatoes that has been stewed with beef.'

       b. Baoyu xiang-qi-le   na   bao [RC dun-le   tudou] de niurou.
          Baoyu recall-INCH-PRF that bag   stew-PRF potato DE beef
          'Baoyu recalled the bag of beef that has been stewed with potatoes.'

Like ordinary A-bar movement, the proposed A-bar movement of the external conjunct in a SAC is not clause-bound, but is subject to island constraints. In (6.18a), *naxie niurou* 'that beef' moves from the embedded clause to the matrix clause, and in (6.18b), *naxie niurou* may not move out of a complex nominal.

(6.18) a. Lian naxie niurou, wo zhidao [Baoyu dou yijing   dun-le   _ tudou].
          even those beef   I know Baoyu also already stew-PRF   potato
          'Even that beef, I know Baoyu has stewed potatoes with.'

       b. *Lian naxie niurou, wo tingshuo [Baoyu dou yijing
          even those beef   I hear   Baoyu also already

          dun-le   _ tudou] de xiaoxi.
          stew-PRF   potato DE news

We now examine the preverbal DPs of SACs that have neither an agent nor *ba*, as in (6.3). If there is only one preverbal nominal in a SAC in Chinese, the nominal, which is a patient, is in a subject position. In Chinese, patient nominals of transitive verbs may occur in a preverbal subject position (Cheng 1988; den Dikken and Sybesma 1998; among others). Such constructions in Chinese can be either property-denoting or episodic-eventuality-denoting, as shown in (6.19a) and (6.19b), respectively.

(6.19) a. Tudou keyi zhu.
          potato can   boil
          'Potatoes can be boiled.'

       b. Tudou yijing   shao-hao-le.
          potato already cook-ready-PRF
          'The potatoes have been cooked already.'

Since the preverbal subject position in Chinese is an available position for patients, it is plausible to assume that the preverbal DP of a Chinese SAC is in the subject position. Here are three further pieces of evidence for this assumption.

First, like an ordinary subject, the preverbal DP in such a construction precedes a modal, and a VP-adverbial. Both types of elements mark the left edge of a predicate.

(6.20) a. Tudou keyi shao niurou.
potato may cook beef
'One may cook potatoes with beef.'

b. Tudou zaojiu shao-le niurou.
potato early cook-PRF beef
'The potatoes were cooked with the beef a long time ago.'

Second, like an ordinary preverbal subject, the preverbal DP of a SAC in Chinese may not be non-specific. The acceptability contrast in the SAC in (6.21b) is parallel to that in (6.21a).

(6.21) a. {Na/*yi} bao tudou yijing huai le ma?
that/one bag potato already bad PRT Q
'Has that bag of potatoes gone bad already?'

b. {Na/*yi} bao tudou yijing dun-le niurou le ma?
that/one bag potato already stew-PRF beef PRT Q
'Has that bag of potatoes been stewed with beef already?'

Third, like an ordinary subject with a quantity reading (Y. A. Li 1998), the preverbal DP of a SAC may also have a quantity reading:

(6.22) Yi gongjin tudou shao-le liang gongjin niurou.
one kg potato cook-PRF two kg beef
'One kg of potatoes has been used to cook with two kg of beef.'

The landing site of the moved conjunct of such a SAC is not a topic position. A topic may precede an overt or implicit agent of a transitive verb, and thus it should license an agent-oriented adverb. Data like (6.23) tell us that no agent-oriented adverbial is allowed in a SAC, although other types of adverbials are allowed (e.g. *yijing* 'already' in (6.21b)). If there were an agent *pro* subject in the construction, an agent-oriented adverb should be licensed.

(6.23) a. *Tudou yukuai de shao-le niurou.
potato happy DE cook-PRF beef

b. *Tudou guyi shao-le niurou.
potato deliberately cook-PRF beef

The exclusion of agent-oriented adverbs also indicates that the preverbal DP of a SAC is not in the position for an instrument adverbial, since such an adverbial may occur with an agent-oriented adverb. In (6.24), *yong guantou* 'with pan' is an instrument and *yukai* 'happily' is an agent-oriented adverbial.

(6.24)   Baoyu yong guantou yukai de zhu-le   yi   guan tang.
          Baoyu with pan   happy DE cook-PRF one can   soup
          'Baoyu cooked a can of soup with a pan happily.'

Of course, like an ordinary subject, the preverbal DP of a SAC may undergo further A-bar movement, to a topic position:

(6.25)   Naxie tudou$_i$, wo tingshuo $_{-i}$ yijing   dun-le   niurou.
          those potato   I   hear   already stew-PRF beef
          'Those potatoes, I heard that they have already been stewed with the beef.'

All of these indicate that the preverbal DP of a SAC is in a position that is derived by A- or A-bar movement.

C.   The syntactic position of the postverbal DP of a SAC
The unraised conjunct of the coordinate DP complex of a SAC remains inside the complex, in a base position decided by the thematic relation between the complex DP and the selecting verb.
    Let us consider the thematic relation between the two DPs and the verb of a SAC in Chinese. It is clear that both DPs have a patient reading. If the two DPs form a complex DP, a plausible hypothesis is that the complex DP is base-generated in the direct object position of the verb, i.e., inside VP (in Chinese at least, postverbal patients must be in direct object position). When the external conjunct is raised, the residue of the complex DP is phonologically realized by the internal conjunct only, and this conjunct thus surfaces in the position of a direct object.
    One may wonder if the verb in a SAC may be passive (as suggested to me by Yang Gu), but the object position of the postverbal DP rules this out. If the verb were passive, the Case of the postverbal DP of a SAC would not be licensed.
    Now let us consider the thematic relation between the DPs and the verb of a SAC in English. The default hypothesis is that the verb in a SAC and the verb in the corresponding non-SAC are the same, and thus they have the same argument structure. For instance, the verb *met* in (6.26a) and the verb *met* in (6.26b) are the same.

(6.26) a. John met Mary.
        b. John and Mary met each other.

(6.27) a. France borders Italy.
        b. France and Italy border each other.

Levin (1993: 37) states that "[T]he action described by the verb in the intransitive [i.e. non-SAC – NZ] variant of this alternation can be roughly paraphrased by the transitive verb when it takes the reciprocal *each other* as object." If the reciprocal *each other* is in direct object position (also see Heim *et al.* 1991), the base position of the coordinate complex *John and Mary* in (6.26b) and *France and Italy* in (6.27b) should be that of external argument of the verb, i.e., Spec of V.

One piece of evidence for the external argument position of the complex nominal in examples like (6.26b) and (6.27b) is that the verb's single argument may not occur postverbally, unlike that of an unaccusative verb.

(6.28) a. There came the sound of gunfire from the street below.
　　　 b. From the street below came the sound of gunfire.

(6.29) a. *There met John and Mary in the street.
　　　 b. *In the street met John and Mary.

Another observation supporting the external argument position of the complex nominal in examples like (6.26b) and (6.27b) is that the argument may not be passivized, unlike the internal arguments of transitive verbs.

(6.30)　*John and Mary were met in the street.
　　　　Intended: "John and Mary met each other in the street."

The verbs in English SACs correspond to reciprocal verbs in other languages. Siloni (2008) reports a detailed study of such verbs and concludes that "cross-linguistic evidence shows that the subject of reciprocals is an external argument."

If the complex nominals in examples like (6.26b) and (6.27b) are base-generated in SpecVP, they undergo A-movement and land at SpecTP. In the SACs in (6.26a) and (6.27a), however, it is the external conjunct of the coordinate DP, rather than the whole coordinate DP, that is raised to SpecTP (see the last subsection). Then the residue of the complex DP, which is phonologically realized by the internal conjunct only, remains in Spec of V. Assuming the verb is always moved out of its base position (see Johnson 1991; Koizumi 1995; Runner 1995; Bowers 2002; and Baltin 2002; 2006 for various implementation of this assumption), we capture the surface order in which the verb precedes the element in Spec V. Moreover, since only the external conjunct is raised to SpecTP, it alone bears nominative Case. Then the Case of the internal conjunct may no longer be nominative, as seen in (6.31). Instead, it may check its Case with V, as the pronoun *other* does in non-SAC constructions like (6.26b) and (6.27b).

(6.31)   Jane married {*he/him}.

This Case checking between V and the post-verbal DP in a SAC may also explain why SACs do not permit reciprocals.

(6.32) a. *John met Mary each other.   (cf. (6.26b))
       b. *France borders Italy each other.   (cf. (6.27b))

In (6.32a), both the pronoun *other* and the postverbal DP *Mary* check their Case features with the single V, which is impossible in English. A similar problem occurs in (6.32b).

Another explanation for the unacceptability of (6.32) comes from the analysis of *each other* in Heim *et al.* (1991). They claim that *each* in *each other* undergoes an LF movement, adjoining to a group-denoting antecedent. Thus in (6.26b), for instance, *each* adjoins to the group-denoting element *John and Mary*. We can now see that in the SAC in (6.26a), after the overt raising of the external conjunct, there is no longer a group-denoting element for *each* to adjoin to. If LF movement occurs after the overt syntactic operations, it is too late for *each* to find any group-denoting element. Consequently, representations such as (6.32), which contain unlicensed *each*, are rejected.

This latter account for the absence of reciprocals in SACs may also explain the absence of reciprocals in comitative constructions in English, a fact noted by Baker (1992: 46):

(6.33) a. John and Mary kissed each other.
       b. *John kissed each other with Mary.

In Chinese, the reciprocal adverb *huxiang* 'mutual' is allowed in comitative coordination if the two conjuncts are not separated, as in (6.34a), but not if the first conjunct moves away, as in (6.34b) (see Chapter 4). In neither the English comitative construction in (6.33b) nor the Chinese comitative construction in (6.34b) is there any group-denoting nominal for the reciprocal to adjoin to at LF, so both are rejected.

(6.34) a. Baoyu gen Daiyu yijing   huxiang wo-shou-le.
          Baoyu and Daiyu already   mutual   grasp-hand-PRF
       b. Baoyu yijing   gen Daiyu (*huxiang) wo-shou-le.
          Baoyu already and Daiyu   mutual   grasp-hand-PRF
          Both: 'Baoyu and Daiyu have shaken their hands.'

I conclude that the preverbal DP of a SAC may occur wherever a language permits an argument to move to. The postverbal DP of a SAC occurs in the base position of the coordinate complex, where its thematic role is assigned by the selecting verb. One consequence is that internal arguments split in SACs in Chinese, whereas external arguments split in SACs in English.

6.2.4   Section summary

We have proposed that SACs are derived by the movement of the external conjunct from a coordinate DP, a proposal that depends on rejecting the CCe. If SACs can be derived syntactically in this way, we solve a variety of puzzles posed by these constructions.

One detail remains neglected in this analysis, namely why, if the derivation of SACs involves a null D in the head position of a coordinate complex, the coordinator must appear overtly in certain other constructions, in both English and Chinese.

In our analysis of SACs in English, the null D heading a coordinate complex licenses single conjunct raising if the conjuncts have a reciprocal relation. But why does the raising of the whole coordinate complex in the corresponding non-SAC require the overt occurrence of the coordinator?

(6.35)   John *(and) Jane married.

Descriptively speaking, null coordinators in ordinary coordinate constructions (i.e. not SACs) are marked in English (Payne 1985: 25), especially for coordinate nominals, though as Kayne (1994: 144 fn.5) notes, null coordinators are possible in coordinate verbal complexes, as in (6.36):

(6.36)   They went, one to Paris, the other to London.

In Chinese, the raising of the external conjuncts is possible even when the coordinator is overt (see Chapter 4), but nothing in the analysis requires it to be overt. Nevertheless, the facts show that the raising of a single conjunct from preverbal position (the cases discussed in Chapter 4) does indeed require the overt appearance of the coordinator:

(6.37) a. Baoyu (gen) Daiyu he-mai-le   yi   zuo fangzi.
            Baoyu and   Daiyu co-buy-PRF one CL   house
            'Baoyu and Daiyu co-bought a house.'

        b. Baoyu yijing   *(gen) Daiyu he-mai-le   yi   zuo fangzi.
            Baoyu already and   Daiyu co-buy-PRF one CL   house
            'Baoyu and Daiyu already co-bought a house.'

Despite this, the English constraint shown in (6.35) is not obeyed in Chinese:

(6.38)   Baoyu (gen) Daiyu xiang-ai-le.
         Baoyu and   Daiyu mutual-love-PRF
         'Baoyu and Daiyu fell in love with each other.'

In this book I focus on the generalization that conjuncts may move if the coordinators have categorial features, regardless of whether the coordinators are overt or covert. Null coordinators with nominal categorial features may occur not only in SACs, but also in the construction to be discussed in next section. It is obvious that not all overt coordinators have a null counterpart, and not all null coordinators have an overt counterpart. At this point the principles accounting for the overtness of coordinators in English and Chinese remain a puzzle to me, and I leave this issue for future research.

6.3   Deriving Modifier-Sharing Constructions by giving up the CC

6.3.1   *The Modifier-Sharing Construction*

In this section, we examine constructions such as (6.39), where a relative clause (RC) seems to be shared by two modified elements (Ross and Perlmutter 1970).

(6.39) a. Mary met a man$_i$ and John met a woman$_j$ [who$_{i\&j}$ knew each other$_{i\&j}$ well].
       b. A man$_i$ came in and a woman$_j$ left [who$_{i\&j}$ were quite similar].
       c. The house has a room$_i$ and the shop has a cellar$_j$ [which$_{i\&j}$ are joined by a small underground passageway].

In (6.39a), for example, the RC, as a modifier, seems to be shared by two modified elements, antecedents, or Heads, namely *a man* and *a woman*.[3] The two DPs are distributed in the two matrix clauses respectively. Each of the two nominals is singular, but the reciprocal *each other*, which requires a plural binder, seems to be licensed by the combination of the two nominals (via the relative pronoun *who*). I call the constructions Modifier-Sharing Constructions (MSC, henceforth).

MSCs have been claimed to pose a serious problem for syntactic theory (Alexiadou *et al.* 2000: 13). The RCs in MSCs are not adjacent to their antecedents, but this separation of the modifier and its modified elements cannot be generated either by extraposition or by deletion of the RC. This is shown by the occurrence of relational expressions such as *similar, each other, join*, which indicate that the RCs must be semantically related to the multiple Heads

---

3 I use "Head" to refer to the modified nominal of a RC, such as *the man* in *the man who came.* Such a nominal is also called antecedent or "Head nominal." I reserve the term "head" for the projecting element of a syntactic constituent.

simultaneously. Syntactically, the RCs must be licensed by a plural nominal, rather than either of the two singular Heads alone. For instance, (6.39a) cannot be derived from either (6.40a) or (6.40b). The extraposition in (6.40a) is not possible because the RC in the gap position _k is not well-formed, given that *each other* is not licensed by any c-commanding plural element in the local domain. The deletion in (6.40b) is not possible for a similar reason.

(6.40) a. *Mary met a man_i _k and John met a woman_j [who knew each other well]_k.
 b. *Mary met a man_i [who knew each other well] and John met a woman_j [who knew each other well].

As claimed by Gazdar (1981: 179), the RCs in MSCs "must be generated in situ." If so, the base position of the RCs and at least one of their antecedents are not adjacent, unlike regular RC constructions. This raises the question of whether MSCs are actually RC constructions at all. If they are not, they might be derived in some other way, such as the way in which a depictive construction is derived. In (6.41), the depictive *young* modifies the subject *he*, but the two elements are not adjacent.

(6.41)   He died young.

In short, we are confronted with an unclear syntactic relation between two separate DPs and their shared modifier.

In this section, I propose that MSCs are derived from ordinary RC constructions. What is special about the constructions is that the two antecedents of an MSC, as conjuncts of a coordinate complex, have undergone sideward movement from the complex. My analysis will show how giving up the CC, and accepting the operation of sideward movement, make it possible to understand this special RC dependency construction, while avoiding problems with an alternative approach.

The structure of this section is as follows. In Section 6.3.2, I argue that the two apparent antecedents of an MSC originally form a coordinate complex, the real antecedent of the RC. In Section 6.3.3, I propose that the observed splitting effects of MSCs are syntactically derived by sideward movement of the conjuncts out of this coordinate complex. In Section 6.3.4, I point out certain disadvantages with an alternative analysis. Finally, Section 6.3.5 is a brief summary.

6.3.2   *MSCs have coordinate antecedents*

I claim that the derivation of an MSC contains a step where the two apparent antecedents are two conjuncts of a coordinate complex, and it is this complex that is the real and unique antecedent of the relative pronoun.

In data like (6.42), RCs take a coordinate Head (Vergnaud 1974; Jackendoff 1977: 190; Link 1984). Such data are different from MSC data in that the antecedents are not "split" into two matrix clauses.

(6.42) a. <u>a man</u>$_i$ and <u>a woman</u>$_j$ [who$_{i\&j}$ knew <u>each other</u>$_{i\&j}$ well]
        b. <u>a room</u>$_i$ and <u>a cellar</u>$_j$ [which$_{i\&j}$ are joined by a small underground] passageway]
        c. <u>the boy</u>$_i$ and <u>the girl</u>$_j$ [who$_{i\&j}$ were in love]
        d. <u>the car</u>$_i$ and <u>the truck</u>$_j$ Op$_{i\&j}$ that collided

Moltmann (1992a) calls both the RC in data such as (6.42) and the RC in MSCs multiply-Headed RCs. We call the construction where a RC takes a coordinate Head, such as those in (6.42), a Coordinate-Head RC Construction (CHC).

I claim that the structure of (6.42a), for instance, is as follows:[4]

(6.43)

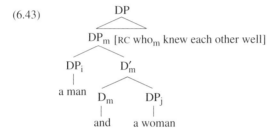

In this structure, DP$_m$ is a coordinate antecedent of the RC. I claim that the antecedent of the RC of an MSC is also a coordinate DP. There are two major differences between MSCs and CHCs. First, D$_m$ in MSCs is realized by a null conjunction, whereas it is realized by *and* in CHCs. Second, the two DP conjuncts are separately re-selected by two verbs in MSCs, but not in CHCs. I will present a full-fledged syntactic derivation of MSCs in Section 6.3.3. In the present section, showing the syntactic similarities between CHCs and MSCs, I present three arguments (A, B, and C) for the claim that in both constructions the RC takes a single coordinate DP complex as its Head, and thus the RC is not syntactically multiply headed.

---

4 In CHCs, the status of the RC as RC is not important. Other types of phrases can also be merged with a coordinate DP. In (i), the phrase to the right of the coordinate DP is a PP modifier; and in (ii), the phrase to the right of the coordinate DP is a complement (Jackendoff 1977: 191–192). The frame of our structure in (6.43) is general enough to cover all of these types of examples.

   (i)   the boy and the girl [with a common background]
   (ii)   three members and two vice-chairmen [of interlocking committees]

A.   Argument A: restrictive modification constructions

A well-established constraint on restrictive RCs in English is that they do not take bare proper names (i.e. without an article) or pronouns as antecedents (see Jackendoff 1977: 171), as shown in (6.44a) through (6.44d). The example in (6.44e) further shows that a pronoun cannot be included in the Head of the RC.

(6.44) a. *Pat {who/that} I like is a genius.   (Sag 1997 (91))
     b. The Pat {who/that} I like is a genius.
     c. *He {who/that} I know is a genius.
     d. *Mary met [him]$_i$ [who$_i$ knew her well].
     e. *I saw [him and the man]$_i$ who$_i$ were late yesterday.

This constraint is not seen in non-RC modifiers such as depictives. In (6.45), the depictive *young* may modify the pronoun *he* or the bare proper name *Pat*.

(6.45)   {The man/He/Pat} died young.

Both CHCs and MSCs are restrictive modification constructions. In English, this means that neither a CHC nor an MSC may allow proper name or pronoun antecedents. Wilder (1999: 2.1) notes that neither of the apparent antecedents of MSCs can be a pronoun, as shown in (6.46a). It is obvious that this is also true of CHCs, as seen in (6.46b).

(6.46) a. *Mary met [him]$_i$ and John met [a woman]$_j$ [who$_{i\&j}$ knew each other well].
     b. *[he]$_i$ and [a woman]$_j$ [who$_{i\&j}$ knew each other well]

Parallel to this pronoun constraint, the antecedents of both CHCs and MSCs obey a proper name constraint:

(6.46) a. *Mary met Bill$_i$ and John met [a woman]$_j$ [who$_{i\&j}$ knew each other well].
     b. *[Bill]$_i$ and [a woman]$_j$ [who$_{i\&j}$ knew each other well].

The impossibility for pronouns and proper names to be antecedents of CHCs and MSCs indicates that the RCs in both constructions are restrictive. If the two types of constructions are derived in a similar way, the sharing of this property is explained.

B.   Argument B: D-features of the modified nominals

Another property shared by CHCs and MSCs is that the determiners of the Head nominals must be identical. Vergnaud (1974) and Link (1984) note that the determiners of the Head nominals must be identical in CHCs, and Moltmann (1992a: 191, 195) further notes that this property is shared by MSCs:

(6.48) a. *a man and the woman who met last year   (CHC)
      b. *the father of John and a woman who know each other well   (CHC)
      c. *A man entered and the woman left who met last year.   (MSC)
      d. *John saw the man and Mary saw a woman who met last year.   (MSC)

In (6.48a), *a man and the woman* is the Head of the RC *who met last year*. Since the determiner *a* and the determiner *the* are not identical, the CHC is not acceptable. Parallel to this, in (6.48c), the two antecedents are *a man* and *the woman*, and again the difference in determiners causes the MSC to be unacceptable. The other examples in (6.48) show the same pattern.

In fact, more precisely, the two modified nominals should share the same definiteness or specificity, rather than the same form. Neal Whitman (p.c.) points out the acceptability of "your piano student and my guitar student turned out to know each other." The two D-elements *your* and *my* are both definite.

Importantly, as pointed out by Moltmann, this restriction on determiners does not hold for simple conjoined nominals, as seen in the following examples (6.49).

(6.49) a. John met a man and the woman he saw yesterday.
      b. John met that man and a woman.

In (6.49a), the coordinate object is composed of two conjuncts: *a man*, and *the woman he saw yesterday*. The former is indefinite and the latter is definite. The two conjuncts in (6.49b) are also different in their determiners, but like (6.49a), the sentence is acceptable.

This restriction on the determiners of the Head nominals of both CHCs and MSCs can be accounted for by our hypothesis that, as in CHCs, the actual Heads of the RCs in MSCs are coordinate complexes. Semantically, RCs are predicates of their Head nominals, and each predicate has only one subject. This is also true of the Head nominal of the RC in a CHC or MSC; it must be a unique nominal, and this unique nominal cannot have two different specificity or quantificational features. In our analysis, the unique nominal is a coordinate DP complex. Thus, the RCs of CHCs and MSCs do not have multiple Heads. In an MSC, the conjuncts of this single complex Head later each undergo certain syntactic operations, splitting the conjuncts into two clauses (see Section 6.3.3). The fact that the determiners of CHCs and MSCs obey the same constraint indicates that the two constructions may undergo certain identical steps in their derivations. In one of these steps, I argue, both constructions have a single coordinate complex as the antecedent of the relative pronoun, as shown in (6.43).

Moltmann (1992a: 191) denies a semantic approach to the condition restricting the determiners of the Head nominals. She argues that (6.50a) could be perfectly interpretable and (almost) equivalent to (6.50b), and similarly for (6.51a) and (6.51b):

(6.50) a. *a man and the woman who met last year
  b. a man$_i$ and the woman that he$_i$ met last year

(6.51) a. *A man entered and the woman left who met last year.
  b. A man$_i$ entered and the woman left who met him$_i$ last year

Indeed, D-feature unification is a formal, not semantic, constraint. A crucial difference between the a- and b-sentences above is that the RC in the latter is the predicate of the simplex nominal, *the woman*. If the RC requires its Head, *the woman*, to have a consistent set of specificity features, so should all other RCs. Accordingly, the a-sentences are unacceptable because *a man* and *the woman* do not provide a consistent set of specificity features for the RC, which takes the combination of the two nominals as its Head (its semantic subject). If the Head of an RC does not exhibit consistent specificity features, there cannot be any predication relation between the Head and the RC.

The D-feature unification of the antecedents of CHCs and MSCs supports our claim that the so-called multiply-headed RCs are actually RCs that take a single-coordinate complex Head.

C. Argument C: licensing reciprocals
One more property shared by CHCs and MSCs is that they both license reciprocals, which need a plural antecedent (see Section 6.2.3C). In the CHC in (6.52a), the reciprocal *each other* is licensed by the coordinate complex *a man and a woman*, via the relative pronoun *who*. In the MSC in (6.52b), there is no plural nominal to serve as the antecedent of the reciprocal, or no plural nominal to ensure that the relative pronoun is plural so that it can license the reciprocal locally, but the sentence is acceptable. If the derivation of (6.52b) involves a representation similar to (6.52a), in which the two singular nominals, *a man* and *a woman* form a coordinate complex, the licensing of the reciprocal is accounted for.

(6.52) a. <u>a man</u> and <u>a woman</u> [who knew <u>each other</u> well] (= (6.42a))
  b. Mary met <u>a man</u> and John met <u>a woman</u> [who knew
    <u>each other</u> well]. (= (6.39a))

I thus claim that the antecedent of the relative pronoun in an MSC is a coordinate complex, and the head of this complex is realized by a null conjunction (the element *e* in (6.53b)). Thus regardless of how the relative clause is derived, at a certain point of the derivation, we are forced to conclude that the structure in (6.53b) is integrated into the derivation of (6.53a):

(6.53) a. Mary met <u>a man</u>$_i$ and John met <u>a woman</u>$_j$ [who$_{i\&j}$ knew <u>each other</u>$_{i\&j}$ well]

b.
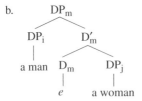

6.3.3   Deriving MSCs by sideward conjunct raising

I have argued for the existence of a coordinate DP in MSCs (DP$_m$ in (6.53b)). I now propose that MSCs are derived by the sideward movement of the conjuncts of this DP.

A.   Sideward movement

Before I spell out my proposal for the derivation of MSCs, I will briefly introduce sideward movement. Generally speaking, the movement of α lands in the same "tree," that is, in a position that c-commands the launching site. The movement from one tree into another tree is sideward movement, as illustrated below.

(6.54) Step 1: α moves from Tree 1 to Tree 2

Tree 2   Tree 1

Step 2: Tree 1 is integrated into Tree 2 by a kind of remnant merger[5]

Since the landing site of sideward movement is in a different tree from that of the launching site, it neither c-commands nor is c-commanded by the

---

5 Remnant merger here is parallel to remnant movement (den Besten and Webelhuth 1990; Müller 1998), in which part of a phrase is extracted, and then the rest of the phrase undergoes further syntactic operation (Move or Merge).

launching site. Moreover, since the element that undergoes sideward movement may be reselected by a verb in the new working site, it may land in a theta position.

Sideward movement is discussed in Bobaljik and Brown (1997), Nunes (2001), Hornstein (2001), and Nunes and Uriagereka (2000). The existence of sideward movement is expected, if Remerge (Move), like Merge, simply sets up new syntactic relations. As pointed out by Hornstein and Nunes (2002: 27), sideward movement does not add any new operation or condition to our current computational system. Instead, it merely removes the stipulation that movement must target the syntactic object that contains the trace. Hornstein and Nunes (2002) claim that such a stipulation is a residue of D-structure, a notion that is not compatible with the Minimalist Program. If no D-structure is assumed and the computational system relies on generalized transformations to build phrasal objects, the landing site of movement may lie beyond the domain that contains the trace. "In other words, in a system that may operate with more than one single-rooted syntactic object at once, as in Chomsky 1995, only brute force would force movement to always target the same tree" (Hornstein and Nunes 2002: 28). Sideward movement "is the result of taking the primitive operations of the system seriously and exploring their full potential" (Boeckx 2007: 896).

Sideward movement has been argued to account for a number of unrelated phenomena, such as adjunct control (Hornstein 2001), issues pertaining to extraction domains (Nunes and Uriagereka 2000), PRO-gate effects (Hornstein and Kiguchi 2003), donkey anaphora (Boeckx 2003), antecedent-resumptive relations (Kayne 2002), binominal *each* (Boeckx and Hornstein 2005), and (pseudo)gapping (Agbayani and Zoerner 2004).

B.   Deriving MSCs by the evacuation of coordinate DP complexes
Rejecting the CC and assuming that conjuncts may move, I propose the following derivations for MSCs: the two antecedents of an MSC are originally two conjuncts of a coordinate nominal, then each undergoes sideward movement, landing in a new working site and being selected by a verb. After that, a coordinate clausal complex is also constructed. In the old working site, a complex nominal is constructed, in which the relative clause takes the remnant coordinate nominal as its antecedent. Finally, the complex nominal adjoins to the coordinate clausal complex. The whole process includes four major steps. I illustrate the derivation of (6.55) as follows.

(6.55)   Mary met <u>a man</u>$_i$ and John met <u>a woman</u>$_j$ [who$_{i\&j}$ knew <u>each other</u>$_{i\&j}$ well]

Step ①: *a man* and *a woman* form a coordinate nominal, with a null D as its head:

(6.56)

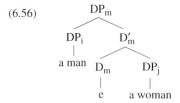

Step ②: the DP *a man* undergoes sideward movement and is selected by *met*. After certain additional syntactic operations, the TP *Mary met a man* is constructed. Similarly, the DP *a woman* undergoes sideward movement and is selected by *met*. After certain further additional syntactic operations, the TP *John met a woman* is constructed. The two TPs and the conjunction *and* form a coordinate clausal complex TP_k (recall that the coordinator *and* itself does not have any categorial features, and it obtains categorial features from conjuncts, which is why it is under T in (6.57)).

(6.57)

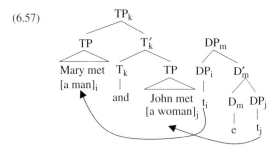

Step ③: In the old working site, a complex nominal DP_n is constructed, which contains the RC and its antecedent, the remnant DP_m:

(6.58)

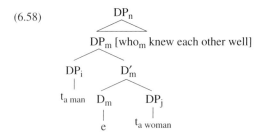

Step ④: DP_n, which was constructed in Step ③, adjoins to TP_k, which was constructed in Step ②:

(6.59)

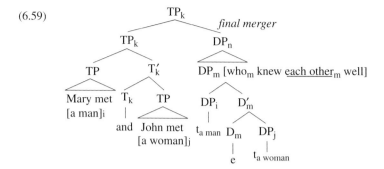

This proposed derivation of the MSC in (6.55) has the following character-istics:

1. DP_i and DP_j form a coordinate complex headed by a null D in their base-positions;
2. Both DP_i and DP_j are conjuncts and they move out of the coordinate complex DP_m;
3. DP_i and DP_j are remerged with the verbs via separate sideward move-ments;
4. DP_n, which hosts the RC and the remnant of the DP_m after the conjunct movement, adjoins to TP_k, as the last step of the derivation.

Consider 1. It is important that the Head of the coordinate nominal is null, rather than an overt conjunction such as *and*. If it were not null, unacceptable forms like the following would be derived:

(6.60)   *Mary met a man and John met a woman <u>and</u> who knew each other well.

This null D is different from the conjunction *and* in two respects. First, it has its own categorial features, and thus it does not get categorial features from any conjunct. Following the arguments in Chapter 4, then, the conjuncts may move. Second, as a null element, the null D does not need any phonological host, and therefore the conjuncts linked by it may move. In other words, given our analysis of the CC, we predict that both the CCe and the CCi may be violated by the coordinate complex DP_m.

Now we turn to 2. In this proposed derivation of (6.55), DP_i and DP_j are conjuncts and they move. Recall that in Chapter 4 and 6.2 of this chapter, I asserted that single conjuncts may move if the conjuncts are semantically related to each other. Since in the derivation of MSCs both conjuncts move, the semantic condition on single conjunct movement does not apply here.

Characteristic 3 can be described as follows. DP_i and DP_j are remerged with the two transitive verbs, respectively. One might wonder whether the proposed derivation violates the Complex NP Constraint (Ross 1967), since the two conjuncts are extracted from a complex nominal. However, sideward movement permits extraction from islands if the islands are not yet integrated into the core structure (see Nunes and Uriagereka 2000; Hornstein 2001; Nunes 2004; Taylor 2006). In my derivation, sideward movement occurs in Step ②, and the complex nominal is constructed in Step ③. Since the sideward movement occurs before any complex nominal exists, it does not violate the Complex NP Constraint. Moreover, in a MSC it is the Head of the complex nominal, rather than any element within the modifier or complement of a complex nominal, that is moved. This kind of movement seems not to be subject to the Complex NP Constraint.

Similarly, when the sideward movement occurs in Step ②, DP_n, which becomes an adjunct in Step ④, does not yet exist, so the sideward movement does not violate any adjunct island constraint.

We now come to 4: DP_n adjoins to TP_k, as the final step of the derivation. DP_n is a complex nominal, containing an RC. There is no constraint on the category of an adjunct, so if there is no illegal integration of the formal features, syntactic merger is permitted.

We conclude this subsection with a description of one more property shared by MSCs and CHCs, providing further support for the unified analysis. Recall that in both CHCs and MSCs the determiners of the Head nominals must be identical (Section 6.3.2B). Link (1984) observes that partitive nominals apparently allow for RCs with multiple Heads, regardless of the differences in the nature of the determiners of the conjunct nominals, as in (6.61a). Such data are in contrast to non-partitive data like (6.61b). Moltmann (1992a: 202) notes that this contrast in CHCs is also seen in MSCs, as shown in (6.62):

(6.61) a. all of the students and several of the professors who have met in secret
      b. *all students and several professors who have met in secret

(6.62) a. John saw all of the students and Mary met most of the professors who have met in secret.
      b. *John saw <u>all men</u>$_i$ and Mary met <u>most women</u>$_j$ who$_{i\&j}$ danced together.

With respect to (6.61a) and (6.62a), Moltmann (1992a: 202) explains that "the reason why the agreement condition on the determiner is met in this case, most plausibly, is that *the students* and *the professors* share definite determiners. If this is true, then apparently the relative clause relates to the lower NPs, rather than to the conjunct partitive NPs." We adopt her account. In our analysis,

accordingly, both (6.61a) and (6.62a) have the following DP as the Head of the
RC *who*$_m$ *have met in secret*:

(6.63)

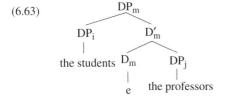

The derivation of (6.61a) is illustrated in (6.64). DP$_i$ *the students* undergoes
sideward movement to be remerged with *of*, and then *of the students* merges
with *all*, building the new nominal *all of the students*. Similarly, DP$_j$ *the
professor* undergoes sideward movement to be remerged with *of*, and then
of the professors is merged with *several*, building the new nominal *several of
the professors*. After that, the two newly built complex nominals merge with
the conjunction *and*, one after the other, forming the coordinate DP complex
all of the students and several of the professors. In the old working site, the
remnant DP$_m$ becomes the Head of the RC, forming DP$_n$. Finally, DP$_n$ adjoins
to the coordinate complex.

(6.64) a. all of the students and several of the professors who have met in secret

b.

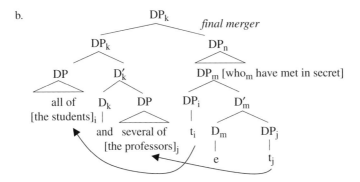

The derivation of (6.62a) is illustrated in (6.65). DP$_i$ *the students* undergoes
sideward movement to be re-merged with *of*, and then *of the students* merges
with *all*. Thus a new nominal *all of the students* is built. Similarly, DP$_j$ *the
professor* undergoes sideward movement to be re-merged with *of*, and then *of
the professors* merges with *most*. Thus a new nominal *most of the professors*
is built. After that, the two newly built complex nominals are selected by the
transitive verbs *saw* and *met*, respectively. Other operations occur to build the

two clauses separately: *John saw all of the students* and *Mary met most of the professors*. Then, a process occurs by which these two clauses merge with the conjunction *and*, one after the other, and form the clausal coordinate complex *John saw all of the students and Mary met most of the professors*. In the old working site, the remnant DP_m becomes the Head of the RC, forming DP_n. Finally, DP_n adjoins to the coordinate clausal complex.

(6.65) a. John saw all of the students and Mary met most of the professors who have met in secret.

b.

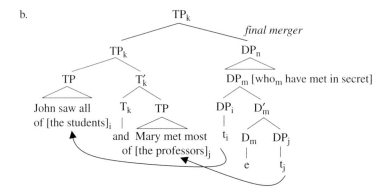

6.3.4   A comparison with the multiple dimensional analysis

We now compare our analysis with Moltmann's (1992a; see also Wilder 2008: 253) multiple dimensional analysis of MSCs. Moltmann (1992a: 147) claims that in the example *A man came and a woman left who knew each other well*, "*a man* and *a woman* are implicitly coordinated." The notion of implicit coordination means that two elements function like a coordinate complex, but do not form a coordinate complex syntactically. This differs from the present proposal, where elements are conjoined by a null conjunction at a certain step in the derivation of MSCs. Moltmann's syntactic representation of (6.66a) is (6.66b):

(6.66) a. A man came and a woman left who knew each other.

b.

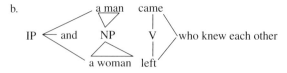

In (6.66b), the two clauses are conjoined, but not the two NPs. Using the same approach, the structure of (6.67a) is given by Wilder (1999) as (6.67b):

(6.67) a. John met a man and Mary met a woman who knew each other well.

b.

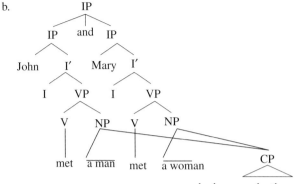

One major difference between our approach and the multiple dimensional analysis is that in the multiple dimensional analysis, the apparent antecedents do not move. Instead, they are linked to the RC by special tree branches.

One disadvantage of the multiple dimensional analysis is that the two overt antecedents of the relative pronoun, *a man* and *a woman* in (6.67), never form a constituent in the derivation, and thus additional constraints are required to cover the facts presented in Section 6.3.2. For instance, if the two objects are selected by two verbs respectively, they need not have the same D-features. Then the unification of D-features discussed in Section 6.3.2B needs to be accounted for. Moltmann (1992a) is indeed forced to stipulate certain constraints in order to restrict the derivations. In my approach, the restrictions are captured naturally: the two nominals originally form a coordinate complex serving as the unique antecedent of the relative pronoun, which does not tolerate internal disagreement in D-features.

Another disadvantage of the multiple dimensional analysis is that it depends on the linearization of multiple-dimensional structures, a more complex operation than linearization from two-dimensional structures. Advocates of the multiple-dimensional analysis have sought to formalize the necessary operation, but if their empirical goals can be met by the simpler two-dimensional approach, I see no advantage to the more complex multiple-dimensional approach.

6.3.5 Section summary

In this section, I have proposed a syntactic derivation for MSCs such as *Mary met a man and John met a woman who knew each other well*. I have claimed that the two modified elements of such a construction are originally two conjuncts of a coordinate nominal. Then each undergoes sideward movement from the original working site to a new one, where it is selected by a verb. The two nominals take part in the building of a coordinate clausal complex. In the old working site, a complex nominal is constructed, in which the relative clause takes the remnant coordinate nominal as its antecedent. Finally, the complex nominal adjoins to the coordinate clausal complex. This analysis shows how the rejection of the CC and the freedom in the selection of landing sites gained from sideward movement make syntactic derivation of this special type of relative clause construction possible, while at the same time avoiding the problems of the alternative multiple-dimensional analysis.

This analysis also shows that the derivation of the relative clauses in MSCs do not pose problems for either of the two major analyses of relative clause constructions, namely the conventional Matching-Adjunction Analysis and the Raising-Complement Analysis (Kayne 1994; Bianchi 1999; among others). In the Matching-Adjunction Analysis, our proposed sideward movement may occur before the adjunction of the relative clause to the Head nominal. In the Raising-Complement Analysis, the relative pronoun and the antecedent DP are initially merged together, and later the antecedent DP moves away from the relative pronoun (Bianchi 1999; Zwart 2000). In this latter analysis, our proposed sideward movement may occur before the antecedent DP is merged with the relative pronoun. Thus just as MSCs do not require special multiple-dimensional structures, RCs in MSCs can be analyzed with either of the two major approaches to relative clause constructions.

6.4   Deriving Interwoven Dependency Constructions by giving up the EC

This section examines the syntactic derivation of a construction that exhibits dependencies between one coordinate complex and two syntactic gaps, with each conjunct of the complex associated with one of the gaps, respectively. The construction is shown in (6.68).

(6.68)   [[Which nurse]$_i$ and [which hostess]$_j$]$_k$ did Fred date $_{\_i}$ and Bob marry $_{\_j}$, respectively?

The construction illustrated in (6.68) is called the Interwoven Dependency Construction (IDC) (Postal 1998). In this construction, conjunct$_i$ and conjunct$_j$ in the coordinate complex$_k$ are associated respectively with gap$_i$ and gap$_j$.

I claim that the construction is derived by sideward movement of elements from conjuncts. My analysis shows how rejecting the EC and accepting sideward movement make it possible to give syntactic derivations for IDCs, while avoiding the problems associated with alternative approaches. This effort shows how the challenges posed by the construction can be faced without giving up key assumptions of generative syntax (cf. Postal 1998).

I first introduce IDC data in Section 6.4.1, summarize previous analyses of the construction in Section 6.4.2, motivate a movement approach in Section 6.4.3, and argue for a sideward movement analysis in Section 6.4.4. A brief summary is given in Section 6.4.5.

6.4.1   The Interwoven Dependency Construction (IDC)

The IDC example introduced above is repeated here as (6.69):

(6.69)   [[Which nurse]$_i$ and [which hostess]$_j$]$_k$ did Fred date _$_i$ and Bob marry _$_j$, respectively?

The IDC contains a coordinate DP-complex, DP$_k$ in (6.69). The construction poses a serious challenge to syntactic theory because each conjunct of the DP-complex has a clear base position, but the complex as a whole does not. If (6.69) is derived via wh-movement, the base position of *which nurse* should be the object position of *date*, which is inside the first clausal conjunct, and that of *which hostess* should be the object position of *marry*, which is inside the second clausal conjunct. However, there doesn't seem to be a launching site for the complex *which nurse and which hostess*.

To the best of my knowledge, IDCs have previously been discussed most fully in Tai (1969: 14), Dougherty (1970a; 1970b), McCawley (1988a), and Postal (1998). IDCs need not involve wh-movement like in (6.69). The examples in (6.70) illustrate IDCs involving subjects that have presumably been base-generated below TP and raised to SpecTP; they too seem to have split launching sites. Note the cross-category nature of the predicates here: they can be PP, AP, and various projections extended from VP (such data are found in Dougherty 1969: 628; 1970a: 527, 544; Scha 1981; Link 1984: 246; McCawley 1988a: 536; Krifka 1990: 165; and Postal 1998: 108, 162):

(6.70)   a. [Hans and Fritz]$_k$ are from Germany and from Switzerland.
         b. [Logical and empirical truth]$_k$ are necessary and contingent, respectively.
         c. [John and Bill]$_k$ were certain to leave and ready to leave respectively.
         d. [John and Bill]$_k$ should go to N.Y. and will go to Chicago respectively.
         e. [Kim and Sandy]$_k$ sang and danced, respectively.
         f. [George and Martha]$_k$ respectively denounced and were denounced by the governor.

IDCs are also found with topicalization. In each of the following examples, if the two PP conjuncts have undergone A-bar fronting from the two predicate conjuncts, the sentence can also be treated as an IDC ((6.71b) is from McCawley 1988a: 538).

(6.71) a. Under the pillow and in the drawer Lulu put her diary and hid her letters,
           respectively.
        b. On Fridays and (on) Saturdays, John respectively teaches and goes surfing.

IDCs are observed cross-linguistically (see Zhang 2007b). Although their syntactic derivations have not been thoroughly studied, they have been claimed to pose a serious challenge to any framework of generative syntax positing movement operations (Postal 1998: 163).

Before I present an analysis of IDCs, I clarify the role of the adverb *respectively* in them.

IDCs, by definition, have a distributive reading, thus permitting the adverb *respectively*. However, it is not obligatory; *respectively* need not occur if the distributive reading is made clear in some other way, as in the following.

(6.72)   [The dogs and the roosters]$_k$ barked and crowed all night.

Nevertheless, in most of the IDC examples discussed here, if the adverb *respectively* is absent, the sentences can be ambiguous between an IDC reading (distributive) and an Across-the-Board dependency reading, if semantically and pragmatically permitted. In the latter reading, the sentence-initial coordinate complex is semantically related to the two clausal or predicate conjuncts simultaneously (Postal 1998: 136). For instance, the Across-the-Board reading of *How many frogs and how many toads did Greg capture and Lucille train?* is a question asking for two numbers, x and y, such that Fred captured x frogs and y toads and Lucille trained x frogs and y toads. Since IDCs are not Across-the-Board constructions, I do not discuss this alternative reading here, but leave Across-the-Board constructions to Chapter 9.

The possibility for *respectively* to occur in IDCs distinguishes them from other constructions. The following coordinate complexes do not allow *respectively* and thus are not IDCs.

(6.73) a. John and Mary are my two best friends and two oldest colleagues
           (*respectively).
        b. I consider John and Mary two excellent philosophers but two lousy parents
           (*respectively).   (see Heycock and Zamparelli 2005: 248)

Semantically, the adverb *respectively* is licensed by a plural element in the context. In IDCs, it is licensed by the two coordinate complexes. Syntactically, the adverb is an adjunct here that can be merged to either the left or the right of VP or at any projection higher than VP. In (6.71b), for instance, it is merged to the left of VP, and thus surfaces between the raised subject *John* and the coordinate predicate *teaches and goes surfing*. In some other IDC examples, the adverb occurs in sentence-final position. In this case, it may be merged to the right of VP or some higher projection. I do not consider the adverb in my proposed syntactic derivations of IDCs, since there is nothing special about the syntax of this adverb.

6.4.2   *Previous analyses*

While Postal (1998) uses IDCs to challenge generative syntactic theory as a whole, Tai (1969: 15) and Dougherty (1970a; 1970b) proposed syntactic derivations for IDCs within generative frameworks. In Tai (1969: 15), (6.74a) is derived from the structure in (6.74b) by the so-called *Respectively* Transformation.

(6.74) a. John and James are eager to please and easy to please, respectively.

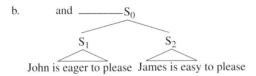

b.

Tai does not give any details about this special syntactic operation, but consistent with much generative theorizing of the time, takes the *Respectively* Transformation as a primitive operation requiring no further elaboration. Since there seems to be no way to decompose this transformation into more basic operations, I do not adopt this analysis.

In Dougherty's approach, IDCs are derived by the so-called *Respectively* Substitution Transformation (Dougherty 1970a: 544; 1970b: 887). In his approach, the subject of the second clausal conjunct moves to the subject of the first clausal conjunct to fill in a dummy element introduced by his phrase structure rules, and the predicate of the second clausal conjunct also moves to the predicate of the first clausal conjunct to fill in another base-generated dummy element. Thus (6.75a) should be derived from the structure in (6.75b):

(6.75) a. Kim and Sandy sang and danced, respectively.

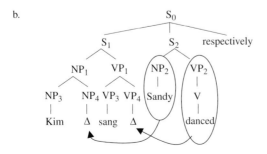

b.

Dougherty (1970b: 887) states that "[t]he *Respectively* Substitution Transformation operates to 'fill in' dummy elements introduced by the phrase-structure rules of the base." In (6.75b), there are two dummy elements, NP_4 and VP_4, each marked by Δ. They are replaced by NP_2 and VP_2, respectively.

The techniques used in Dougherty's derivation are problematic, from the viewpoint of contemporary syntactic theory. In particular, the generation of the dummy elements is not justified locally, but they are created merely in order to be replaced later. We must thus pursue a new analysis of IDCs.

6.4.3   IDCs exhibit parallel movement dependencies

I argue that IDCs should be analyzed by movement originating from the clausal conjuncts. I have four arguments for this movement approach, and against the hypothesis that the coordinate nominal complexes in IDCs are base-generated in their surface positions.

First, in varieties of English disallowing extraction of an indirect object (including standard varieties) such extraction is also disallowed in IDCs (Postal 1998: 135).[6] In (6.76a), the object of the preposition *to* is moved, whereas in (6.76b), the indirect object is moved. The parallel acceptability pattern in (6.77a,b) shows that the IDCs in (6.77) obey the same constraint on movement seen in (6.76).

(6.76) a. [Which nurse] did Ernest sell cocaine to _ (and George sell heroin to _)?
     b. *[Which nurse] did Ernest sell _ cocaine (and George sell _ heroin)?

(6.77) a. [[Which nurse]$_i$ and [which hostess]$_j$]$_k$ did Ernest sell cocaine to $_{-i}$ and George sell heroin to $_{-j}$, respectively?
     b. *[[Which nurse]$_i$ and [which hostess]$_j$]$_k$ did Ernest sell $_{-i}$ cocaine and George sell $_{-j}$ heroin, respectively?

Second, if reflexive binding is a local structural relation, Postal's (1998: 161) analysis of examples like the following implies that the two wh-conjuncts of the IDC show the same movement dependencies, since each wh-phrase can license its reflexive before moving:

(6.78)   [Which man]$_i$ and [which woman]$_j$ did respectively I talk to $_{-i}$ about himself$_i$, and you talk to $_{-j}$ about herself$_j$?

The reflexive binding here follows the strict gender and number agreement restrictions between antecedents and reflexives.

---

6 See Bruening (2001: 236 fn. 5) for a discussion of dialect variation in whether indirect objects can be moved.

Third, if s-selection is also a local structural relation, we infer that in the following IDC, *how many cakes* is base-generated in the VP headed by *bake*, since the latter s-selects the former. Similarly, we infer that *how many letters* is base-generated in the VP headed by *write*, since the latter s-selects the former.

(6.79)   How many cakes and how many letters, respectively, did Mary
         bake _ and John write _ this morning?

The s-selection relations between the predicates (*barked, crowed*) and the subjects (*the dogs, the roosters*) in (6.72) demonstrate the same point.

Fourth, the gaps in IDCs cannot be bound variable *pro*s, since such *pro*s are not available for PPs, in data like (6.71).

I conclude that the left-peripheral coordinate complexes in IDCs are not base-generated in their surface positions.

6.4.4   *Deriving IDCs by sideward extraction from conjuncts*

Postal (1998: 160–162) has argued that it is impossible to move the whole coordinate wh-complex in examples like (6.69) from the gap position of either or both of the clausal conjuncts. We have seen that this is intuitively right: one gap is semantically related to one conjunct of the wh-complex, and the other gap is semantically related to the other conjunct of the wh-complex. There is no source position for the whole coordinate wh-complex in the two clausal conjuncts.

This conclusion is consistent with the arguments given in the previous section that IDCs involve multiple movement dependencies. Since these dependencies seem to involve extraction from clausal conjuncts, accounting for them requires rejecting the EC. I now propose a derivation for IDCs incorporating these insights. The sentence in (6.80a), for instance, is derived from the steps in (6.80b) and the structure in (6.80c). The important steps are marked by ①, ②, and ③ (as stated in Section 6.4.1, we ignore the adverb *respectively* in our representations).

(6.80) a. Kim and Sandy sang and danced, respectively.

        b. Assemble: [$_{VP}$ Sandy danced];
            ① The nominal *Sandy* undergoes sideward movement and is remerged with
            and in the new working site, forming [*and Sandy*];
            Assemble: [$_{VP}$ Kim sang];
            ②The nominal *Kim* undergoes sideward movement and is remerged with
            [*and Sandy*], building [$_{DP}$ *Kim and Sandy*];
            The two VPs and the conjunction *and* form a coordinate VP complex;
            The coordinate VP complex is merged with T and T′ is projected;
            ③The complex [$_{DP}$*Kim and Sandy*] is merged with T′, appearing at SpecTP.

c.

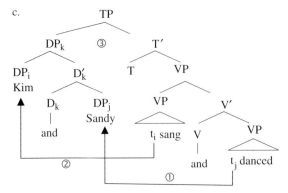

Keep in mind that when *Sandy* undergoes sideward movement, DP$_k$ does not yet exist, and the merger of DP$_k$ with T$'$ occurs even later. Thus, from the local perspective, the sideward movement of *Sandy* does not violate the Extension Condition, the requirement that substitution operations in overt syntax always extend their target (Chomsky 1993).

Similarly, (6.81a) is derived from the steps in (6.81b) and the structure in (6.81c).

(6.81) a. [[Which nurse]$_i$ and [which hostess]$_j$]$_k$ did Fred date t$_i$ and Bob marry t$_j$, respectively?

   b. Assemble: [$_{TP}$ Bob marry which hostess];
       ①The phrase *which hostess* undergoes sideward movement and is remerged with *and* in the new working site, forming [*and which hostess*];
       Assemble: [$_{TP}$ Fred date which nurse];
       ② The phrase *which nurse* undergoes sideward movement and is remerged with [*and which hostess*], building [$_{DP}$ *which nurse and which hostess*];
       The two TPs and the conjunction *and* form a coordinate TP complex;
       The coordinate TP complex is merged with *did* at C;
       ③ The complex [$_{DP}$ *which nurse and which hostess*] is merged with C$'$ and appears at the SpecCP.

   c.

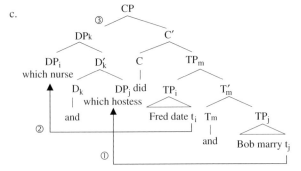

In this proposed derivation, there are two parallel movement dependencies, each with its own landing and launching sites. Specifically, each DP traveler undergoes a sideward movement, landing at a position that neither c-commands nor is c-commanded by the launching site. The landing site is in the working site of the coordinating head of DP_k, whereas the launching site is in the working site of a VP. In the derivations illustrated above, the movement in step ② is not blocked by the movement in step ①, because the landing site of the movement in step ① does not c-command the launching site of the movement in step ②. The two positions are in different working sites.

In Chapter 5, I concluded that elements may be extracted from single conjuncts if the conjuncts are semantically related to each other, i.e., in AC. In the derivation of IDCs, however, elements are extracted from both conjuncts. As with MSCs, which also involve movement of both conjuncts, this semantic condition does not apply here. I will say more about where such semantic constraints do and do not apply in the next chapter.

6.4.5   Section summary

IDCs have been claimed to pose a serious challenge to generative syntax. I have responded to this challenge by arguing that the two conjuncts of the left coordinate complex in an IDC independently undergo sideward movement from the gap positions, forming a coordinate complex with a conjunction, and later the newly built coordinate complex is integrated into the complex clause.[7]

The analysis here shows how rejection of the EC and the landing site freedom gained from sideward movement makes the syntactic derivation of certain

---

7 One might wonder whether IDCs display island effects. It has been claimed in the literature that sideward movement permits extraction from islands if the islands are not yet integrated into the core structure (see Nunes and Uriagereka 2000; Hornstein 2001; Nunes 2004; Taylor 2006). Although de Vos and Vicente (2005: 103 (21)) report some island effects in IDCs, my own investigation does not give a consistent result. In October 2002, I asked six native English speakers to judge the following adjunct island and tensed wh-island sentences:

(i) a.   How many frogs and how many toads, respectively, did Greg get a prize after capturing and Lucille get a prize after training?
   b.   How many frogs and how many toads, respectively, did Greg ask who has captured and Lucille ask who has trained?

Three of the informants accepted both sentences and the remaining three rejected both. This inconsistency in acceptability hints that IDCs may not display clear island effects, though a larger judgment experiment would be needed to detect any subtle pattern that may exist (Myers 2009).

special constructions possible, while avoiding the problems associated with alternative approaches proposed in the literature.[8]

6.5   Chapter summary

In the previous two chapters, I have argued that neither the CC nor the EC is a syntactic constraint on the derivation of coordinate complexes. In this chapter, I have presented derivations for three constructions that crucially rely on rejecting the CSC. Indeed, if the CSC is truly a syntactic constraint, these constructions seem to be difficult if not impossible to derive. This chapter has thus demonstrated the empirical advantages of abandoning the CSC, already shown to be problematic in earlier chapters.

In my proposed derivation for SACs, single conjuncts are moved from non-distributive coordinate structures. In other words, the two conjuncts must be semantically related. In my proposed derivations for MSCs and IDCs, however, both conjuncts of coordinate constructions are affected by movement, and so are not subject to this semantic constraint.

In the proposed derivations, the CC is ignored in SACs and MSCs and the EC is ignored in IDCs. EC-like effects only arise in certain semantic, pragmatic, or processing contexts, as explained in Chapter 7; there is thus no constraint in syntax to block the derivations proposed here for IDCs. CC-like effects are partially phonological and morphosyntactic, but since the coordinators assumed in SACs and MSCs are null, the relevant lexical properties exhibited by *and* do not exist. That is, no conjunct needs to serve as phonological host of a coordinator, since the coordinator is null, and no conjunct needs to provide categorial features to the coordinator, since the coordinator is assumed to be a (null) D with its intrinsic D-features. Therefore, the conjunct movements posited for SACs and MSCS are licensed.

---

8 The explanatory power of sideward movement might also benefit the analysis of other constructions, such as a split variable construction discussed in Zhang (2008b) and a Japanese construction discussed in Takano (2002), which, consistent with this study, concludes that "UG has a way of conjoining derived constituents, in addition to base-generated ones" (p. 275).

7 *Relativized parallelism in syntactic complexes*

7.1   Introduction

In Chapters 4 and 5, I linked the effects of the CSC to the lexical–syntactic properties of coordinators and the semantic relations between conjuncts. In this chapter I examine the CSC together with some other constraints which have also been claimed to apply exclusively in coordinate complexes.

Many authors consider Ross's CSC to be related to or covered by the Parallelism Requirement (PR). The PR is a label for the generally recognized requirement that the syntactic and semantic representations of the components in syntactic complexes must not only be well-formed independently, but also symmetrical or parallel to each other. In particular, it has long been realized that the conjuncts in a coordinate complex obey something like the PR. However, it is not clear what part of the cognitive system is responsible for the PR, nor how far coordinate complexes actually obey it.

Moreover, although many authors have attempted to account for the CSC in terms of some version of PR, or at least to link the two notions, the implementation of the PR itself remains a controversial issue. As a type of PR, the CSC has been analyzed as a trigger of movement (Hornstein and Nunes 2002), a constraint on movement (Williams 1978: 37; Pesetsky 1982; and Postal 1998), and as a constraint on merge (Johnson 2002a). However, it has also been claimed in the literature that the CSC is not a constraint on syntactic operations at all (e.g. Ruys 1992; Munn 1993; Rögnvaldssen 1993: Section 3.4; Heycock and Kroch 1994: 271–273; Levine 2001; Lin 2001; Kehler 2002: 141; Potts 2002).

In this chapter I argue that (beyond the lexical–syntactic properties of coordinators discussed in Chapter 4) all apparently coordination-specific constraints (including, but not restricted to, the CSC) can be covered by a general relativized parallelism filter. Clarifying the key issues in the PR literature, I show that this filter is applied to linguistic representations rather than syntactic operations, and that it is motivated by economy considerations in processing.

The chapter is organized as follows. In Section 7.2, I first review four coordination-specific constraints in addition to the CSC, and propose my own generalization, the Relativized PR (RPR), to cover all of the relevant observations. Then in Section 7.3 I unpack the components of the RPR and illustrate them with examples. In Section 7.4, I review some experimental results compatible with my conclusions. In Section 7.5, I show that the RPR does not affect syntactic operations and that it is motivated by economy in processing. Finally, based on a summary of this book's argument so far, in Section 7.6 I conclude that there is no coordination-specific constraint on syntactic operations.

7.2   The Relativized Parallelism Requirement (RPR)

7.2.1   *The Coordination of Likes Constraint and other similar constraints*
In this section, we review some problems with five constraints that have been proposed exclusively for coordinate complexes, and propose our own unified generalization for the relevant facts.

Ross's (1967) CSC was designed to constrain the syntactic operation Move, in coordinate constructions exclusively. Ten years before the CSC was proposed, a different constraint had been proposed to restrict the syntactic operation Merge, also exclusively in coordinate constructions. Consider the following data:

(7.1) a.   the scene [$_{PP}$ of the movie] and [$_{PP}$ of the play]
        b.   *the scene [$_{PP}$ of the movie] and [that I wrote]

In (7.1a), both conjuncts are PPs. In (7.1b), however, the first conjunct is a PP and the second one is a clause. In order to account for the unacceptability of data like (7.1b), Chomsky (1957: 36; 1965: 212 fn. 9) claims that syntactically different categories cannot be conjoined. This constraint has been referred to as the Coordination of Likes Constraint (CLC) (see also Williams's (1978) "Law of Coordination of Likes," and Gazdar 1981: 172 "only items of the *same* syntactic category can be conjoined").

Ten years after the CSC, Schachter (1977) proposed another constraint, the Coordinate Constituent Constraint (CCC), which states that conjuncts must not only belong to the same syntactic category but also have the same semantic function. Unlike the CLC and CSC, the CCC is a constraint on surface representations rather than on syntactic operations. The CCC is supposed to cover the effects of both the CLC and the CSC. Let us see how.

On the one hand, Schachter points out that although the CLC can account for (7.1b) above, it cannot explain data like (7.2) below. Both of the conjuncts are clauses in (7.2a), and adverbs in (7.2b), satisfying the CLC. However, the sentences are still not acceptable (Gleitman 1965: 263; Schachter 1977: 89; similar data can be found in Haspelmath 2007: (54)).

(7.2) a. *What are you doing and shut the door.
     b. *John probably and unwillingly went to bed.

   Schachter observes that the semantic functions of the two conjuncts in the sentences in (7.2) are different. In (7.2a), one is a question and the other is a command, and in (7.2b), one adverb is speaker-oriented (*probably*) and the other is subject-oriented (*unwillingly*) (p. 89). Accordingly, he claims that the CCC, which requires conjuncts to have the same semantic function, can explain what the CLC cannot explain. Thus the CCC seems to be superior to the CLC. The relationship between the CLC and "semantic categories" has also been discussed by Sag *et al.* (1985: 143), Goodall (1987), and Munn (1993: 113–120; 1996: Section 3).

   At the same time, Schachter claims that the CCC can also cover the CSC. This is because extraction of a conjunct (the CC part of the CSC) or an element from a conjunct (the EC part of the CSC) creates a syntactic representation in which the two conjuncts are neither identical in syntactic category nor identical in semantic function.

(7.3) a. *Who did John kiss _ and Mary?   (CC)
     b. *The lute which Henry [plays _ and sings madrigals] is warped.   (EC)

   In Schachter's approach, after the movement of the first conjunct in (7.3a), the two conjuncts of the coordinate complex become Ø and *Mary*, which are claimed to differ in both syntactic category and semantic function (Schachter 1977: 95). Similarly, after the extraction from the first conjunct in (7.3b), the two conjuncts become [*plays*] and [*sings madrigals*]. "*Plays* is functioning as a relation between *Henry* and *lute*; *sings madrigals*, on the other hand, is functioning as a property of *Henry*. Relations and properties – or two-place predicates and one-place predicates – are distinct semantic functions, and their conjunction is prohibited by the CCC." (See Gazdar 1981: 173 fn. 25 for a similar claim about the CSC.) The CCC thus takes a representational approach to the facts ascribed by the CSC to constraints on movement.

   Since Schachter believes that the CCC entails the CSC, he assumes that the CSC is descriptively valid. Thus despite acknowledging the acceptability of extraction in AC, he claims that such examples are not instances of coordination at all, since the word *and* in AC could be a kind of complementizer, rather than conjunction (p. 94) (see arguments against this assumption in Section 2.4).

In previous chapters we have supported Culicover and Jackendoff's (1997) claim that AC is true coordination, and have shown that both the CC and the EC can be violated in natural coordination. Two examples where the CSC is violated are listed in (7.4). Since violations of the CSC create representations that violate the CCC, the acceptability of examples like (7.4) indicates that like the CSC, the CCC is too strong.

(7.4) a. What kind of herb can you [eat __ and not get cancer]?   (EC violation)

   b. Baoyu yijing [__ gen Daiyu] he-mai-le yi   zuo fangzi.   (CC violation)
      Baoyu already   and Daiyu co-buy-PRF one CL   house
      'Baoyu and Daiyu already co-bought a house.'

Unlike Schachter (1977), who replaces the CLC (sensitive to syntax) with the more restrictive CCC (sensitive to both syntax and semantics), Sag *et al.* (1985: 143), Goodall (1987: 43), and Munn (1993) instead advocate a less restrictive constraint requiring conjuncts to be identical only in semantic types. For instance, two conjuncts of a coordinate complex must both denote [+ manner], or both denote [+ temporal], and so on. This semantic constraint successfully captures the acceptability of data like the following, which cannot be accounted for by either the CLC or the CCC:

(7.5)   Jermaine is boring and a fool.   (Sag *et al.* 1985) (AP & NP)

In (7.5), the two conjuncts are not identical in their categories: one is an AP and the other is an NP, violating the CLC and the CCC. But both denote negative properties of a person. Let us call this semantic constraint CLCsem.

However, this constraint cannot account for examples like (7.6):

(7.6)   Do that and I'll give you $10.   (Wilder 1999: 9)

In (7.6), the two conjuncts are not identical in their semantic type: one is a command and the other is not.

In order to cover data like (7.5), Peterson (2004: 650) claims that conjuncts should be identical in grammatical functions (such as OBJECT, ADJUNCT, and PREDICATE). Let us call this constraint CLCfunc. However, this constraint doesn't work either, since it cannot account for data like (7.2b), where the two conjuncts are both ADJUNCTS but the coordinate complex is still not acceptable.

Various versions of the CLC have been also proposed in other works, such as Dik (1968: 25), Hudson (1972: 28), Pullum and Zwicky (1986), and Gazdar *et al.* (1985).

We summarize the five constraints introduced so far in (7.7). The symbol "+" marks the type of sentences for which judgments are predicted by the constraint, and the symbol "−" marks the type of sentences for which judgments are not predicted by the constraint.

(7.7)	(7.1)	(7.2a)	(7.2b)	(7.3)	(7.4)	(7.5)	(7.6)
the CLC	+					-	
the CLCsem						+	-
the CLCfunc			-			+	
the CCC		+	+	+	-	-	-
the CSC				+	-		

Since each of the five constraints fails to account for certain types of data, we conclude that none of them is desirable.

7.2.2   *The RPR: conjuncts must hold a coherence relation*

I propose the following filter on the representations of syntactic complexes:

(7.8)   Conjuncts of a coordinate complex must hold a coherence relation in terms of:

    a.   Relatedness: they must be related to each other semantically, as in natural coordination; or

    b.   Resemblance (Parallelism Requirement): they must hold a resemblance relation in terms of both their semantic type and their dependency chains.

This filter states a symmetrically and inclusively disjunctive coherence relation between conjuncts. The inclusive disjunctive nature of this filter is that conjuncts must satisfy either the relatedness stated in (7.8a) or the resemblance stated in (7.8b), or both. The symmetrical nature of this filter is that the two kinds of coherence relation are independent of each other and equally important.

The notion of coherence is adapted from Kehler (2002). Developing proposals of David Hume, Kehler distinguishes three general classes of coherence relations: Cause–Effect, Contiguity, and Resemblance. I group the first two classes, together with other relations such as the conditional relation (as in (7.6)), into my general Relatedness relation. This is what is exhibited in natural coordination, in contrast to accidental coordination. One conjunct is related to another conjunct in a context to the extent that its contextual effects in this context are large (cf. Sperber & Wilson 1995: 125).

Kehler states that the EC cannot be violated when the Resemblance relation is operative, whereas it can be violated when the other two classes of coherence relations are operative (p. 116). Examples like (7.3b) show the former case and examples like (7.4a) show the latter case. Empirically, both Kehler's theory and my (7.8) capture the acceptability pattern of the relevant data. In (7.8), I make explicit the disjunctive nature of the relation between Resemblance and other kinds of coherence relations. Precisely speaking, I propose it is the absence of Relatedness as defined in (7.8) that makes the Resemblance relation become obligatory. Therefore, EC effects correlate with the absence of Relatedness.

If the resemblance requirement is a Parallelism Requirement (PR), the coherence filter in (7.8) should be understood as a relativized PR. I thus call this filter the Relativized Parallelism Requirement (the RPR).

Let us now see how the RPR covers the representative data listed above:

(7.9)	(7.1)	(7.2a)	(7.2b)	(7.3)	(7.4)	(7.5)	(7.6)
(7.8a): Relatedness					+		+
(7.8b): Resemblance in semantic type	+	+	+	+		+	
(7.8b): Resemblance in movement history		+		+			

In the data in (7.1) through (7.3), no semantic relation between the conjuncts is seen. Thus (7.8a) does not apply. However, (7.8b) does apply here. In the acceptable example (7.1a), the conjuncts are of the same semantic type, whereas in the unacceptable (7.1b), (7.2a), and (7.2b), the conjuncts are of different semantic types. In (7.1b), the PP *of the movie* is the semantic licensor of the relational noun *scene*, whereas the RC *that I wrote* is a modifier. In (7.2a), the first conjunct is a question and the second one is an order. In (7.2b), the speaking-oriented adverb *probably* and the subject-oriented adverb *willingly* are of different semantic types. The first component of (7.8b) alone rules out these examples. Moreover, in (7.2a), (7.3a) and (7.3b), movement occurs in one conjunct, but not in the other. The second component of (7.8b) alone can also account for their unacceptability.

In (7.4a) and (7.4b), a movement chain starts from a single conjunct. The examples are acceptable, because the conjuncts in each coordinate complex are related to each other. (7.4a) expresses a "nevertheless" relation between the two conjuncts, and (7.4b) expresses a togetherness relation between the two conjuncts, and so their acceptability is predicted by (7.8a). The conjuncts in (7.5) are of the same semantic type (negative properties of persons), and so the acceptability of (7.5) is predicted by (7.8b). The example in (7.6) is acceptable, because the two conjuncts are semantically related to each other via a condition – result relation, and so the acceptability of (7.6) is predicted by (7.8a).

One characteristic of the RPR is that syntactic category is not considered. As shown in Chapter 3, generalizations relating to the syntactic categories of conjuncts and coordinate complex have already been taken care of independently. The RPR does not impose any new constraints in this regard.

Another characteristic of the RPR is that the coherence requirement is also found in larger linguistic representations such as narratives (Kehler 2002). Thus elements linked by overt coordinators and those that show conjunctive relations but are not linked by overt coordinators are, plausibly, subject to the same filter.

7.3   The components of the RPR

The RPR states that if the conjuncts of a coordinate complex are neither related to each other semantically, nor similar to each other in terms of semantic type and dependency chains, the complex is not acceptable. In this section, I elaborate on these two components of the RPR: relatedness and resemblance.

7.3.1   *Examples of the semantic relatedness between conjuncts*
A.   AC

If the encoded eventualities of two conjuncts are related to each other, the coordinate complexes are generally acceptable, regardless of whether the conjuncts show resemblance in syntactic category, semantic type, or movement history. This is the case with AC. In Section 5.2.2 I mentioned a few examples of AC, and Huddleston and Pullum (2002: 1299–1304) provide a systematic classification. In this subsection, I show how the RPR is superior to other proposed constraints in handling various types of AC.

Interrogatives and declaratives   In (7.10a), the first clausal conjunct is interrogative and the second one is declarative. In (7.10b), the first clausal conjunct is declarative and the second one is interrogative.

(7.10) a. How much wine can you drink and still stay sober?
       b. Big Louie sees this mess and who's going to be in trouble?   (Culicover
          and Jackendoff 1997: 210)

In each example above, there is a certain semantic relation between the conjuncts. In (7.10b), for instance, the first conjunct encodes a condition for the eventuality encoded by the second conjunct. In each case, the two conjuncts are of different types semantically. They are also different in their movement history: one conjunct contains a wh-movement chain, whereas the other does not. It is Relatedness (7.8a), rather than Resemblance (7.8b), that accounts for the acceptability of such examples.

In contrast to the above examples, the conjuncts of the following hold neither a relatedness nor a resemblance relation.

(7.11) a. *[What has Bill seen] and [he has heard the bad news]?   (Culicover and
       Jackendoff 1997: 211)
     b. *[Bill has seen the broken window] and [what has he heard]?
     c. *John asked me for a dollar and why the sky is blue.

In the examples in (7.11), one conjunct is a question and the other is not. In none of these examples do the conjuncts belong to the same semantic type, failing to satisfy (7.8b). At the same time, the two conjuncts in each coordinate complex do not have any semantic relation, failing to satisfy (7.8a). Thus the RPR is violated.

An EC-like effect is also observed in IDCs:

(7.12) a. What book and what magazine did John buy and Bill read respectively?
     b. *What book and what magazine did John buy, [Sue write the novel], and
       Bill read respectively?   (Kehler 2002: 125)

In (7.12a), both clausal conjuncts are interrogative. In (7.12b), however, among the three clausal conjuncts, two are interrogative while the middle one, *Sue write the novel,* is not. Thus in (7.12b), the conjuncts do not satisfy the resemblance condition.

The coordination in IDCs is accidental, as signaled by the word *respectively*, and so the conjuncts cannot satisfy Relatedness. IDCs are therefore only acceptable if they satisfy Resemblance, as (7.12a) does by having conjuncts of the same semantic type (interrogative).

Interrogatives and imperatives   In examples like (7.13), an imperative expression is coordinated with an interrogative one (Huddleston and Pullum 2002: 1332). Though the two conjuncts in (7.13a) are of different semantic types, they are nevertheless semantically related: the speaker uses the second conjunct to ask the hearer to respond to the content expressed in the first conjunct. However, in (7.13b), the two conjuncts are both of different semantic types and unrelated to each other. Thus, it is not acceptable.

(7.13) a. Come around six, or is that too early?
     b. *What are you doing and shut the door.

Interrogatives and exclamatives   In examples like (7.14), an interrogative expression is conjoined with an exclamative one (Huddleston and Pullum 2002: 1332). The two conjuncts both describe the same event, and thus they are semantically related, making the sentence acceptable.

(7.14)   I remember who was there and what a success it was.

Imperatives and declaratives   In (7.15a) and (7.15b), the first clause is imperative and the second one is declarative. Semantically, the first conjunct encodes a condition for the second conjunct, and thus the two conjuncts are semantically related to each other.

(7.15) a. Do that and I'll give you $10.   (= (7.6))
        b. Be there or I'll get angry.

Declaratives and exclamatives   In examples like (7.16), an exclamative expression is conjoined with a declarative one (Huddleston and Pullum 2002: 1332). The two conjuncts seem to have a "nevertheless" relation.[1]

(7.16)   What a disaster it was and yet no one seemed to mind.

Passives and actives   Passive and active constructions can also be conjoined. In examples like (7.17), the first conjunct is a passive clause and the second one is an active clause. The coordination is an AC. The two conjuncts in (7.17) exhibit Cause-Effect and Contiguity relations (Kehler 2002).

(7.17)   I was criticized yesterday and thus I criticized others today.

According to the RPR, the data in (7.10) through (7.17) are acceptable because the two conjuncts are semantically related to each other.

B.   Co-reference with whole conjuncts
Relatedness is also exhibited in co-reference. Coordinate complexes can be acceptable without sharing semantic type across conjuncts, if one conjunct is co-referential with an element inside the other conjunct.

(7.18)   Let us examine [this alternative possibility] and [how it affects the
          predictions of the LF Identity Condition].   (Heim and Kratzer 1998: 255)

In (7.18), the pronoun *it* in the second conjunct is co-referential with the first conjunct *this alternative possibility*. This makes the two conjuncts semantically related, and thus the coordinate complex satisfies (7.8a) and by extension, the RPR. This is so even though the two conjuncts are not of the same semantic

---

1 This is a counterexample to the claim that the nevertheless-type of AC tends to have a modal or to be non-episodic (see Kehler 2002: 140).

type (the second conjunct is a question whereas the first one is not) and hence violates (7.8b).

Another type of example showing co-reference between one whole conjunct and an element of the other conjunct is represented by the following (Zoerner 1995: 94; Progovac 1998b: 6).

(7.19) a. John read the book and quickly.
      b. Robin knows Kim and intimately!

It is possible that they are derived from (7.20) by PF-deletion of the verb-object string in the second conjunct (the underlined part). Since the content of the deleted string can be recovered from the first conjunct, the deletion follows Chomsky's (1965: 144) recoverability condition on deletion.[2]

(7.20) a. John [read the book]   and   [read it quickly].
      b. Robin [knows Kim]   and   [knows her intimately]!

In each example in (7.19), the whole first conjunct is co-referential with the gap between the coordinator and the adverb in (7.20). Thus the two conjuncts are semantically related.

7.3.2   *Examples of the resemblance between conjuncts in semantic types*

In this subsection we show that if conjuncts are of the same semantic type, the coordinate complexes are generally acceptable, regardless of whether the conjuncts are semantically related to each other or show any resemblance in syntactic category.

A.   Conjuncts of the same force

Question clauses and question words can conjoin since they share question features, although their syntactic categories are different.

(7.21) a. [What and when] does John (normally) eat?
      b. John asked [the time and where the bathroom was].   (Munn 1993: 119)

The two conjuncts in (7.21a) are both question words, and thus belong to the same semantic type (see Zhang 2007b for a syntactic analysis of the construction). In (7.21b), the two conjuncts of the coordinate complex belong to different syntactic categories. One is a DP, and the other is a clause. However,

---

2 In (7.20), the pronoun *it* is structurally equivalent to the antecedent *the book*, and in (7.20), the pronoun *her* is structurally equivalent to the antecedent *Kim* (see Elbourne 2005 and Kratzer 2009 for recent defenses of this analysis of pronouns).

they are of the same semantic type. The DP *the time* in these examples is an implicit question, meaning "what time was it," satisfying the s-selection of *ask* in (7.21b) (see Grimshaw 1981; Pesetsky 1982).

Exclamative clauses and non-clausal exclamative expressions can also conjoin (Munn 1996: 4):

(7.22)   It's amazing how tall he is and the things he can do.

B.   Focus feature-bearing conjuncts

If some focus-marking element is present in both conjuncts, such as the words *only* and *even* and the degree words *more* and *most*, elements that are categorially different can also be conjoined. We have seen examples like the following in Chapter 3 (Grosu 1985, where parallel examples are given from Finnish, Modern Hebrew, Kikuriya (Bantu), and Joluo (Nilotic)).

(7.23) a. John eats only pork and only at home.
       b. *John eats pork and at home.

(7.24) a. John eats the most unlikely things and at the most unlikely hours.
       b. John has stolen more watches and from more unsuspecting victims than anybody else ever will.
       c. I eat [neither meat nor at restaurants].   (Chris Wilder, p.c.)

If both conjuncts are foci, they are of the same semantic type. Similarly, if both conjuncts contain the same degree word, they can also be of the same semantic type. The above examples thus satisfy (7.8b), and so their acceptability is predicted by the RPR. Since the two conjuncts in (7.23b) are neither of the same semantic type nor semantically related to each other, its unacceptability is also predicted by the RPR.

C.   Circumstantials (time and location)

Temporal expressions can be conjoined, as can locative expressions, regardless of their syntactic categories, since they are of the same semantic type. In (7.25a) and (7.25b), two temporal expressions are conjoined, although one conjunct is a nominal while the other is a PP.

(7.25) a. John went to the library [yesterday] and [on Tuesday].   (NP & PP)
       b. John plays at night and every Sunday.   (Moltmann 1992a: 25) (PP & NP)

D.   Other semantic types

Other types of semantic resemblance, not fitting into the above categories, permit satisfaction of (7.8b) of the RPR. We have seen one such example in (7.5), where the semantic type involves negative properties of persons. Further examples illustrating the wide range of semantic types satisfying the RPR can be found in Dik (1968: 28), Sag *et al.* (1985: 117f.), Gazdar *et al.* (1985: 174), Zoerner (1995), Munn (1996: 4), Huddleston and Pullum (2002: 1335), among other places. Consider the following.

(7.26) a. John is sick and in a foul mood.   (AP & PP)
        b. *John is sick and in the park.   (Munn 1993: 117)

(7.27) a. *Dogs are mammals and are barking right now in front of my window.
        b. *A dog is a mammal and is barking right now in front of my window.

(7.28)   *Liz made out Mason to be intelligent and Sarah to be angry.

    In both (7.26a) and (7.26b), an AP is conjoined with a PP. The former is acceptable, since both conjuncts denote properties of a person, the same semantic type. The latter is not acceptable, since one conjunct denotes a property and the other a location, different semantic types. Once more, we see that the RPR captures the acceptability contrast while the CLC cannot. In (7.27) (taken from Manfred Krifka's talk at ZAS-Berlin, June 16, 2003), the two predicate conjuncts are not of the same semantic type: one is generic and the other is episodic, and they are not related to each other, either. In (7.28), the predicate in the first conjunct, *intelligent*, denotes an individual-level property, whereas that in the second conjunct, *angry*, denotes a stage-level property. In this example, the conjuncts are not of the same semantic type, nor are they related to each other.

    The unacceptability of (7.26b) and (7.27) is not predicted by Sag *et al.*'s (1985: 119) structural rule that coordinate complexes introduced by the verb *be* allow conjuncts of any type. These examples also challenge CLCfunc, as well as a predicate approach to the CLC (Sag *et al.* 1985; Chametzky 1987; Morrill 1990; Zoerner 1995; cf. Munn 1993). It is not true that coordination is always possible with elements that can be used as predicates. Such approaches are inadequate because they neglect semantics.

    The RPR is exhibited not only in the non-modifier type of coordinate complexes, as in (7.26) through (7.28), but also in the modifier type of coordinate complexes, including adverbials and modifiers of DPs (some of the examples in (7.29) are from Peterson 2004: 650).

(7.29) a. John ran down the path, <u>a marked man</u> and <u>desperately afraid</u>. (NP & AP)

    b. In jeans and a T-shirt and <u>sporting two days' growth on his chin</u>, John presented a less than inspiring figure. (PP & VP)

    c. <u>Late for a meeting</u> and <u>growing impatient</u>, the woman got out and glowered down at the man as he struggled with a wrench. (AP & VP)

    d. Anyone <u>knowing the whereabouts of John Smith</u> and <u>afraid to tell the police</u> should contact the following emergency number. (VP & AP)

    e. John walked [slowly] and [with great care]. (Adv & PP)

    f. na   ge landuo erqie jingchang chidao   de xuesheng (AP & RC)
       that CL lazy   and often   late.come DE student
       'that student that is lazy and often comes late'

(7.30) a. *I sat [on the couch] and [with fever]. (Progovac 1998b: 6)

    b. *Jessie believes Tracy [to be happy and walks] (Pollard and Sag 1994: 204)

In (7.29a), the nominal conjunct *a marked man* and the adjectival conjunct *desperately afraid* both express mental states. They can conjoin since they are of the same semantic type. The other examples in (7.29) also contain conjuncts of the same semantic type. However, the conjuncts in the examples in (7.30) are neither semantically related to each other nor of the same semantic type. In (7.30a), for instance, *on the couch* refers to a location, whereas *with fever* refers to a state.

Note that the coordinate complexes in both (7.29) and (7.30) are syntactically adjuncts. Hence their acceptability contrasts cannot be covered by Peterson's (2004: 650) CLCfunc.

The acceptable coordinate complexes in (7.23) through (7.29) all satisfy (7.8b), regardless of whether they are modifiers or predicates, since the conjuncts in each complex are of the same semantic type, and they do not contain any unlike movement chains.

Not only are forms that do not satisfy the RPR judged unacceptable, but the same holds for interpretations. For instance, the adverb *clearly* in (7.31a) is ambiguous between a manner reading and an evidential reading (synonymous with *obviously*). In (7.31b), this adverb is coordinated with the adverb *loudly*, which has only a manner reading. The evidential reading of *clearly* in the conjoined structure is no longer available, as correctly predicted by the RPR.

(7.31) a. Eve was clearly singing a lullaby.

    b. Eve was clearly and loudly singing a lullaby.

The construction in (7.31b) is only possible because of the ambiguity of *clearly*. With adverbs of unambiguously distinct types, conjunction is not possible at all, as in (7.2b), repeated here as (7.32):

(7.32)   *John probably and unwillingly went to bed.

The effect of the PR on interpretation has been extensively discussed in Lang (1984) and Fox (2000) (see also Potts's 2002 review of Fox 2000). It thus will not be addressed any more in this book.

7.3.3   The CLC: two further issues
A.   Against a gapping account of CLC violations

The coordination of unlike categories is not consistent with a verb gapping analysis.

It has often been assumed that sentences like (7.33a) (= (7.5)) are derived from sentences like (7.33b), after deletion of the second copula.

(7.33) a. Jermaine is boring and a fool.
       b. Jermaine is boring and ~~is~~ a fool.

If all cases of coordination of unlike categories were derived by copula-deletion, the contrast in (7.34) would not be accounted for.

(7.34) a. The bouncer was muscular and was a guitarist.   (Goodall 1987: 34)
       b. *The bouncer was muscular and a guitarist.

By contrast, in the RPR analysis, (7.34a) is fine because each conjunct encodes a proposition about the same person, satisfying (7.8b). (7.34b) is deviant because the two conjuncts are neither semantically related to each other nor semantically of the same type: *muscular* denotes a physical property but *a guitarist* denotes an occupation.

Another argument against the gapping approach is the fact that acceptable unlike coordination constructions need not have any corresponding "full-fledged" forms with syntactically like conjuncts (Munn 1996: 4). For instance, (7.35a) cannot be derived from the unacceptable (7.35b) or (7.35c). Similarly, (7.36a) cannot be derived from the unacceptable (7.36b) (see Munn 1993: 120; Wilder 1999: 10; Peterson 2004: 648 for more discussion of problems with the copula-gapping analysis).

(7.35) a. John knows neither the murderer, nor where the body is.
       b. *John knows neither the murderer, nor knows where the body is.
       c. *John knows neither the murderer, nor John knows where the body is.

(7.36) a. Slowly and with great care, was how John walked.
　　　b. *Walk slowly and walk with great care, was how John walked.

B.　　　Coordinate complexes in predicate and subject positions

The present analysis also allows us to account for a puzzle posed by unlike conjuncts that has not previously been solved in the literature of coordination. Starting with Gazdar (1981: 172 fn. 24) it has been noted that although an adjective and a noun can form a coordinate complex in a predicate position, as in (7.37a), such a complex cannot occur in a subject position, as in (7.37b) and (7.37c).

(7.37) a. Jermaine is boring and a fool.
　　　b. *Boring and a fool entered the restaurant.
　　　c. *A fool and boring entered the restaurant.

In fact, (7.37b) can be independently ruled out. In Chapter 3, I showed that in English, the category of the external conjunct, here *boring*, determines the category of the coordinate complex as a whole, here *boring and a fool*. Since the complex in (7.37b) occurs as the subject of an eventive predicate, it must be a DP, but it cannot be, because *boring* is not a DP.

(7.38)　　*Boring entered the restaurant.

As is well known, nominals are property-denoting in predicate positions, but individual-denoting in the argument positions of eventive verbs. However, the semantic types of adjectives are consistent. (7.37a) is fine because the predicate nominal *a fool* denotes a property, and the word *boring* also denotes a property. The two conjuncts are thus of the same semantic type. The two conjuncts of (7.37c), however, are not of the same semantic type, since the first conjunct, the nominal *a fool*, must be individual-denoting in the position of the subject of the eventive verb *enter*, whereas the second conjunct, *boring*, is not individual-denoting. Therefore, (7.8b) is not satisfied. Moreover, nothing indicates that the two conjuncts are semantically related (a fool is not necessarily boring). Thus (7.8a) is not satisfied, either. Therefore, the unacceptability of (7.37c) is predicted by the RPR.

We can explain the following examples in a similar way (data from Gazdar *et al.* 1985: 174; Borsley 1994: 231; Higginbotham 1987: 52):

(7.39) a. He is a sick man and suffering from fever.
　　　b. *[A sick man and suffering from fever] needs rest.

(7.40) a. His father was well known to the police and a devout Catholic.
       b. *The [well known and a Catholic] man was my father.
       c. *Soon [a Catholic and well known] started shouting again.

(7.41) a. John is a linguist and proud of it.
       b. *John met a linguist and proud of it.
       c. *He took offense and coffee.

If nominals such as *a sick man, a Catholic, a linguist,* and *coffee* are individual- or entity-denoting in argument positions, they cannot be conjoined with property-denoting elements, such as *suffering from fever, well known,* and *proud of it*, or abstract notions such as *offense*, in these positions. Similarly, the semantics of the adjective *stupid* and that of the proper noun *John* are different, therefore they cannot be conjoined:

(7.42)   *He is stupid and John.   (Higginbotham 1987: 52)

The RPR explains these data (and similar examples in Sag *et al.* 1985: 141).

7.3.4   *Examples of the resemblance between conjuncts in dependency chains*

If conjuncts do not exhibit relatedness, they show resemblance in dependency chains such as movement chains in terms of the semantic features and the phonological realization of the chain links.

A.   The semantic features of the links of dependency chains
If both conjuncts have dependency chains, they share a resemblance in the thematic features of the chain links. Let us start with MSCs. In the two clausal conjuncts of an MSC, the link of a dependency in one clausal conjunct must have the same thematic features as the link of the parallel dependency in the other clausal conjunct. For instance, they must both be themes, as in (7.43a), or patients, as in (7.43b). But the pattern in (7.43c), in which one link in the first conjunct is a patient but the parallel link in the second conjunct is an agent, is not acceptable (more examples can be found in Moltmann 1992b: 175 (58)):

(7.43) a. [A man]$_i$ came and [a woman]$_j$ left [who$_{i\&j}$ knew each other well].
       b. John met [a man]$_i$ and Mary met [a woman]$_j$ [who$_{i\&j}$ knew each other well].
       c. *John saw [a man]$_i$ and [a woman]$_j$ saw Mary [who$_{i\&j}$ were wanted by the police].

The RPR can be satisfied even when theta roles are merely similar, rather than identical. Thus the MSC in (7.44) is acceptable, even though *a man* is a theme and *a woman* is a goal.

(7.44)   John saw <u>a man</u> and Mary talked to <u>a woman</u> who were wanted by the police.

There are two ways to analyze the non-contrastiveness of *a man* and *a woman* in (7.44). According to Reinhart (2002), only the features of agent and patient are contrastive, whereas the features of other theta roles are not. Thus *a man* and *a woman* in (7.44) have sufficiently similar thematic features to satisfy the resemblence condition of the RPR. According to the typology in Platzack (2008), the thematic roles of both *a man* and *a woman* in (7.44) belong to family C (not inherently affected, e.g. path, theme), as opposed to family B (inherently affected, e.g. undergoer, experiencer), as well as family A (e.g. agent, instrument).

IDCs obey a similar constraint. In the two clausal conjuncts of an IDC, the gap in one must be in a syntactic position similar to the gap of the parallel dependency in the other. In other words, the gaps must be associated with similar thematic roles. For instance, they must be either both agents or both patients, as in (7.45a) and (7.45b), respectively. In (7.45c), the gap in one conjunct is a patient whereas the gap in the other conjunct is an agent, and so is not acceptable.

(7.45) a. [[Which nurse]$_i$ and [which hostess]$_j$]$_k$ $_{-i}$ dated Fred and $_{-j}$ married Bob respectively?
    b. [[Which nurse]$_i$ and [which hostess]$_j$]$_k$ did Fred date $_{-i}$ and Bob marry $_{-j}$, respectively?
    c. *[[Which nurse]$_i$ and [which hostess]$_j$]$_k$ did Fred date $_{-i}$ and $_{-j}$ marry Bob, respectively?

B.   The phonological realization of the links of dependency chains
Conjuncts also show resemblances in how the links of dependency chains are realized phonologically. Namely, they must be both silent or both overt (e.g. expressed by a pronoun). Consider the wh-movement construction in (7.46a) and the Chinese topicalization construction in (7.46b). In neither of these examples does a gap in one conjunct occur with a pronoun in the other conjunct.

(7.46) a. Which book$_i$ did Mary like $_{-i}$ and John review (*it$_i$)?

    b. Na ge ren$_i$,   Baoyu xihuan $_{-i}$, Daiyu taoyan (*ta$_i$).
       that CL person Baoyu like   Daiyu dislike   he
       'That person, Baoyu likes and Daiyu dislikes.'

Unlike the gaps in (7.46), parasitic gaps are not obligatory:

(7.47)   Which paper$_i$ did Mary file $_{-i}$ without reading (it$_i$)?

The obligatory gapping in (7.46) is covered by the second part of the Resemblance condition of the RPR, relating to the resemblance of the phonological realizations of dependency chain links. Specifically, no overt element internal to the right conjunct may be co-indexed with a gap or silent element in the left conjunct. The following examples are cited from Wilder (1997: 59, 60, 67, 94).

(7.48) a. *[_$_i$ came in] and [{Mary$_i$/she$_i$} sat down].
    b. *[John _$_i$ wine], but [Mary drinks$_i$ beer].
    c. *[John ~~likes Beethoven~~] and [Mary likes Beethoven].

We can see that the constraint is also seen in ellipsis constructions, and the offending overt forms in the second conjuncts are not restricted to pro-forms.

RNR constructions like (7.49) are fine because it is a gap rather than an overt form in the second conjunct that is related to the gap in the first conjunct, and the "shared" element (underlined in (7.49)) is outside the coordinate complex (see Postal 1998; among others).

(7.49)   John offered _, and Mary actually gave _, a gold Cadillac to Billy Schwartz.

This and the previous subsection show that conjuncts must show resemblance in dependency chains. This can be covered by the following condition of Lang (1984: 22):[3]

(7.50)   Given some coordinate construction divided by a connector into two sub-structures s1, s2, then for the specification of a pair cj1, cj2 within s1 and s2 respectively as conjuncts, it holds that
    (a) as to their format, cj1, cj2 are delimited by the set of parallel-structured matching constituents in s1, s2
    (b) cj1 and cj2 must display parallel stress patterns
    (c) cj1 and cj2 must be contrastable constituentwise

Item (a) of (7.50) explains the acceptability patterns of (7.43) and (7.45). This is a PR effect. Moreover, from the perspectives of PF and information structure, items (b) and (c) of (7.50) are valid as well. We can add another item: between cj1 and cj2, it is impossible for one to be silent and the other to be realized phonologically.

3 Zoerner (1995: 61) proposes a similar condition, the Condition on Index Association (CIA): In a series of parallel index sequences, the *nth* term of one sequence associates syntactically and semantically only with the *nth* of any other sequence.

7.4   The RPR in language processing

In this section, we review three types of processing research which show that syntactically well-built representations are not processed equally. Rather, processing is easier if the subcomponents of the representations have a tighter semantic relation, or have parallel merged structures, or have parallel dependency chains. The results of these processing studies are therefore compatible with the RPR.

7.4.1   The more tightly semantically connected, the easier to process
It is generally recognized that elements that are more readily integrated into the sentence are processed faster than elements that are not so readily integrated into the sentence. For instance, the arguments of a verb are easier to process than adjuncts of the verb. Thus Speer and Clifton (1998) found that readers read the same prepositional phrases faster when they were arguments of a verb than when they were adjuncts. A similar conclusion follows from the finding that prepositional phrases that can function either as arguments or as adjuncts tend to be understood as arguments (Schütze and Gibson 1999). Furthermore, an experiment reported by Lin (2007) found that the possessors of inalienable nouns (including kinship terms and body parts) were read significantly faster than their alienable counterparts.

   Conjuncts of natural coordination are more readily integrated into the sentence than conjuncts of accidental coordination, so we expect that natural coordination constructions should be processed more easily than accidental coordination constructions. This is indeed the case. First, if a coordinate complex is ambiguous between natural and accidental coordination readings, the default is the former reading. We have seen the examples in (7.51) in Chapter 5. For (7.51a), the collective reading is the default one, whereas the distributive reading is marked. For (7.51b), the AC reading is the default one, whereas the non-AC reading is marked.

(7.51) a. Baoyu {he/gen} Daiyu dingqin-le.
             Baoyu and/and   Daiyu engage-PRF
             'Baoyu and Daiyu are engaged.'

       b. John went to the store and bought some ice cream.

   As pointed out by Carston (1993: 29), the natural coordination reading "is overwhelmingly more likely to be recovered by the hearer, and to have been intended by the speaker," than the accidental coordination reading. Second, the experimental studies reported in Frazier *et al.* (1999) on English and Yu

(2008) on Chinese also show that natural coordination is processed faster than accidental coordination.

The fact that natural coordination reading is the default reading of a coordinate construction has been discussed from a pragmatic perspective since Grice (1967), and accounted for by the pragmatic notion of relevance by Carston, which he claims minimizes processing effort (p. 29; see also Sperber and Wilson 1995: 260). Relevance is subsumed under the relatedness condition of the RPR.

7.4.2   *The more parallel in merged structures, the easier to process*

Frazier *et al.* (2000) find that the coordination of syntactically like categories, as in (7.52a), is processed faster than coordination of unlike categories, as in (7.52b).

(7.52) a. John walked <u>slowly</u> and <u>carefully</u>, avoiding the broken glass.
     b. John walked <u>slowly</u> and <u>with great care</u>, avoiding the broken glass.

Likewise, Frazier and Clifton (2001) and Carlson (2002) find that a conjunct is read faster if it is structurally parallel to the preceding conjunct than if it is not. (7.53a) was read more quickly than (7.53b), and the sentences in (7.54) were read more quickly than those in (7.55).

(7.53) a. Hilda noticed <u>a strange man</u> and <u>a tall woman</u> when she entered the house.
     b. Hilda noticed <u>a man</u> and <u>a tall woman</u> when she entered the house.

(7.54) a. Jim believed all Tom's stories and Sue believed Jim's stories.
     b. Jim believed all Tom's stories were literally true and Sue believed Jim's stories were fictitious.

(7.55) a. Jim believed all Tom's stories and Sue believed Jim's stories were fictitious.
     b. Jim believed all Tom's stories were literally true and Sue believed Jim's stories.

In (7.53a), both conjuncts have a [D A N] construction, whereas in (7.53b), the first conjunct has a [D N] construction and the second conjunct has a [D A N] construction. We can see that in (7.53a), the two conjuncts are identical in their structure, and thus the sentence is read faster. In (7.53b), the two conjuncts are not identical in their structure, and thus the sentence is read slower. Similarly, in (7.54a) the object of each conjunct is a DP. The two conjuncts thus have similar structures. In (7.54b), the object of each conjunct is a clause. The two conjuncts thus also have similar structures. In contrast, in (7.55a) and (7.55b), one of the two conjuncts has a nominal complement and the other conjunct has a clause complement. Since these data are minimal pairs, the contrast in their reading speed is directly related to the contrast in the degree of parallelism in the conjuncts.

Parallelism makes processing easier and more efficient. However, the forms that show more parallelism and those that show less parallelism are both syntactically well-formed.

A similar experiment is reported in Luka and Barsalou (2005). It is observed that grammaticality ratings are increased for sentences that share representational structures with those read earlier. Again, the more parallel, the easier to process. This is covered by the resemblance condition of the RPR.

7.4.3   The more parallel in dependency chains, the easier to process
A final example showing the role of the RPR in processing is the following. If each clausal conjunct contains a dependency chain, coordinate complexes with non-parallel gaps are not acceptable.

(7.56) a. I know a man who [Bill likes _ and [Mary hates _].
     b. *I know a man who [Bill saw _] and [_ likes Mary].   (Williams 1978: 34)

In (7.56a), the gaps in both conjuncts are object gaps, and thus they are parallel. In the unacceptable (7.56b), however, the gap in the first conjunct is an object gap, whereas the gap in the second conjunct is a subject gap. The gaps in the conjuncts are not parallel and since they also show no semantic relation, the sentence is unacceptable.

However, the following examples, which also have non-parallel gaps, are fine, because they are saved by having semantically related conjuncts:

(7.57) a. This is the dress which Mary bought _ and _ cost $6,000.   (Goodall
     1987: 72)[4]
     b. That's the candidate who the unions endorsed _ and _ was the
     overwhelming favorite of the Democrats.   (Goodall 1987: 75)

Anderson (1983) reports from her experimental study that non-adjacent gaps are more acceptable than adjacent ones. In (7.56b), (7.57a), and (7.57b), for instance, the gaps are adjacent; in (7.56a), however, the gaps are not adjacent. Generally speaking, the degree of route parallelism is lower when the two gaps are adjacent than when the two gaps are not adjacent. The fact that the two conjuncts in (7.57a) in (7.57b) are semantically related may reduce the processing difficulty caused by the non-parallel dependency chains.

---

4 Zoerner (1995: 82) points out that (i) is natural only with heavy phonological stress on the
  conjunction.

  (i) Mary wore a dress that Ungaro designed and cost a fortune.

7.5   The nature of the RPR

7.5.1   *The RPR is a filter on representations of syntactic complexes*

Based on the relativized nature of the RPR, in this section we first examine what the RPR cannot be. Then we will claim that the RPR is a filter on the syntactic and semantic representations of syntactic complexes.

It has been generally recognized that all five of the constraints discussed in Section 7.2.1 are related to the PR. In our approach, only the morphological component of the CC, which is lexical-item-specific, is captured by mechanisms other than the RPR (see Chapter 4). However, the RPR is responsible for all the rest of the CSC, as well as all of the other constraints proposed for coordination.

A.   Against a pure syntactic approach to the RPR

The RPR is not a syntactic operation   In order to explain the processing contrast between (7.53a) and (7.53b), Frazier and Clifton (2001) claim that an operation of Copy α is present in (7.53a) but absent in (7.53b), and this copy operation is cheaper than the regular step by step operation. If the PR is a Copy α operation, what is copied is a syntactic category in (7.52a), a structure in (7.53a), and a semantic feature in (7.31b).

However, the relativized nature of the RPR suggests that the PR is a global evaluation: the RPR compares two conjuncts that have already been built. If the two conjuncts are of semantically different types, they must be semantically related; if the two conjuncts are semantically related, they are allowed to have non-parallel representations. If neither the relatedness nor the resemblance condition is satisfied, the coordinate complex is not acceptable. Such an evaluation cannot be implemented at a point in the derivation where only one conjunct has been built. Thus after we have built the internal conjunct, we cannot know whether the proposed Copy α is operative or not. In other words, the proposed Copy α is not motivated by any local formal requirement, unlike well-recognized operations like Merge and Move. I therefore do not think that the PR is a syntactic operation. Frazier and Clifton state in their footnote 11: "In fact we suspect that Copy α is just the linguistic reflex of a more general cognitive ability that we dub 'ditto.'" It is possible that what they revealed in their study is a PR filter, which reflects a general law of economy in language processing.

The RPR is not a trigger of syntactic operations   Can the RPR be a feature built inside coordinators to trigger syntactic operations? On the one hand, Hornstein and Nunes (2002) claim that the PR is an interface requirement (p. 28) or a bare output condition (p. 37), while on the other hand, they emphasize that "the Parallelism Requirement demands that movement apply to all the conjuncts if it applies to any (Ross's [1967] Coordinate Structure Constraint)" (p. 37). They make the following claim (p. 41):

> [A]fter a coordinating head merges with a given constituent X, it signals that the computational system should proceed to build a constituent Y parallel to X, with the lexical items available at the relevant derivational step. If the available lexical material does not yield a (semantically) parallel structure, then the Parallelism Requirement, locally enforced by the coordinating head (or by the label of the syntactic object it heads), licenses the copying of constituents of X in order to build Y.

In other words, they claim that if one of the conjuncts is syntactically legal, parallelism alone can trigger an otherwise unlikely operation in building the other conjunct. They further claim (p. 47) that in an ATB dependency, launching movement from the late-merged conjunct can be driven by parallelism alone.

It is generally assumed that the properties or features of syntactic elements trigger syntactic operations (following Collins 2002a we assume that Merge is also triggered by checking selectional features). One might assume that the PR is a feature of coordinators and can trigger syntactic operations, so that the two conjuncts have similar representations (see the above claim of Hornstein and Nunes 2002 and their claim [p. 40] that "the Copy operation must be licensed either by Last Resort or the Parallelism Requirement"; similarly, Nunes 2001: 336 claims that "the Parallelism Requirement functions as an enabling condition that authorizes movement operations that otherwise would not be licensed by Last Resort"). The observed relativity of the PR, however, falsifies this assumption. The global nature of the RPR means that the PR cannot structurally manipulate the building of the external conjunct. After we merge the internal conjunct with a coordinator like *and*, there is no way for the coordinator to signal whether or not the computational system should proceed to build the external conjunct parallel to the internal conjunct already available in the structure. I thus do not think that after the Merger of one conjunct, parallelism alone can trigger an otherwise unlikely operation in building the other conjunct. A more plausible possibility is that the two conjuncts and the whole coordinate complex are built without any PR guidance, but the acceptability of the complex is evaluated by the RPR, which is a filter on language processing.[5]

---

5 While some people have assumed the PR to be a trigger of syntactic operations, others have posited an anti-PR as a trigger of syntactic operations. Thus Moro (1997; 2000) claims that syntactic operations may be triggered in order to change a symmetrical relation into an asymmetrical one.

The PR is not a constraint on syntactic operations   Ross (1967) and most advocates of the CSC, including Moltmann (1992b: 36, 41), believe that the CSC is a constraint on movement operations. In Johnson (2002), the CSC, assumed to reflect the PR, is taken as a constraint on structural building (Merge), determining whether small or large conjuncts should be built. However, as we have seen throughout this book, it has also been pointed out that the CSC is not a constraint on movement (Ruys 1992; Munn 1993: 62, 97; and V. Lin 2001: 366). More generally, Potts (2002: 16) states that the CSC is "not a narrowly grammatical restriction." Our study supports the view adopted by this latter group of authors.

More specifically, the arguments given above against the trigger status of the PR can be used to argue against the syntactic constraint status of the PR, since the RPR has no effect on the building of conjuncts. Instead, the evidence suggests that the RPR evaluates representations rather than restricting syntactic operations.

The CSC and CLC should not be used to make any claims about syntactic structures   Since the CSC and CLC are not syntactic constraints, we cannot use them to make any claims about syntactic structures. In particular, we need to clarify two issues regarding the EC and the CLC, respectively.

First, the EC part of the CSC has been one of the major arguments used to support the VP-Internal Subject Hypothesis (Burton and Grimshaw 1992; McNally 1992). Fortunately, the EC is not the sole argument for the hypothesis, so giving up the EC need not have any effect on it.

Second, taking the CLC for granted, Bowers (1993; 2001) uses data like (7.58a) to argue for the existence of PrP, which is a covering category for all categories that can encode a predication relation.

(7.58) a. Jermaine is boring and a fool.   [AP & NP]   (= (7.5))
   b. I want to emphasize {this point/this} and also that you should never forget what your father told you.   (Dik 1968: 28)   [DP & CP]
   c. You can depend on my assistance and that he will be on time.
   d. [The death of his wife and that he is in prison now] worry me.

In this proposed PrP, the Spec of Pr is assumed to be a subject position, and the complement is a predicate position (an earlier proposal of the category PRED is seen in Jacobson 1987). However, if we follow this line of reasoning, examples like (7.58b), (7.58c), and (7.58d) might be used to argue for V-ObjP, Prep-ObjP, and SubjP, respectively. Although Subject and Object have indeed been analyzed as syntactic features in Jackendoff (1977: 32) and Borsley (1983), they are not regarded as syntactic categories independent of other categories such as DP and CP. In fact, what Bowers calls PrP has been covered by VP (or other extended projections, or den Dikken's 2006 RelatorP or RP) (see Munn 1993: 117 for arguments against the syntactic feature Predicate), and the evidence for the existence of VP is independent of the CLC.

B.   The RPR is a filter on representations of syntactic complexes

Since the PR simply evaluates the syntactic and semantic representations of complexes, we can regard it as a representational filter, rather than a syntactic operation, a trigger of syntactic operations, or a constraint on syntactic operations. One difference between a filter and the other choices is the timing of the application: the former applies after the syntactic derivation is completed, whereas the latter applies before or during syntactic operations.

7.5.2   The general economy motivation of the RPR

So far, what we have shown is that if the subcomponents of a syntactic complex deviate from parallelism in their semantic types and movement links, without any semantic relation to integrate them, the complex is too difficult to process, and thus is rejected as unacceptable. The RPR is thus the result of a general economy principle of processing.

Unlike this general principle, the five coordinate construction-specific constraints, the CLC, CLCsem, CLCfunc, CCC, and CSC, are ad hoc. Given the general operations of Merge and Move, unlike categories can conjoin, and conjuncts and their internal elements can move, as direct consequences of the complementation structure of coordinate complexes argued for in Chapter 2. There is no special categorial constraint on a complementation structure; external and internal conjuncts are simply in a Spec-Complement relation. There are also no special restrictions on movement for complementation structures; specifiers and complements may move, and elements may be extracted from them. As correctly pointed out by Anandan (1993: 33), "As there are no rules for particular constructions such as interrogative, relative, passive and so on, there are no rules for coordinate constructions also."

I conclude that both parts of the RPR, Relatedness and Resemblance, reflect economy in processing.

7.6   Chapter summary and conclusions for Part III

Empirically, I have shown that on the one hand, each of the five coordinate construction-specific constraints proposed in the literature, namely the CLC, CLCsem, CLCfunc, CCC, and CSC, can be violated. On the other hand, the observed effects of these constraints can be accounted for in terms of two independently motivated mechanisms: morphological constraints on the behavior of (certain) conjunctions, and the RPR, which is a filter on linguistic representations in processing. The morphological constraints were addressed in Chapter 4, where I showed, first, that coordinators, like some other types of head elements, do not allow null complements, so if an internal conjunct moves, the surface representation is not acceptable (accounting for the CCi), and second, that if the coordinator does not have categorial features, it will take them from the external conjunct, which will then be unable to move (accounting for the CCe). As for the RPR, it is repeated as follows:

(7.60) Conjuncts of a coordinate complex must hold a coherence relation in terms of:
    a. Relatedness: they must be either related to each other semantically, as in natural coordination; or
    b. Resemblance (Parallelism Requirement): they must hold a resemblance relation in terms of both their semantic type and their dependency chains.

A theoretical consequence of my arguments is that we must remove these five coordinate construction-specific constraints from the syntactic computational system, since they are both ad hoc and empirically falsified. Moreover, they should not be used as diagnostics when testing syntactic hypotheses of any kind.

We now reach the third major conclusion of this book:

> THERE IS NO SPECIAL SYNTACTIC CONSTRAINT ON THE DERIVA-
> TIONS OF COORDINATE COMPLEXES.

Before I end my discussion of the CSC, it seems fair to consider the questions of why the CSC was developed in the first place, and why it has been so influential in syntactic research for more than forty years. As an answer, recall the following facts. First, the EC part of the CSC is seen in accidental rather than natural coordination. Second, the CCe part of the CSC is seen in two situations: in accidental coordination and in coordinate complexes where overt coordinators do not have any categorial features, as is typically found in European languages. Third, the CCi part of the CSC follows from the fact that coordinators are like various other head elements in taking their complement as phonological host. Thus each piece of the putative CSC is due to a completely different factor. The CSC only looks like a unified construction-specific constraint due to the coincidental confluence of these distinct factors in the coordinate complex, a primitive notion in traditional grammar. However, when one takes the broader view demanded by contemporary syntactic theory – considering other head elements, the semantic relations between conjuncts, and coordinators in a wider range of languages – one sees the CSC melting away.

IV No special syntactic operation

8 *The derivation of coordinate clauses with identity adjectives*

8.1 Introduction

Across-the-Board (ATB) constructions are coordinate constructions in which each conjunct contains a gap, like the following example.

(8.1)   Who$_i$ did you say that Carrie likes $_{-i}$ and Sarah hates $_{-i}$?

The goal of this chapter and the next is to propose a new analysis of the syntactic derivation of ATB constructions. It is generally assumed that the constructions are derived by a kind of operation called ATB movement, which "move[s] a constituent out of all the conjuncts of a coordinate structure" (Ross 1967: 107; see also Williams 1977; 1978). In other words, the single extracted element in this construction has been assumed to move simultaneously from multiple gaps. Such movement chains are called "forking chains," and are assumed to occur only in coordinate constructions.

In this book, however, I advocate the position, first stated in George (1980), that ATB movement does not exist at all (see also Franks 1992; Munn 1992, 1993; Bošković and Franks 2000; and Hornstein and Nunes 2002). Moreover, I support Munn's (1992; 1993) claim that the extracted element in ATB constructions originates in the first conjunct only, and show that there is a binding dependency between the extracted element and a silent pro-form in the second conjunct. Both the extraction operation and the pro-form binding dependency are motivated independently of coordinate constructions. The proposed derivation thus does not require any ad hoc forking chains.

The claims about ATB constructions that I make in this chapter are based on an analysis of identity adjectives, such as English *same*, aiming to show the parallelism between *same* constructions and ATB constructions. In my proposed analysis, (8.2a) is derived from (8.2b):

(8.2) a.   The same man Mary helped and Jane ruined.

   b.   [Mary helped [$_{DP_i}$ the same man]$_i$] and [Jane ruined *pro-ϕP_i*].

To anticipate, I will argue that in (8.2b), the pro-form in the second conjunct takes the nominal *the same man* as its antecedent. The category of the pro-form is pro-φP, which shares its gender, number, and person features with its antecedent (see Déchaine and Wiltschko 2002). The pro-φP in *same* constructions is silent at PF. Moreover, I will argue that a similarity expression such as *the same man* in (8.2a) must be licensed by a plural element, which here is the coordinate complex. This expression must move out of the coordinate complex, simply because similarity expressions must be outside their licensing elements (see G. Carlson 1987: 540).

The syntax of *same* gives us clues about the derivation of ATB constructions. In the next chapter, I will demonstrate the similarities between ATB constructions and *same* constructions, and extend my analysis of the latter to the former. Thus, ATB constructions are derived without any forking movement.

In Section 8.2, I review certain syntactic properties of *same* constructions and the important syntactic questions raised by sentences like (8.2a). These questions form the research goals for the following two sections. In Section 8.3, I argue for the existence of a null pro-form in the second conjunct in sentences like (8.2a). In Section 8.4, I argue that a similarity expression like *the same man* in (8.2a) must move from the first conjunct and land outside the coordinate complex. Section 8.5 gives a summary of the chapter.

8.2   The identity adjective *same*

Adjectives such as *same, similar, equal*, and *different* express similarity relations. Among them, *different* expresses a negative value of similarity and *same* expresses a positive and superlative value of similarity, namely identity. I call expressions that host a similarity adjective Similarity Expressions (SE). In (8.2a), for instance, *same* is an identity adjective and *the same man* is an SE.

8.2.1   *The general plural-α licensing of identity adjectives*

Some elements need licensors in their context. For instance, a negative polarity item such as *any* is licensed in a negative context. The licensor can be an independent negation word such as *not* (e.g. *He did not eat any candy*) or a negative feature expressed in a negative word such as *refuse* (e.g. *He refused to eat any candy*). Similarly, verbs such as *combine*, predicates such as *collide*, and adverbs such as *respectively* are all licensed in a plural context. A plural context has two or more eventuality participants or two or more eventualities (we will see examples later). Again, the forms of the licensors can vary (a plural nominal or a coordinate complex). I call this general plural context a plural-α context.

Like other similarity adjectives, identity adjectives must be licensed by a plural-α context. Semantically, this is expected from the notion of similarity, which presupposes the existence of multiple entities or multiple parts of wholes so that a certain kind of "implicit comparison" (Carlson 1987: 531) can be established. I divide plural-α contexts into three basic types. In the first type, the SE is thematically related to the multiple verbal phrases, while in the latter two types it is not.

A.   The Thematic Licensing *same* Construction (TLC)
In the first type of plural-α contexts, the SE seems to get its theta role from the multiple verbal phrases. I call identity adjective constructions of this type the Thematic Licensing *same* Construction (TLC).

The examples in (8.3) represent the TLC. In each example, the coordinate clausal complex provides a context of plural eventualities. In (8.3a), for instance, it is the combination of the helping eventuality and the ruining eventuality that licenses the SE *the same man*. Moreover, in these examples each conjunct of the coordinate complex seems to assign a theta role to the SE, if we ignore the word *same*. In (8.3a) for instance, *helped* in the first conjunct assigns a theta role to its object, and it seems that *the (same) man* is this object; similarly, *ruined* in the second conjunct also assigns a theta role to its object, which also seems to be *the (same) man*.

(8.3) a. The same man Mary helped and Jane ruined.   (= (8.2a))
      b. The same man got drunk and was arrested by the cops.
      c. The same man praised you and seemed to hate you.
      d. The same brush, John used for cleaning the toilet and Mary used for cleaning the kitchen.

Putting aside the role of the identity adjective (*same*), this type of construction intuitively seems to be defined in such a way that the relation between the whole SE and the verb (or verb phrase) of each conjunct is a thematic licensing relation.

The TLC has another version in which the *same*-phrase, the SE, occurs in the right-peripheral position of the sentence.

(8.4)   John avoided and Bill ignored the same man.   (Jackendoff 1977: 192)

I do not discuss such right-edge *same*-constructions (see Hartmann 2000: 78; Abels 2003: 127; Barker 2007; Johnson 2007 for some discussion). I assume that the constructions belong to or should be dealt together with RNR

constructions, in the sense of Postal (1974) and Abbott (1976). It has been recognized that there are systematic syntactic differences between left-peripheral
argument-sharing constructions (ATB constructions) and RNR constructions
(e.g. the right-edge constraint on gap positions is seen in the latter but not in
the former) (Ross 1967; Wilder 1997; Sabbagh 2007; among others). For this
reason, I do not assume that the leftward dependency and the rightward dependency can be derived in a unified way, and so I leave the "right" constructions
for future research.

   Since theta-role relations are syntactic relations, the relation in a TLC
between the SE and its licensor (plural-α), the coordinate verbal phrase, is
a syntactic licensing relation. By contrast, in the two types of SE constructions
introduced in the following two subsections, the relation between the SE and
its licensor (plural-α) is not syntactic.

B.   The Paired Pronoun *same* Construction (PPC)

One construction in which the relation between the SE and the plural-α is not
thematic is the Paired Pronoun *same* Construction (PPC). As in a TLC, in a PPC
the SE is licensed by a context of plural eventualities. In (8.5a), for instance,
it is the combination of the coming eventuality and the leaving eventuality
that licenses the SE *the same man*. In a PPC, the thematic licensing relation is
satisfied by a pronoun in each conjunct, and the two pronouns both take the SE
as their antecedent. In (8.5a), for example, the thematic licensing relation of
came and *left* are satisfied by the first *he* and by the second *he*, respectively, and
both pronouns take *the same man* as their antecedent. (8.5b) and the Chinese
example in (8.5c) show the same point.

(8.5) a.   The same man, he came and he left.
      b.   The same brush, John used it to clean the toilet and Mary used it to
           clean the kitchen.
      c.   Tong yi   ge nühair, Baoyu gei <u>ta</u>   xie-le
           same one CL girl   Baoyu to   her write-PRF

           qing-shu,   Fanjin gei <u>ta</u>   song-le   jiezhi.
           love-letter   Fanjin to   her send-PRF   ring
           'The same girl, Baoyu wrote love letters to her and Fanjin sent a ring to her.'

   This construction can be regarded as a gapless TLC. Semantically, in a TLC,
the missing argument in each conjunct must have the same interpretation as the
referent of the SE. Similarly, in a PPC, the pronoun in each conjunct must have
the same interpretation as the referent of the SE. Neither of the two pronouns
can refer to anyone else other than the referent of the SE. The relationship

between the SE and the two gaps in a TLC is similar to the bound pronoun binding between the nominal *some sheep* and the two pronouns in (8.6) (Evans 1980: 339).

(8.6)   Some sheep are such that John owns them and Harry vaccinates them in the spring.

Similarly, the relationship between the SE and the two pronouns in a PPC is like the bound pronoun binding between *some sheep* and the two pronouns in (8.6). Therefore, in this semantic sense, PPCs are similar to TLCs.

Syntactically, however, the formal features of the verb in each conjunct are saturated by the pronoun in a PPC. No thematic or Case relation exists between the SE and the coordinate complex, unlike the situation in a TLC. The gapless TLC data are similar either to the construction in (8.7a), where one nominal is the antecedent of the two resumptive pronouns, or to the construction in (8.7b), where one nominal is the antecedent of the two relative pronouns distributed in the two conjuncts:

(8.7) a.   Na ge nühair, Baoyu gei <u>ta</u>   xie-le   qing-shu, Fanjin gei <u>ta</u>
            that CL girl   Baoyu to   her write-PRF love-letter Fanjin to   her

            song-le   jiezhi
            send-PRF   ring
            'That girl, Baoyu wrote love-letters to her and Fanjin sent a ring to her.'

     b.   The manuscript [[the letter on the front of <u>which</u> and the scribbling
           on the back of <u>which</u>] Harry deciphered] was in Gwambamamban.
                                                                (Postal 1972: 132)

C.   The Non-Thematic Licensing *same* Construction (Non-TLC)
Another type of construction in which the relation between the SE and the plural-α is not thematic is the Non-Thematic Licensing *same* Construction (Non-TLC), which has four subtypes.[1]

       Discourse plural licensing   *Same* may have an indexical reading, as in (8.8).

(8.8)   John saw the same tree.

As described in G. Carlson (1987: 532), the most natural interpretation for sentences like (8.8) involves a covert comparison between something referred to in the sentence (a certain tree) and something that is understood by the listener

---

1 The adjective *same* can also appear in comparatives, as in *John found the same solution as Mary*. Since the syntax of comparatives is not yet clear to me, I do not discuss this construction here.

as having already been contextually defined. The speaker is considering both the current eventuality and a previous one in which a tree was mentioned. It is this plurality of eventualities that licenses the identity adjective.

In (8.8), the SE *the same tree* has a thematic relation with the selecting verb *saw*. The discourse licensing of the SE does not involve any thematic relation.

Quantifier presupposition plural licensing   *Same* may be licensed by a universal quantifier. In (8.9a), *same* is licensed by *everyone*, and in (8.9b), *same* is licensed by *all the furniture*.

(8.9) a. Everyone saw the same tree.   (Moltmann 1997: 136)
　　　b. All the furniture is of the same color.

As is well known, when a universal quantifier is used with an individual-denoting nominal in an episodic context, a group of individuals is presupposed so that we can mention every item of the group. In (8.9a), the existence of two or more persons is implied, and in (8.9b), the existence of several pieces of furniture is implied. It is this implied plurality that licenses the identity adjective.

Since a quantified nominal is not a verb or predicate, it does not have any thematic relation with the SE.

Plural licensing with restrictive relative clauses   *Same* may appear in restrictive relative clause constructions, as in (8.10).

(8.10)   The same man {that/who} we saw yesterday came today.

The semantic function of restrictive relative clauses is to restrict the referent in a set of elements. Thus relative clauses also presuppose the existence of plural elements. It is this presupposed plurality that licenses the identity adjective.

In (8.10), the SE *the same man* has a theta relation with the matrix predicate *came*, rather than with its licenser, the relative clause. Within the relative clause, *we* and the relative pronoun *who* (or a null operator) satisfy all the thematic checking requirements.

Clause-internal plural licensing   *Same* may occur in a construction where an explicit plural-α occurs. This plural-α is realized by plural morphemes, coordinate complexes, or plural numerals. The examples in (8.11) represent this type of construction. The plural elements are underlined. These can be either a plural nominal, like *the students*, or a coordinate complex, like *John and Mary*, as seen in (8.11a). Keep in mind that unlike in TLCs, there is no thematic relation between the SE and the plural-α in this construction (i.e. the plural-α does not assign a theta role to the SE). In (8.11a), for instance, the object *the same picture* is an SE and the plural subject *the students* licenses the SE. However, unlike the situation in a TLC, the SE gets its theta role from the verb *saw*, rather than its licensor, the subject. Likewise, the subject gets its theta role from the whole predicate *saw the same picture*, rather than the SE. Since the SE and its licensor are both arguments, neither assigns any theta role to the other, so there is no thematic relation between them.

(8.11) a. {The students/John and Mary} saw the same picture.
      b. The same salesman sold me these two magazine subscriptions.   (G.
         Carlson 1987: 532)
      c. The same child slept in the bed and on the floor.
      d. John played the same sonata slow and fast.   (Moltmann 1992b: 231)

Since the plural-α is not a verbal element in these examples, it does not have any thematic relation with the SE in the sentence. Note that the distinction between this construction and TLCs is the latter property (thematic relations), not the former (whether the plural-α is a verbal element). In the following example, the SE adverbial is base-generated out of a coordinate verbal complex and is directly licensed by it. Nevertheless, these examples are Non-TLCs because the formal features of the verbs in the conjuncts are satisfied locally, so there is no thematic relation between the SEs and their licensors.

(8.12)   Zai tong yi   tian, Baoyu wancheng-le boshi lunwen, Daiyu
          at   same one day   Baoyu finish-PRF   PhD   thesis   Daiyu

          sheng-le haizi.
          bore-PRF child
          'On the same day, Baoyu finished a PhD thesis and Daiyu gave birth
          to a child.'

8.2.2   *Major questions about the syntax of TLCs*

After distinguishing TLCs from other SE constructions, we are now ready to examine the syntactic properties of TLCs. TLCs have been regarded by Jackendoff (1977: 192–194), Abbott (1976: 642), Gazdar (1981: 180), Gazdar *et al.* (1982: 664), and Postal (1998: 137) as a challenge to generative syntax. Such data are special in that, if the SE is "reconstructed" into each clausal conjunct, the sentence either becomes unacceptable or does not have the intended reading. For instance, if no man has been mentioned previously in the discourse, (8.13b) is not acceptable. One cannot use this sentence to initiate a description of two events in which a single specific man had been involved. If someone has been previously mentioned in the discourse, (8.13b) is acceptable, but then the two occurrences of *the same man* both refer to the previously mentioned man (i.e., the reading is changed into that of the discourse plural licensing type of Non-TLCs).

(8.13) a. The same man Mary helped and Jane ruined.   (= (8.3a))
        b. (*)Mary helped the same man and Jane ruined the same man.

Why is it that the SE in TLCs cannot surface inside the coordinate complex? I call this the Question of the Surface Position of SEs.

This question in fact requires us to solve another basic syntactic question, the Question of the Base Position of SEs: where are the SEs in the constructions base-generated? This second question entails questions like the following: Why do we interpret SEs as having the same theta role expected for the missing part in the conjuncts? How is the formal feature licensing of the verbal element achieved if the argument that can implement the licensing is missing in each conjunct of a TLC? For instance, in (8.13a), both *helped* and *ruined* are transitive. The agent of the former is *Mary* and the agent in the latter is *John*. According to the Projection Principle (Chomsky 1981; among others), in the presence of the agent, the transitive verb in each conjunct must have an object. The verb and the object need to have formal feature relations (selection, theta role, Case, and so on). But what is the object in each conjunct of the sentence?

In addition to the above two basic syntactic questions, one more fact is in need of explanation, namely why the gap position in the second conjunct of a TLC cannot be filled with an overt pronoun, as shown in (8.14). I call this the Question of Overt Right Link of a Dependency.

(8.14) a. The same man Mary helped and Jane ruined (*him).
        b. The same man Mary helped and (*him) Jane ruined.

All of these questions will be answered in sections 8.3 and 8.4.

8.3   Building well-formed conjuncts of TLCs

This section aims to answer the Question of the Base Position of SEs.

8.3.1   *The existence of a silent nominal in the second conjunct*
We can see that an SE functions as an argument of the predicate or verb in each conjunct of a TLC, although it does not occur in either conjunct. However, no single nominal may satisfy the formal requirements of two predicates or verbs (e.g., selection, theta role, Case). Moreover, any (sideward) movement chain relation between the two conjuncts is unlikely, since the tail and the head links need not have identical forms. In (8.15), for instance, if the gap position in the

second conjunct were the base position of the SE *the same picture of herself,* the derivation would crash, since the feminine reflexive *herself* would not be licensed in the conjunct.

(8.15)   The same picture of herself, Mary painted yesterday and John bought today.

A plausible response to these problems is to hypothesize that the SE is base-generated as an argument in the first conjunct only, and there is another nominal, which is silent, in the second conjunct.

In each conjunct of a TLC, the existence of a nominal related to the argument gap is first of all required by the general formal feature licensing, as stated above. Second, it can also be seen in examples like (8.16), where the reflexive in each finite clausal conjunct must be licensed by a local antecedent. Note that the occurrence of the auxiliary *has* in each conjunct indicates that the construction is a clause, not a VP, since auxiliaries surface at T and TP is a clause. If the reflexive of the first clausal conjunct in (8.16) is licensed by *the same guy*, the reflexive of the second clausal conjunct must be licensed by a different nominal base-generated inside the clausal conjunct.

(8.16)   The same guy has constrained himself in public and has indulged himself
           in his home.

8.3.2   *The interpretation of the silent argument in the second conjunct*

After demonstrating the existence of an argument in the gap position of the second conjunct of a TLC, we now determine its interpretation.

First of all, the φ-features of the assumed silent argument in the second conjunct must be identical to that of the SE. The unacceptability of (8.17) shows that the φ-features of the silent argument are not underspecified, since they may not be different from those of the SE.

(8.17)   *The same guy has constrained himself in public and has indulged herself
           in her home.

Secondly, this assumed argument in the second conjunct of a TLC may not have an independent referent. For instance, the TLC in (8.18) may not be followed by the plural pronoun *they*, taking as its antecedent the combination of the SE and the silent argument.

(8.18)   The same man came today and will come tomorrow. {He/*They} had a
           cold yesterday.

Semantically, the relationship between the silent argument and the SE is like that between an anaphor or a resumptive pronoun and its antecedent. The former has an unvalued [ID] (identification) feature, which is valued by its antecedent (see Adger and Ramchand 2005: 173 and Harley 2005: Section 7 for formalization of the [ID] feature).

8.3.3   *The syntactic category of the silent argument in the second conjunct*

I now identify the syntactic category of the assumed silent argument in the second conjunct of a TLC. I claim that the argument is a pro-form, rather than a copy of the SE. I have shown in (8.17) that the φ-features of the silent argument are identical to those of the SE, i.e., those of the head of the SE only. In (8.19), for instance, the silent argument in the second conjunct must be a pro-form. If the conjunct contained a copy of the SE, *the same picture of herself,* in any step of the derivation, the feminine reflexive *herself* would not be licensed in the conjunct.

(8.19)   The same picture of herself, Mary painted yesterday and John bought
            today.   (= (8.15))

We can further identify the anaphor-like pro-form in the second conjunct of a TLC as a pro-φP, defined in Déchaine and Wiltschko (2002) on the basis of a cross-linguistic survey (including English) as never having independent referents. This kind of (silent) pro-form for the lower link of A-bar dependencies is also argued for in Adger and Ramchand (2005).

I thus conclude that the argument in the second conjunct of a TLC is a silent pro-form, taking the SE as its antecedent. I leave the issue of why this pro-form is silent to Section 8.4.3.

I can now answer the Question of the Base Position of SEs. An SE is base-generated as an argument in the first conjunct, where it satisfies local formal requirements like theta role and Case feature checking. In the second conjunct, in the gap position there is a silent pro-φP satisfying its own local formal requirements. Note that this conclusion depends on the assumption that the verb or predicate of the second conjunct assigns its relevant theta role to a nominal distinct from that of the first conjunct.

I have now established the existence of a silent argument in the second conjunct of a TLC, as well as its interpretation and category. The SE and this silent argument guarantee the syntactic well-formedness of each conjunct in the TLC.

8.4   Extraction of SEs out of their licensing coordinate complexes

So far, I have demonstrated two dependencies in a TLC, namely the binding relation between the SE and a silent pro-φP, and the licensing of the SE by a plural-α. Each of these dependencies is independently motivated. Reflexives encode the former dependency only, whereas relational nominals encode the latter dependency only. Relational nominals such as *combination, mixture, marriage, comrade,* or *friend* express relations between multiple individuals and thus require a plural-α licensor, but they do not encode any binding relation. The SEs that host the word *same* in TLCs are special in that they encode both dependencies. For the binding relation, the SEs satisfy the formal conditions of the pro-ϕP, whereas for the licensing relations, their own formal conditions are satisfied by a plural context.

I have discussed the licensing of SEs of TLCs via the coordination of two clausal conjuncts in Section 8.2.1A, and the binding relation in TLCs in Section 8.3. In this section, I show that it is the plural-α SE licensing relation that forces the SE to move out of the coordinate complex. This obligatory raising also correlates with the obligatory silence of the pro-form in the second conjunct. We will thus be able to answer both the Question of the Surface Position of SEs and the Question of Overt Right Link of a Dependency, raised in Section 8.2.2.

8.4.1   The extraction of SEs out of first conjuncts

I argued in Section 8.3 that the SE of a TLC is base-generated in the first conjunct of the construction. Recall that the SE of a TLC cannot be "reconstructed" back into both conjuncts (see (8.13)). I now argue that the association between the SE and the gap in the first conjunct of a TLC is a movement chain. In other words, the left-edge position of the SE of a TLC is derived by movement. My first argument for the movement analysis comes from island effects.

(8.20) a. *The same person, Bill lost business because he hired and Mary praised
          a lot.
      b. *The same person, Bill lost business after he hired and Mary praised a lot.
      c. *The same student, the teachers who often praise are functionalists, and the
          formalist teachers often criticize.
      d. *The same nurse, John is still wondering whether he should date and
          Jack has dated.

In the above unacceptable examples, the SEs originate in islands. In (8.20a), the SE *the same person* is related to the object of the verb *hired*, which is inside a *because*-adverbial clause. In (8.20b), the SE *the same person* is related to the object of the verb *hired*, which is inside an *after*-adverbial clause. The impossibility of these dependencies can be covered by the adjunct island effect. In (8.20c), the SE *the same student* is related to the object of the verb *praise* inside the relative clause of the first conjunct, so the impossibility of this dependency can be covered by the complex definite DP island effect. Finally, in (8.20d), the SE *the same nurse* is related to the object of the verb *date*, which is inside a question initiated with the word *whether*, so the impossibility of this dependency can be covered by the wh-island effect.

I argued in Section 8.3 that the gap in the second conjunct of a TLC is a silent pro-form, which is not formed by movement. Hence we do not expect it to show any island effects, and this is indeed the case. Setting aside the marked nature of topicalization in English, my English-speaking informants confirm the relative acceptability of (8.21a,b), in contrast to (8.20a,d), respectively.

(8.21) a. The same person, Bill praised a lot and Mary lost business because she hired.
       b. The same nurse, John has dated and Jack is still wondering whether he should date.

The unacceptable TLC examples in (8.20) also stand in contrast to the following acceptable PPC examples. Since there is no movement chain in deriving the surface positions of the SE and the pronouns in a PPC, the acceptability of the sentences is expected.

(8.22) a. The same person, Bill lost business because he hired him and Mary praised him a lot.
       b. The same person, Bill lost business after he hired him and Mary praised him a lot.
       c. The same student, the teachers who often praise him are functionalists, and the formalist teachers often criticize him.
       d. The same nurse, John is still wondering whether he should date her and Jack has dated her.

My second argument for the movement approach is that an SE may contain a reflexive bound by the subject of the first conjunct, as shown in (8.23a), but may not contain a reflexive bound by the subject of the second conjunct, as shown in (8.23b).

(8.23) a The same picture of herself, Mary painted yesterday and John bought today.   (= (8.19))
       b. *The same picture of himself, Mary painted and John bought.

The reconstruction effect of the reflexive indicates that movement has occurred in the first conjunct.

8.4.2   *Carlson's constraint and the motivation for SE extraction*

In this subsection I explain the motivation for the observed movement of SEs in TLCs. For instance, what drives the SE *the same man* in (8.24a) to move out of the coordinate complex?

(8.24) a. The same man Mary helped and Jane ruined.   (= (8.13a))
  b. (*)Mary helped the same man and Jane ruined the same man.   (= (8.13b))

Recall that there are two dependencies in TLCs: the binding of the silent pro-ϕP by the SE and the licensing of the SE by a plural-α. It is the latter dependency that requires the extraction of SE out of the coordinate complex. The requirement comes from a constraint noted by G. Carlson (1987: 540), whereby the similarity adjectives *same* and *different* cannot surface inside their licensing complexes. Examples like the following are unacceptable as TLCs (they are only acceptable as the first type of Non-TLCs, with indexical SEs licensed by the discourse context).

(8.25) a. *John [spilled his milk and poached the <u>same</u> egg].
  b. *Brer Rabbit ran [into the briar patch and away from <u>different</u> enemies].

Carlson's constraint is in fact not restricted to *same* and *different* constructions. Consider the following:

(8.26) a. the meeting of {John and Mary/the boys/*the boy}
  b. *John and the meeting of Mary

(8.27) a. the mixture of the wine and oil
  b. *the wine and the mixture of oil

Collective expressions such as *meeting, mixture*, and *combination* are licensed by non-singular arguments. In (8.26a), for instance, the word *meeting* requires its argument to be plural. Either the coordinate complex *John and Mary*, or the plural nominal *the boys* satisfies this requirement. The singular countable DP *the boy*, however, does not. (8.26a) shows that collective expressions can also be licensed by a coordinate complex. Why then are the coordinate contexts in (8.26b) and (8.27b) unable to license the collective expressions? Carlson's constraint can provide the answer: such expressions cannot occur inside their licensing coordinate complexes. For the same reason, the extraction of SEs out of coordinate complexes is obligatory in TLCs.

I claim that SEs and collective expressions can be licensed in a derivational way. After an SE or a collective expression moves out of a coordinate complex, the complex is able to license the SE or the collective expression. In particular, in TLCs, SEs are licensed by the coordinate verbal complexes that they move out of. In (8.24a), for instance, the SE *the same man* is licensed after it moves out of the coordinate complex.

If an SE or collective expression cannot be licensed at any step of the derivation, the derivation will crash. (8.24b), (8.25), (8.26b) and (8.27b) all illustrate this.

All of the examples that Carlson discusses are the fourth type of Non-TLCs. In this type, an SE and its licensor are both in the same clause but there is no thematic relation between them. Even though the SE in a TLC does have a thematic relation with a conjunct of the licensing coordinate complex, Carlson's constraint can still be used to account for why the SE must be moved out of its licensing coordinate complex in a TLC.

One may formalize this constraint in terms of feature-checking or some other licensing relation. I will not commit myself to any specific formalization here, since my approach depends only on the empirical observations motivating the constraint.

This answers the Question of the Surface Position of SEs posed in Section 8.2.2. Why must the SE in a TLC be outside the coordinate complex? My answer is that the coordinate complex is the licensor of the SE, and no SE can be contained in its licensor, according to G. Carlson's (1987: 540) constraint on SEs. By contrast, in a PPC, the SE is already outside the licensing coordinate complex, and so it does not move.

8.4.3   The silence of the pro-form in the second conjunct of a TLC

In Section 8.3, we determined that the null argument in the second conjunct is a pro-form, rather than a full-fledged DP. We now need to explain why this pro-form must be silent. For instance, why does the overt pronoun *he* in (8.28) make the sentence unacceptable?

(8.28)   *The same man came and he sat down.

If the gap in each conjunct of a TLC is replaced by a pronoun, the construction becomes a PPC (see Section 8.2.1B).

(8.29)   The same man, he came and he sat down.

The constraint seen in (8.28) indicates that when an SE is related to two gap positions (as in a TLC) or two pronouns (as in a PPC), the sentence is fine; however, if it is simultaneously related to a gap in one conjunct and a pronoun in another (as in (8.28)), the sentence is not acceptable. In Section 7.3.4B, we saw that conjuncts show resemblance in the phonological realization of the links of dependency chains. If each conjunct contains a link of a certain dependency chain, the links in the two conjuncts must be both silent or both realized phonologically (e.g. by a pronoun). This PR therefore answers the Question of Overt Right Link of a Dependency, posed in Section 8.2.2.

An independent issue is how the required silence of the pro-forms in TLCs is achieved. On the one hand, the pro-forms may be inherently null pronouns, like one version of pro in Japanese (Tomioka 2003). On the other hand, the silence of the pro-forms may be the result of phonological deletion of an overt pro-ϕP (Déchaine and Wiltschko 2002). Potentially, different languages may choose different strategies to achieve silence of the pro-forms in TLCs required by the PR, but I will leave this issue to future research.

Regarding the derivation of the TLC, I conclude that syntactically, an SE is raised from the first conjunct and a silent pro-form is present in the second conjunct, and semantically, as I mentioned in Section 8.2.1B, the relation between the raised SE and the gap positions is similar to bound pronoun binding (see Evans 1980: 339).[2]

8.5   Chapter summary

In this chapter, I have presented a new approach to coordinate clauses with identity adjectives constructions. I have examined the syntactic properties of *same* constructions and proposed a new analysis for the syntactic derivation of constructions of type TLC, like *The same man Mary helped and Jane ruined*. In the proposed derivation, the similarity nominal that contains the adjective *same* is base-generated in the first conjunct, and moves out of the coordinate complex. The raised relational nominal binds a silent pro-form, a pro-ϕP, in the second conjunct. Thus the derivation of a TLC involves two major dependencies: a movement chain and a binding dependency, and the raised SE c-commands both gaps. These properties will then provide a new analysis for ATB constructions, as shown in the following chapter.

---

2 The issue of pro-form binding with respect to the adjective *same* is discussed in Moltmann (1992b), but she does not discuss TLCs. Comparing sentences like *John and Mary bought the same book* (a Non-TLC, similar to my examples in (8.11)) with sentences like *John and Mary think they love each other*, she analyzes the nominal containing the word *same* as a bound element similar to a reciprocal. Her analysis thus covers certain types of Non-TLCs, which are not the focus of this chapter.

9 *Forming Across-the-Board constructions without forking movement*

9.1   Introduction

Across-the-Board (ATB) constructions are coordinate constructions in which each conjunct contains a gap, like the following wh-question in (9.1a) and relative clause construction in (9.1b):

(9.1) a.   Who$_i$ did you say that Lulu likes $_i$ and Tubby hates $_i$?
     b.   I saw the person who$_i$ Lulu likes $_i$ and Tubby hates $_i$.

ATB constructions have been claimed to be universal (Goodall 1987: 77). In this chapter, I present a new analysis of the constructions. In the previous chapter, I discussed the syntax of the identity adjective *same*. In my proposed analysis, (9.2a) is derived from (9.2b) by the movement of the SE *the same man* from the external conjunct:

(9.2) a.   The same man Mary helped and Jane ruined.
     b.   [[Mary helped [$_{DP_1}$ the same man]$_i$] and [Jane ruined *pro-ϕP_i*]].

In this chapter, I will demonstrate the properties shared by *same* constructions and ATB constructions, and propose a syntactic derivation for ATB constructions similar to (9.2b). This proposed derivation does not require any ad hoc forking chains of movement.

In Section 9.2, I apply my analysis of *same* constructions to ATB constructions. In Section 9.3, I address the issue of the *respectively* reading of ATB constructions. In Section 9.4, I compare my new analysis of ATB constructions with other analyses. Section 9.5 gives a summary of the chapter and Part IV of the book.

9.2   ATB constructions as TLCs

So-called ATB constructions are in fact identity constructions, although there is no explicit identity adjective. I claim that all argumental ATB constructions are derived in the same way as proposed for TLCs in Chapter 8. This means that the apparently shared arguments in ATB constructions are SEs with an implicit morpheme meaning "same." My derivation of (9.3a) is illustrated in (9.3b).[1]

(9.3) a. Which picture of himself did Tom paint and Mary buy?

    b. ▲ [[$_{DP_2}$ which Ø $_{<same>}$ picture of himself] did Tom paint t$_{DP_2}$ and *pro-* ϕP_i ~~did~~ Mary

        buy t$_i$]

In (9.3b), the DP2 *which Ø$_{<same>}$ picture of himself*, which is base-generated in the first conjunct, moves out of the coordinate complex, and binds a wh pro-ϕP in the second conjunct.

In this section, I present arguments for this TLC approach to ATB constructions. This approach is motivated by three observations about ATB constructions, which will be presented in the three subsections of this section. First, such constructions always have an identity reading (Section 9.2.1); second, there is a silent argument in the gap position of the second conjunct (Section 9.2.2); and third, there is a correspondence between wh-extraction and identity reading in wh-*in situ* languages (Section 9.2.3). These observations, along with Munn's (1992; 1993) observation that movement in ATB constructions launches from the first conjunct only, lead me to the new analysis of ATB construction illustrated in (9.3b).

9.2.1 *The identity readings of ATB constructions*

The extension of the analysis of TLCs to ATB constructions is first of all motivated by a well-recognized observation: ATB constructions are always permitted to have an identity reading. As described by Moltmann (1992b: 126, 132), (9.4a) implies that the person that John married is also the person that Bill proposed to, and (9.4b) can only concern a single man who both walked down the street and was killed.

(9.4) a. Which woman did John marry and Bill propose to?

    b. A man walked down the street and was killed.

The identity reading of ATB constructions is confirmed by the parallel semantic anomalousness of (9.5a) (Heycock and Zamparelli 2000: 351) and (9.5b):

(9.5) a. # Tell me which documents John wrote today and Mary filed yesterday.

    b. #The same documents, John wrote today and Mary filed yesterday.

---

1 In Section 9.3.2, I will claim that adjunct ATB constructions in English are not TLCs, but Non-TLCs.

The oddness of both (9.5a) and (9.5b) is accounted for by the common sense that the same documents cannot be written today after being filed yesterday.

The left-peripheral nominal in ATB constructions can also be kind-denoting:

(9.6)   Xiao mao, Baoyu xihuan, Daiyu taoyan.
        small cat   Baoyu like   Daiyu dislike
        'Small cats, Baoyu likes and Daiyu dislikes.'

The Chinese sentence in (9.6) does not allow the reading that Baoyu likes small cat A, while Daiyu dislikes small cat B. Instead, it means that Baoyu likes all small cats and Daiyu dislikes all small cats.

Moreover, if the extracted argument of an ATB construction is definite, adding (*the*) *same* to the argument does not change the meaning of the construction. The two sentences of each pair below are synonymous.

(9.7) a.   John robbed the bank and ran for president.
      b.   The same John robbed the bank and ran for president.

(9.8) a.   The man robbed the bank and ran for president.
      b.   The same man robbed the bank and ran for president.

(9.7a) and (9.8a) are ATB constructions, whereas (9.7b) and (9.8b) are TLCs. It seems plausible to posit that the ATB constructions are TLCs with an implicit identity adjective.[2]

Identity readings are available for all types of ATB constructions. However, Munn (1999) claims that some ATB constructions may also have *respectively* readings, a possibility I will address in Section 9.3.

---

2 One difference between this assumed silent identity adjective and the overt form *same* is that the latter generally needs to occur with the article *the*, a fact emphasized by Lasersohn (2000: 86). *Same* may occur neither with the determiner *a*, nor in a determinerless nominal, as shown in (ia) and (iia). This is different from the adjective *different*, which can occur with the determiner *a*, as in (ib), and in a determinerless nominal, as in (iib).

(i) a.   Ada and I have {the/*a} same hobby.
     b.   She is wearing a different dress every time I see her.
(ii) a.   Meet friends with {the/*Ø} same hobbies.
     b.   All the men are from different towns.

Similarly, the German *gleich* 'same' must occur with a definite determiner. It cannot occur with an indefinite determiner, nor in a determinerless nominal.

The silent identity adjective probably does not have this morphological property. For example, the wh-phrases in (9.4a) and the indefinite nominals *a man* in (9.4b) are clearly not compatible with *the*. Thus in examples like (9.4), the silence of the assumed identity adjective must be an inherent property of this morpheme, rather than the result of phonological deletion of the word *same*.

One intriguing case that needs to be clarified is represented by examples like (9.9) (such data are reported in Moltmann 1992b: 137; Fox 2000).

(9.9) a. I would like to know how many books every student liked and every professor disliked.
    b. A guard is standing in front of every church and sitting at the side of every mosque.

Among the several readings of (9.9a), we care about the one in which *how many books* takes wide scope over *every* and an appropriate answer has to specify the quantity of books x such that every student liked x and every professor disliked x (see Moltmann 1992a: 137 for a discussion of the other possible readings). It is in this sense that the sentence is an ATB construction, where the wh-phrase takes scope over the conjunction. Here, the identity reading is associated with the quantity x.

In (9.9b), it is the quantity and property reading of *a guard* that is "shared" by the two conjuncts. Our world knowledge rules out the individual reading of *a guard*, since the same person cannot appear in different locations at the same time. The sentence makes sense only in the quantity and property reading (see Li 1998 for the claim that quantity-denoting indefinite nominals are NumPs rather than DPs). In this kind of ATB construction, then, the identity reading is associated with quantity and property.

9.2.2   *The syntactic reality of a silent argument in the second conjunct*

The extension of the analysis of TLCs to ATB constructions is also motivated by the following observations: the left-peripheral extracted element is not moved from the second conjunct, and there is a silent argument nominal related to the gap position of the second conjunct.

Extracted reflexives in ATB constructions cannot be reconstructed into the internal conjunct either semantically or syntactically. Citing Haïk (1985), Moltmann (1992a: 126) claims that (9.10) could mean "John likes himself and Bill hates himself" if the reflexive were reconstructed into the second conjunct, but most speakers can interpret (9.10) only as "John likes himself and Bill hates John."

(9.10)   Himself, John likes _ and Bill hates _.

The following examples of Munn (1992: 10) illustrate the same generalization:

(9.11) a. Which picture of {himself/*herself} did John buy and Mary paint?
    b. Which pictures of himself$_{i/*j}$ did John$_i$ buy and Bill$_j$ paint?

In (9.11a), the extracted element, *which picture of himself*, cannot originate in the second conjunct. If the derivation of this sentence contained the representation of (9.12) at any step, it should have crashed immediately after this step, thus making the assumed ATB movement impossible.

(9.12)   *Mary painted which picture of himself

We conclude that the wh-phrase in (9.11) can only be base-generated in the first conjunct, where the anaphor *himself* is licensed by the c-commanding and local *John*.

Moreover, there are island effects for the gap in the first but not the second conjunct of an ATB construction. In (9.13a), the gap in the first conjunct is in an adjunct island, and the sentence is not acceptable, whereas in (9.13b), the gap in the second conjunct is in the same adjunct island, but the sentence is acceptable.

(9.13) a. *Who did Bill lose business because he hired and Mary praise a lot?
        b. Who did Bill praise a lot and Mary lose business because she hired?

Furthermore, if elements were extracted from two conjuncts at the same time, one would expect it to be possible to extract a distinct wh-element from each conjunct, at least in multiple wh-fronting languages. However, this is never the case:

(9.14) a. *Koga$_i$ sta$_j$ on [vidi_$_i$] i   [jede_$_j$]?
            whom what he sees   and eats
            'Whom what does he see and eat?'   (Russian, Kasai 2004: 169)

        b. *Kogo$_i$ kogo$_j$ Jan lubi _$_i$ a Maria kocha _$_j$?
            whom whom Jan likes and Maria loves
            'Whom does Jan like and Maria love?'   (Polish, Citko 2003: (7))

In (9.14a), for instance, *koga* 'whom' is extracted from the first conjunct and *sta* 'what' is extracted from the second conjunct. Though Russian permits multiple wh-fronting in general, these multiple extraction operations are impossible. In such operations, each wh-element is supposed to move to the same C-domain in one fell swoop (cf. the derivation of IDCs).

Now I turn to the claim that there is a silent argument nominal in the gap position of the second conjunct of ATB constructions. This claim is supported by the following observations.

First, in examples like (9.15a), the predicate of the second conjunct requires an external argument to check the relevant theta-features, and a silent argument nominal will satisfy this requirement. *Entertaining* requires an external argument, a requirement satisfied by the assumed silent pro-φP. Second, in examples like (9.15b), the reflexive *himself* in the second clausal conjunct needs a local licensor in the tensed clause, and a silent argument nominal can serve as this licensor.

(9.15) a. Who brought his guitar here and is entertaining himself now?
    b. Mary$_i$ has invited John$_j$ and will ask about {herself$_i$/*himself$_j$}.

Cross-linguistically, the following Icelandic examples (Rögnvaldsson 1982; 1993: (17)) also suggest that the missing argument in the second conjunct exists syntactically:

(9.16) a. Margir stúdentar náðu   prófinu og   var   hrósað fyrirþað.   [Icelandic]
        many   students   passed test-the and   were   praised for it
        'Many students passed the test and were praised for it.'

    b. Margir stúdentar náðu   prófinu og   þeim   var   hrósað fyrirþað.
        many   students   passed test-the and   they.D were   praised for it
        'Many students passed the test and they were praised for it.'

The syntactic contrast between (9.16a) and (9.16b) is that the former has no overt subject in the second conjunct, whereas the latter has the dative subject *þeim* 'they.' Rögnvaldsson describes the above examples (= his (17)) as follows.

> Note that the argument which is missing from the second conjunct in (17a) should have dative case, as shown in (17b)... [T]his means that the second conjunct must have a separate subject position, even when the subject is not phonologically realized, as in (17a). This is shown by the fact that the verb and the participle in (17a) have disagreeing forms, *var* and *hrósað*, instead of the forms *voru* and *hrósaðir*, which would be expected if the overt nominative subject *Margir stúdentar* were the only available subject at all levels of derivation.[3]

I thus claim that parallel to TLCs, in ATB constructions the second conjunct has a silent argument, which is a silent pro-φP that takes the extracted DP as its antecedent. The extracted DP is base-generated in the first conjunct, e.g. *who* in (9.15a), and *Mary* in (9.15b).

---

3 In addition to demonstrating the syntactic reality of the null argument in the second conjunct in ATB constructions, the Icelandic data in (9.16) also provide morphological evidence for the claim that the conjuncts in sentences like (9.15b) cannot be intermediate projections. Instead, each conjunct must be a full-fledged TP, with a subject in SpecT. This implies that there is no conjunct of intermediate projection, consistent with the arguments in Chapter 2 (see Borsley 2005 for discussion of this issue).

In the literature on ATB constructions, it has been proposed by some that there is a pro in the gap position of the second conjunct (see McNally 1992: 337 for a review). The main argument given by others against the pro approach is the following: unlike the more familiar sort of pro, which can have an independent referent, the gap in the second conjunct of ATB constructions cannot have a referent independent of the extracted nominal. Godard (1989) and McNally (1992: 338) correctly point out that filling the gap in an ATB construction with an overt pronoun changes the meaning:

(9.17) a. Few politicians behave morally and are rewarded for doing so.
      b. Few politicians behave morally and they are rewarded for doing so.

Note that (9.17a) means that there are few politicians who both behave morally and are rewarded for doing so, but it is possible that there are also some politicians who behave morally but are not rewarded for doing so. The implicit theme of the second conjunct is bound by the quantifier phrase *few politicians*. On the other hand, (9.17b) means that few politicians behave morally and all of them are rewarded for doing so. In this sentence, the quantificational nominal is not able to bind the pronominal subject of the second conjunct. In (9.17a), the quantificational DP takes scope over both conjuncts, whereas in (9.17b), the quantificational DP scopes over the first conjunct only (see Evans 1980: 339; a similar contrast was first noted by Partee 1970). The pro analysis wrongly predicts that (9.17a) will have a reading identical to (9.17b).

The contrast between (9.17a) and (9.17b) is accounted for in my TLC approach to ATB constructions. I claim that (9.17a) patterns with a TLC in the following ways. First, *few politicians* is moved out of the coordinate complex, and that is why the quantifier scopes over the second conjunct. Second, the silent pro-form in the second conjunct is a variable, not an independent pro, that must be bound by the raised *few politicians*. This is similar to the silent argument of a TLC identified in Section 8.3.2. Third, this pro-form is co-indexed with the gap in the first conjunct, and thus as discussed in Section 8.4.3, its silence is not optional, unlike a pro.[4] In (9.17b), by contrast, the overt pronoun *they* gives this sentence a different structure from a TLC. Specifically, in (9.17b), *few politicians* remains in the first conjunct, and that is why the quantifier fails to scope over the second conjunct. If *few politicians* remains in the first conjunct, the construction is not an ATB construction, and thus it does not have to have an identity reading.

---

4 We can see that in addition to pro, PRO, and the lower occurrence of a movement chain, the inventory of null elements also includes a null variable (see Tomioka 2003).

9.2.3   The correspondence between extraction and identity readings

The extension of the analysis of TLCs to ATB constructions is further motivated by the hitherto unnoted correspondence between wh-extraction and identity readings in wh-*in situ* languages.

I showed in Section 8.4 that an SE must be separated from its licensing coordinate complex, regardless of whether it has a thematic relation with any conjunct of the complex. In ATB constructions, it is recognized that the left-peripheral element is outside of the coordinate clausal complex. In this subsection, I present a correlation between the extraction of wh-elements in ATB constructions and the presence of an identity reading. Thus parallel conjunct-internal wh-phrases do not have an identity reading, while at the same time, the extraction of wh-phrases out of coordinate complexes is obligatory for an identity reading.

Identical wh-expressions distributed in two conjuncts do not have an identity reading, cross-linguistically. Such constructions are either unacceptable, as in (9.18a) (Bošković and Franks 2000: 110), or must have *respectively* readings, as shown by (9.18b) and (9.18c) (Bošković and Franks 2000: 111–112; Moltmann 1992b: 126). Exclusively *respectively* readings are also seen in the Korean and Japanese examples in (9.19a) and (9.19b) (Cho and Zhou 2000).

(9.18) a. *Who said that John bought <u>what</u> and that Peter sold <u>what</u>?
       b. Which man said that John bought <u>which house</u> and that Peter sold <u>which house</u>?
       c. <u>Which woman</u> did John marry and <u>which woman</u> did Bill propose to?

(9.19) a. John-i <u>enu</u>   <u>salam-ul</u>   salangha-ko Mary-ka <u>enu</u>   <u>salam-ul</u>
        J-NOM which person-ACC like-and   M-NOM which person-ACC

        miweha-ni?
        hate-Q
        'Which person x, John loves x and which person y, Mary hates y?'
        Not: 'which person x, John loves x and Mary hates x'   (Korean)

       b. John-ga <u>dono hito-o</u>   aisitei-te Mary-ga <u>dono</u>   <u>hito-o</u>
         J.-NOM   which person-ACC love-and M.-NOM which person-ACC

         nikundeiru-no?
         hate-Q
         'Which person x, John loves x and which person y, Mary hates y?'
         Not: 'which person x, John loves x and Mary hates x'   (Japanese)

Similarly, in Chinese, *in situ* wh-phrases distributed in conjuncts do not have an identity reading either, but instead have a *respectively* reading.

(9.20) a. Zhangsan xihuan <u>shenme</u>, Lisi bu xihuan <u>shenme</u>?   (Wu 1999: 16)
    Zhangsan like   what   Lisi not like   what
    'What does Zhangsan like and what does Lisi like, respectively?'

   b. Baoyu <u>zenme</u> qipian ni, Daiyu you <u>zenme</u> weixie ni?
    Baoyu how   cheat you Daiyu also how   threaten you
    'How did Baoyu cheat you and how did Daiyu threaten you, respectively?'

   c. Baoyu <u>weishenme</u> qipian ni, Daiyu <u>weishenme</u> weixie ni?
    Baoyu why   cheat you Daiyu why   threaten you
    'Why did Baoyu cheat you and why did Daiyu threaten you, respectively?'

The ban on SE wh-phrases in conjuncts is parallel to what we see in (9.21) (see Section 8.2.2):[5]

(9.21)   (*)Mary helped the same man and Jane ruined the same man.

In contrast to the above type of data, the identity reading emerges when a wh-phrase is moved out of the coordinate complex in wh-*in situ* languages (see Hoh and Chiang 1990 for arguments for the focus-driven movement of clause-initial wh-elements in wh-*in situ* languages). In this case, there is only one overt wh-phrase. The construction is just like ATB constructions in English: the wh-phrase is an SE, extracted from the first conjunct only.

(9.22) a. <u>Enu</u>   <u>salam-ul</u>   John-i salangha-ko Mary-ka
    which person-ACC J-NOM like-and   M-NOM

    miweha-ni?   (Korean)
    hate-Q
    'Which person x, John loves x and Mary hates x?'
    Not: 'which person x, John loves x and which person y, Mary hates y'

   b. <u>Dono hito-o</u>   John-ga aisitei-te Mary-ga nikundeiru-no? (Japanese)
    which person-ACC J.-NOM love-and M.-NOM hate-Q
    'Which person x, John loves x and Mary hates x?'
    Not: 'which person x, John loves x and which person y, Mary hates y'

---

5 A related fact is the following. Heim (1982: 150) observes that (ia) cannot mean that he likes a cat and she hates the same cat. The Chinese version of the sentence in (ib) cannot have an identity reading either. Similarly, as noted by van Oirsouw (1987: 32), the co-referential reading of the two *someone*s in (ic) is not preferred.

(i) a.   He likes <u>a cat</u> and she hates <u>a cat</u>.
   b.   Baoyu xihuan <u>yi</u>   <u>zhi</u> <u>mao</u>, Daiyu taoyan <u>yi</u>   <u>zhi</u> <u>mao</u>.
        Baoyu like   one CL cat   Daiyu dislike one CL cat
        'Baoyu likes a cat, and Daiyu dislikes a cat.'
   c.   <u>Someone</u> bought a box of cigars and <u>someone</u> bought a bottle of gin.

c. <u>Shenme</u>, Zhangsan xihuan Lisi bu xihuan?　　(Wu 1999: 17) (Chinese)
   what　　　Zhangsan like　Lisi not like
   'What does Zhangsan like but Lisi does not like?'

d. <u>Weishenme</u> Baoyu qipian ni,　Daiyu weixie　ni?
   why　　　　Baoyu cheat　you Daiyu threaten you
   'Why did Baoyu cheat you and Daiyu threaten you?'

I conclude that wh-phrases with an implicit identity adjective, like other SEs, must be raised out of the related coordinate complexes, cross-linguistically.

Recall that SEs may not be reconstructed into their licensing coordinate complexes. If they did, the sentences would not be acceptable (see (9.21) above). Now in ATB constructions, I have claimed that the extracted wh-elements are SEs, and we have seen that if the SEs are not extracted out of the coordinate complexes, no identity reading will be available. The correlation in ATB constructions between the extraction of wh-elements and the presence of an identity reading is expected under my TLC approach to ATB constructions.

I have presented three observations that led me to extend the analysis of TLCs proposed in Chapter 8 to ATB constructions, which, I conclude, also have an adjective (here implicit) meaning "same."

9.2.4　The compatibility between two types of wh-expressions

In this subsection I present evidence that wh-expressions with an implicit identity adjective and wh-expressions without an implicit identity adjective can co-occur. Thus they are not in complementary distribution. Unlike the latter type, the former type needs a plural-α licensor. All of these indicate that they are different types of wh-expressions.

A.　In multiple wh-fronting languages

The following data from Bošković and Franks (2000: 111) show that the wh-element of the matrix clause and the raised wh-element from an embedded coordinate complex can occur side by side.

(9.23) a. Koj$_i$ kakvo$_j$ $_{-i}$ kaza [ce Ivan e kupil $_{-j}$] i　[ce Petâr e prodal $_{-j}$].
   who what　　said that Ivan is bought　and that Peter is sold
   'Which person x, which stuff y, x said that Ivan bought y and that
   Peter sold y?'　　(Bulgarian)

   b. Ko$_i$　šta$_j$ $_{-i}$ tvrdi　[da Jovan kupuje $_{-j}$] i　[da Petar projaje $_{-j}$]?
   who what　asserts that John buys　　and that Peter sells
   'Which person x, which stuff y, x asserts that John buys y and that
   Peter sells y?'　　(Serbo-Croatian)

In these examples, the theta position of the first wh-word is in the matrix clause. The second wh-word is an SE, introducing a binding dependency inside the coordinate complex. This latter wh-word is extracted from the TLC, which is selected by the matrix verb *kaza* 'said' in (9.23a) and *tvrdi* 'asserts' in (9.23b).

B.   In Chinese

The following Chinese examples show that the *in situ* wh-element of the matrix clause can also occur with the wh-element raised from the embedded coordinate complex.

(9.24) a. Shei zhidao shenme [Zhangsan xihuan Lisi bu   xihuan]?
          who   know   what   Zhangsan   like   Lisi not   like
          'Who knows what Zhangsan likes but Lisi does not like?'

       b. Shei zhidao weishenme [zaochen taiyang _ zai dongbian], [xiawu
          who   know   why   morning sun   at   east   afternoon

          taiyang _ zai xibian]?
          sun   at   west
          'Who knows why the sun is in the east in the morning and is in the west in the afternoon?'

       c. Ni   zenme zhidao weishenme [Baoyu _ jie-le   jiu]   [Daiyu _
          you   how   know   why   Baoyu   stop-PRF alcohol Daiyu

          jie-le   yan]?
          stop-PRF smoking
          'How do you know why Baoyu stopped drinking and Daiyu stopped smoking?'

In (9.24a), the theta position of the first wh-word *shei* 'who' is in the matrix clause. This wh-word is not an SE. However, the second wh-word *shenme* 'what' is an SE, inquiring about an identical entity for the two states expressed by the two conjuncts. In (9.24b), *shei* is also in the matrix clause, and is not an SE, either. However, the second wh-word *weishenme* 'why' is an SE, inquiring about an identical reason for the two states expressed by the two conjuncts. Similarly, in (9.24c), the base-position of the first wh-word *zenme* 'how' is in the matrix clause. This wh-word is not an SE. However, the second wh-word *weishenme* 'why' is an SE, inquiring about an identical reason for the two eventualities expressed by the two conjuncts.

The above observations about ATB constructions and the observations about TLCs presented in Chapter 8 compel me to extend my analysis of TLCs to ATB constructions. The lack of an overt adjective like *same* in ATB constructions makes it superficially tempting to suppose that the extracted elements are moved from both conjuncts simultaneously. TLCs cannot be analyzed in this way, however, and their deep syntactic and semantic parallels with ATB constructions suggests that so-called ATB movement is merely an illusion.[6]

9.3   The *respectively* readings of certain ATB constructions

In this section, I divide ATB constructions into two types, modification constructions and formal-feature saturation constructions, and argue that since the former are not TLCs, they allow both identity readings and *respectively* readings.

9.3.1   *Munn's* respectively *readings*

Munn (1999) claims that some ATB constructions in English may allow *respectively* readings. For instance, (9.25a) can be answered by (9.25b), which presumes a *respectively* reading.

(9.25) a. Where did Mary vacation and Bill decide to live?
         b. Mary vacationed in Paris and Bill decided to live in Toronto.

We should note at the outset that *respectively* readings for ATB constructions are not available to all speakers, as observed by Moltmann (1992b: 131). In fact, none of my English informants were able to get such readings for the examples in Munn (1999). There may be some dialect variation here. Assuming, however, that some speakers can get *respectively* readings for ATB constructions, how do we account for them?

Gawron and Kehler (2004) point out that the *respectively* readings are unavailable with unambiguously singular nominals. They show the contrast between (9.26) and (9.27) below:

(9.26) a. In what <u>city</u> did Mary vacation and Bill decide to live?
         b. #Mary vacationed in Paris and Bill decided to live in Toronto.

(9.27) a. In what <u>cities</u> did Mary vacation and Bill decide to live?
         b. Mary vacationed in Paris and Bill decided to live in Toronto.

---

6 The putative ATB movement of head elements cannot be captured in terms of TLC, but there is actually no compelling reason to believe that such movement exists. Consider gapping data like (i), where the auxiliary *will* seems to be shared by the two conjuncts.

(i)   I will buy a house and he Ø sell his flat   (Ø = will)

Although gapping has been seen as the result of head-ATB movement or VP-ATB movement (Johnson 1996; 2009), it is however hard to exclude a null head analysis proposed by Hernández (2007).

(9.26b) cannot be an answer to (9.26a), where the question expression *what city* is singular. However, (9.27b) can be an answer to (9.27a), where the question expression *what cities* is plural. Gawron and Kehler state that if a plural reading is not excluded, an ATB construction might have a *respectively* reading (they then present a semantic analysis of the readings, not relevant to our purposes here; see Zhang 2008b for a syntactic analysis of the *respectively* construction).

Munn (1999: 424; 2001: 383) reports that in examples like (9.28a) and (9.29a), where the extracted element is a subject in the first conjunct, no *respectively* reading is possible, and thus (9.28b) and (9.29b) cannot be their answers.

(9.28) a. Which man murdered Sam and wounded Bill?
      b. #Fred murdered Sam and Joe wounded Bill.

(9.29) a. Which restaurant _ was reviewed _ by Bill and criticized _ by Fred?
      b. #His first restaurant was reviewed by Bill and his second restaurant was criticized by Fred.

We can see that in (9.28a) and (9.29a), the extracted wh-nominal is also singular. The obligatory identity reading is thus correctly predicted by Gawron and Kehler (2004).

However, not all left-peripheral plural elements permit *respectively* readings. In examples like (9.30), although the extracted nominal *which documents* is plural, the *respectively* reading is still impossible.

(9.30)   #Tell me which documents John wrote today and Mary filed yesterday.   (= (9.5a))

It seems that non-singularity of the left-peripheral element is not sufficient to ensure the availability of a *respectively* reading for ATB constructions. I present another condition in Section 9.3.2.

9.3.2   The availability of respectively *readings in modification constructions*

In this subsection I contrast modification and formal-feature saturation constructions with respect to the availability of *respectively* readings of ATB constructions.

It seems that there are two cases in which *respectively* readings are possible.

A.   The left-peripheral phrase as a modifier
If the left-peripheral phrase is an adjunct, a *respectively* reading is possible. The following examples are cited from Moltmann (1992b: 185, 233):

(9.31) a. In these two rooms, John died and Mary was born.
        b. I can't remember in which two rooms John died and Mary was born.

Moltmann reports that "most speakers get the reading of (81a) [= (9.31a)] and of (81b) [= (9.31b)] in which John died in one of the two rooms and Mary was born in the other one." Munn (1999) also reports that *respectively* readings are more likely in adverbial constructions.

B.   The left-peripheral phrase as modified element
Respectively readings are also possible if the conjoined clauses are relative clauses. The following examples are again from Moltmann (1992b: 233) (for more examples, see Gawron and Kehler 2004 (47) and (48)).

(9.32) a. These are the masterworks that Bill painted and John composed.
        b. The two masterworks that Bill painted and John drew are in this room.
        c. These are the two women that Bill married and John proposed to.

The respectively readings remain available if the relative clauses are replaced with PPs:

(9.33) a. the man and the woman with the two black dogs   (Moltmann 1992b: 185)
        b. the blue carpet and the red carpet in the bedroom and the living room
        c. a man and a woman from two remote islands

C.   Generalization
We thus see that if a plural expression is a modifier of a coordinate complex, and if a plural expression is modified by a coordinate complex, a *respectively* reading is possible. There is a contrast between modification and formal-feature saturation constructions with respect to the availability of *respectively* readings of ATB constructions.

The above data lead me to the following generalization: a *respectively* reading is available in a modification relation between two plural elements. In other words, Gawron and Kehler's (2004) plurality condition and a modification relation together may license a *respectively* reading of ATB constructions.

We now consider (9.27a) again. A *respectively* reading is possible because the left-peripheral element *in what cities* is firstly plural and second has a modification relation with the coordinate complex. In (9.30), however, although *which documents* is plural, it has a thematic rather than modification relation with the verb inside the coordinate complex. According to my generalization, this sentence cannot have a *respectively* reading.

One account of the generalization could be that if there is no relation involving formal features (e.g. Case or theta-role) between the left peripheral element and the coordinate complex, the construction is not a TLC. If it is not a TLC, the two possible readings of the construction, an identity reading and a *respectively* reading, can be captured as follows.

With the *respectively* reading, the left-peripheral element is not an SE. Instead, the construction is interpreted as if an implicit adverb *respectively* is present.

With the identity reading, the left-peripheral element may still be an SE, which has an implicit *same*, as in other ATB constructions. However, in this case, the construction is parallel to type IV of the non-TLCs (see Section 8.2.1C). The SE and the coordinate complex are base-generated independently of each other. The relationship between the SE and the complex is just like that between *on the same day* and *three brothers* in (9.34):

(9.34)   Three brothers reached the summit of Everest on the same day.

In other words, in (9.27a), for instance, *in what cities* is base-generated outside of the coordinate complex. An analysis like this has already been proposed for adjunct ATB constructions by Woolford (1987: 168).

9.4   A comparison with other approaches

Our approach to ATB constructions in terms of null pronoun binding and SE raising is different from all previous approaches. Munn (1993) and Zhang (2004b), among others, argue against the forking movement chain approach, but competing alternatives to this approach have been given in the literature, including the following: (a) Munn's (1992) null operator approach, where an element in the second conjunct moves locally and never keeps company with any element in the first conjunct; (b) the multiple dimensional analysis, presented by Goodall (1987), Muadz (1991), Moltmann (1992b), Wilder (1999), Citko (2003), and Gracanin-Yuksek (2007); (c) the deletion approach of George (1980); and (d) the sideward movement approach, where a single element moves from one conjunct to the other, and then out of the coordinate complex, advocated by Hornstein and Nunes (2002).

9.4.1   The characteristics of our approach

A.   No special operation in coordination

I have argued that the overt extracted element in ATB constructions has a movement chain relation only with the gap in the external conjunct. This means that ATB constructions do not require any special movement mode. Thus coordinate constructions, the only contexts in which ATB patterns are found, do not introduce any construction-specific type of movement to the computational system.

Similar claims have formed part of other analyses of ATB constructions, and though I will argue that my analysis is superior, I agree with their rejection of the ad hoc notion of forking movement chains. I endorse the following statement of Munn (2001: 370): "one nonetheless can (and in fact must) dispense with a separate mechanism for ATB movement."

B.   Extraction from first conjuncts only

Like SEs in TLCs, the extracted elements of ATB constructions do not originate in the two conjuncts at the same time. They are instead extracted from the external conjuncts only. The silent pro-ϕP argument in the internal conjunct never moves out of the conjunct.

C.   ATB constructions are syntactically related to other constructions

(a) My analysis of ATB constructions is based on my solution to the problem of TLCs. TLCs have been considered a serious challenge to generative syntax since Jackendoff (1977: 192–194) (see Section 8.2.2), and as far as I know, this book is the first effort to respond to the challenge. I have been able to show not only that the well-established devices of syntactic theory are sufficient to derive TLCs, but that the same devices can handle ATB constructions as well, without the need for construction-specific operations. As a further benefit, the approach advocated here also deepens our understanding of the syntactic and semantic relations between these two constructions, hitherto considered independent.

(b) My analysis accounts for the raising of wh-phrases in coordinate constructions in wh-*in situ* languages, by showing that the raising is required for the licensing of an identity reading. Thus, the approach advocated here also deepens our understanding of the cross-linguistic syntactic properties of ATB constructions.

9.4.2   The null operator approach

Munn (1992; 1993; see also Franks 1992; 1993) proposes a null operator approach, also adopted by Bošković and Franks (2000). As shown in Munn's proposed structure in (9.35), there is no forking movement chain. Instead, a null operator moves from the second conjunct and lands in the Specifier position of the conjunction. The projection headed by the conjunction is a right-adjunct of the first conjunct. The wh-word in the first conjunct alone moves to the CP.

(9.35)   I wonder [$_{CP}$ who$_i$ [Jane detests t$_i$] [O$_{pi}$ and [Harry adores t$_i$]]]

This approach shares characteristics A and B of my analysis (see above), but it does not have characteristic C. Thus it misses the deep parallels between ATB constructions and TLCs. We also cannot accept Munn's hypothesis that the second conjunct is an adjunct of the first conjunct (see Chapter 2). Furthermore, I have argued that the second conjunct of an ATB construction is part of a licenser of an implicit relational word hosted in the extracted element, and is therefore necessary for the identity reading of the construction.

9.4.3   The multiple-dimensional approach

The multiple-dimensional analysis, presented by Goodall (1987), Muadz (1991), Moltmann (1992b), Grootveld (1994), Wilder (1999), Citko (2003), and Gracanin-Yuksek (2007), tries to legalize the forking chain of the assumed ATB movement. Moltmann (1992b: 121–122) claims that (9.36a) is derived from the D-structure in (9.36b) and the S-structure in (9.36c). She claims that the shared part, *what* in (9.36b), represents an implicit coordination, which, according to my understanding, is not a syntactic coordination.

(9.36) a. What did John give _ to Bill and Sue show _ to Mary?

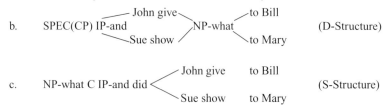

In addition to the problems with the multiple-dimensional approach noted in Section 6.3.4, the main challenge to its application here is its assumption that a single nominal can satisfy two sets of formal features of two verbs at the same time (see my Section 9.2.2). Moltmann (1992a: 121) states that "In this treatment of ATB extraction, for (241a) [= our (9.36a)] never more than one occurrence of *what* has to be represented at any syntactic level. The reason is that the NP node and hence every node it dominates are shared nodes; that is, they are nodes that belong to both planes." Yet it is not clear how the unique *what* in the representation is related to both sets of thematic and Case relations associated with the two clausal conjuncts. This is the same problem faced by the earlier proposal of forking movement (also called factorization extraction) (Ross 1967; Williams 1977; 1978).

The problem is also seen in so-called mixed-movement constructions (Moltmann 1992a: 124):

(9.37) a. Who _ laughed and _ seemed _ to be happy.

   b.
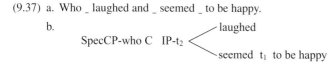

In (9.37b), t_2 is at SpecIP. It seems that there is only one subject position for both *laughed* and *seemed to be happy*. The existence of t_1 indicates that there is an independent theta role bearing nominal originating in the second conjunct. Yet it is a mystery how this nominal and the nominal that gets its theta role from, *laughed*, are squeezed into the single position of t_2.

The multiple-dimensional analysis is costly not only in adding a new type of structure (and dimension) to syntactic computation. It also invokes the notion of implicit coordination, so-called m-planes (meaningful planes) and f-planes (formal planes) (Moltmann 1992b: 36), and constraints such as CSR (Condition on Required Syntactic Relations in multiple-dimensional phrase markers, Moltmann 1992b: 127). Moreover, f-planes are not always interpretable. For instance, the sentence *John compared the picture and the photograph* has two f-planes, where one is *John compared the picture* and the other is *John compared the photograph* (Moltmann 1992b: 42–43). Neither is interpretable.

Everything else being equal, the analysis presented in this book should be preferred because it is grounded on the well-established and simpler two-dimensional structural configuration. Overall, the multiple dimensional analysis has none of the characteristics listed in 9.4.1. For instance, it cannot explain the fact that extraction occurs only in the first conjunct in ATB constructions.

The following comment of Dik (1968: 5) seems to be applicable to this multiple-dimensional analysis:

> Premature formalization . . . has certain dangers of its own, since formalized systems tend to develop into self-contained organisms, independent of the facts they were designed to account for. The simple fact that within such systems a multitude of formal operations and manipulations is possible is then easily taken as a proof of their scientific adequacy. But the only test of the validity of a linguistic theory is whether it provides the means for a satisfactory description and explanation of the facts of language.

9.4.4   The deletion approach

Another alternative approach is deletion of identical elements in conjuncts (see George 1980; Hendriks 1991). However, as pointed out by Gazdar *et al.* (1982: 675), the representations before the assumed deletion and the one after the deletion do not have the same meaning. They demonstrate this with the following two sentences.

(9.38)   a. Who does everyone like and no one respect?
        b. Who does everyone like and who does no one respect?

(9.38a) has an identity reading, whereas (9.38b) does not. If (9.38a) is derived from (9.38b) by deletion of the second *who*, the deletion violates the recoverability condition on deletion (see Chomsky 1965: 144–145), which bans deletions causing a meaning change. Therefore, the deletion approach is not plausible here.

The contrast between (9.38a) and (9.38b) shows that ATB constructions have an identity reading, or equivalently, such a reading is present if a wh-phrase occurs outside the coordinate complex, and is absent if the wh-phrase occurs conjunct-internally (see Section 9.2.3). This pattern is hard to explain in a deletion approach.

Nevertheless, we still allow some kind of deletion in our proposed derivations of TLCs and ATB constructions, namely deletion of pro-ϕPs in second conjuncts (see Section 8.4.3 for arguments relating to TLCs, which carry over to ATB constructions). The pro-ϕPs that are affected by the deletion, however, do not have the same forms with their binders (the SEs), nor does the deletion affect the interpretations.

9.4.5   The sideward movement approach

The sideward movement approach of Hornstein and Nunes (2002; also Nunes 2001: 336–339) assumes that one element moves from one conjunct to the other, and then moves out of the first conjunct. This approach has a major inadequacy: it cannot cover the facts described in Section 9.2.2. For instance, it does not account for the binding pattern in (9.39) noted by Munn (1992):

(9.39)   Which picture of {himself/*herself} did John paint and Mary buy?

In this sentence, the merger of *which picture of himself* in the second conjunct, where it is c-commanded by *Mary*, is illegal.

By contrast, in my approach the gap of the second conjunct in (9.39) is not a trace, but a bound pronoun (syntactically, a pro-ϕP), and therefore it contains no reflexive. This pronoun shares its ϕ-features with the head of its binder, and is either deleted at PF or is in a null phonological form. Thus the above problem is avoided.

This sideward movement approach shares characteristic A with our approach (see Section 9.4.1), but it lacks the other two characteristics B and C.

In fact, none of these alternative approaches to ATB constructions exhibits characteristic C. That is, none of them considers the relationship between TLCs (identity adjectives) and ATB constructions, either syntactically or semantically. Moreover, none of them considers the syntactic issues of ATB constructions in wh-*in situ* languages.

9.5   Chapter summary and conclusions of Part IV

In this chapter, I have presented a new approach to ATB constructions without resorting to ATB movement. I reached the following conclusions.

(a) ATB constructions are TLCs, cross-linguistically. The two constructions share deep syntactic and semantic properties.

(b) There is no forking movement chain in human language, and thus there is no syntactic operation that is exclusively used in coordination. I have argued that the overt extracted element of ATB constructions has a movement chain relation with only the gap in the external conjunct; like SEs, the extracted elements in ATB constructions cannot originate in the two conjuncts at the same time. I have argued that the silent pro-φP argument in the internal conjunct never moves out of the conjunct.

This part of the book (this and the previous chapter) shows that forking chains, which have been stipulated for coordinate constructions only, do not actually exist. Thus coordinate constructions do not introduce any special type of movement to the computational system. This is the fourth (and last) major claim of this book:

> No special operation exists in the computation of co-ordinate complexes.

10 *Conclusions*

In this monograph, I have answered the four fundamental questions listed in the introduction.

A. Does the derivation of coordinate constructions create any special syntactic configuration, other than the general binary complementation and adjunction configuration?

I argued that the structure of coordinate complexes is not different from that of other syntactic constructions. First, I presented new arguments to support the claim that a coordinate complex has a binary-branching structure, with one conjunct internal and the other external to the coordinator. Second, I argued against any adjunction structure for coordination. Instead, I advocated the complementation structure in (10.1), where the coordinator heads a projection and the relation between the external and internal conjunct is a Spec-Comp relation. In this structure, the combination of the coordinator and the internal conjunct is an intermediate projection, which is not able to move.

(10.1)

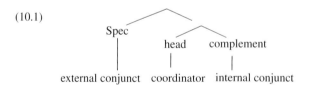

Third, I clarified that although coordination does not have an adjunction structure, it still may express a semantic modification relation. Fourth, I examined an issue with respect to the projectivity of coordinate complexes, namely the issue of word and word fragment conjuncts. Chomsky's (1994) bare phrase structure hypothesis, which abandons bar-levels for syntactic elements, provides us with a simple and thus desirable analysis of coordination of elements of various constituency levels. Thus, one should not use the existence of non-phrasal conjuncts to argue against the complementation structure of coordinate

242

complexes. Fifth, I claimed that when there is only one coordinator and three or more conjuncts, only one conjunct is in the complement position and the remaining conjuncts are in multiple Spec positions.

Overall, the structure of coordination is complementation. The theoretical implication of this conclusion is that the notion "coordination" is not a primitive syntactic relation, but rather instantiates the more general complementation relation.

B. Does the derivation of coordinate constructions require any special syntactic category, other than NP, VP, and so on?

I presented cross-linguistic data showing that coordinators can c-select conjuncts, and may have ordinary categorial features. I concluded that if a coordinator does not have any intrinsic categorial features, the coordinate complex shares its category with the external conjunct; thus there is no special category like &P. Coordinate complexes do not exhibit any distribution other than that of the currently recognized categories, nor do they "bleach" the contrasts among the currently recognized categories. Therefore, they cannot represent an independent syntactic category.

C. Does the derivation of coordinate constructions require any special constraint on syntactic operations, other than general conditions such as the locality condition?

The classic coordination-specific constraint is Ross's (1967) Coordinate Structure Constraint (CSC). This constraint disallows the movement of whole conjuncts (the CC part of the CSC) and the extraction of any element from conjuncts (the EC part of the CSC).

I concluded that the effects of the CC on external conjuncts can be accounted for by the morphological properties of coordinators like *and*. I argued that such elements have no intrinsic categorial features, although they are heads of coordinate complexes. In order for a coordinate complex headed by such a coordinator to take part in any syntactic computation, the categorial features of the external conjunct must be transferred to the coordinator. External conjuncts in *and*-coordinate complexes thus cannot move, having lost their categorial features. This analysis is supported by my study of *de* constructions in Chinese. As in *and*-constructions, the constituent that provides the whole complex with categorial features in *de* constructions may not move. As for internal conjuncts, I argued that they may not move because they are the phonological hosts of the coordinators.

The observed CSC effects are accounted for not only by the morphological properties of conjunctions, but also by the semantic relation between conjuncts. The latter aspect was spelled out in the following two steps.

First, I demonstrated the distinction between accidental coordination and natural coordination: in the former, conjuncts are not semantically related, whereas in the latter they are. This distinction is encoded by language-specific syntactic and morphological strategies. In particular, the bare *and* in English and the conjunctions *he*, *gen*, and *erqie* in Chinese can occur in either accidental coordination or natural coordination, whereas the conjunction *ji* in Chinese occurs only in accidental coordination.

Second, I showed that the possibility of violating the CSC is correlated with natural coordination. Cross-linguistically, the EC part of the CSC can be violated in asymmetrical coordination constructions, but not in symmetrical or accidental coordinate constructions. In Chinese, the CC part of the CSC can be violated in comitative coordination constructions, but not in distributive or accidental coordination constructions. In both asymmetrical coordination and comitative coordination, conjuncts are semantically related to each other, thus they both are natural coordination. The fact that the CSC can be violated in natural coordination reveals a semantic aspect of the generalizations originally motivating the constraint.

I thus investigated two factors related to the CSC: the morphological properties of coordinators, and the semantic distinctions between natural coordination and accidental coordination. Neither factor requires the CSC as a constraint on syntactic operations.

While I argued against the CSC as a syntactic constraint on the operation of Move, I also argued against other constraints on the operation of Merge in building of coordinate constructions. I showed that each of the following constraints can be violated under the proper conditions: the Coordination of Likes Constraint with respect to syntactic categories, the Coordination of Likes Constraint with respect to grammatical functions, the Coordination of Likes Constraint with respect to semantic types, and the Coordinate Constituent Constraint. The observed effects of these constraints can be covered by my Relativized Parallelism Requirement, which is a filter on syntactic representations in language processing. The filter is repeated as follows:

(10.2)   Conjuncts of a coordinate complex must hold a coherence relation in terms of:
    a. Relatedness: they must be related to each other semantically, as in natural coordination;
    or
    b. Resemblance (Parallelism Requirement): they must hold a resemblance relation in terms of both their semantic type and their dependency chains.

The theoretical consequence is that, by accounting for the CSC and other coordinate construction-specific constraints in terms of the morphological properties of coordinators and a processing filter, we remove all of these constraints from the syntactic computational system. Empirically, rejecting the CSC makes it possible to derive three hitherto recalcitrant constructions: the Split Argument Construction, the Modifier-Sharing Construction, and the Interwoven Dependency Construction, as represented by (10.3a), (10.3b), and (10.3c), respectively.

(10.3) a. Italy borders France.
     b. A man came in and a woman left who were quite similar.
     c. Which nurse and which hostess did Fred date and Bob marry, respectively?

I proposed that in Split Argument Constructions and Modifier-Sharing Constructions, conjuncts undergo movement, and in Interwoven Dependency Constructions, elements are extracted from conjuncts.

D. Finally, does the derivation of coordinate constructions require any special type of syntactic operations, other than Merge and the step-by-step, one-tail-one-head chains of Move?

In the generative syntactic literature, it has often been assumed that a special forking movement is required to derive a certain type of coordinate construction, namely Across-the-Board (ATB) constructions. Under this traditional assumption, (10.4a) is derived by the movement chain in (10.4b), in which one head link has two tail links.

(10.4) a. Who did Jim like and Jane hate?
     b.   Who did Jim like __ and Jane hate __ ?   (ATB movement)

In order to find out whether the forking movement exists, I studied the syntactic derivation of *same* constructions such as (10.5a). I found that the relational nominal that contains the adjective *same* is base-generated in the first conjunct, moves out of the coordinate complex, and binds a silent pro-form in the second conjunct. My derivation of (10.5a) is illustrated in (10.5b).

(10.5) a. The same man Mary helped and Jane ruined.
     b. [Mary helped [$_{DP_1}$ the same man]$_i$] and [Jane ruined *pro-ϕP_i*].

I argued that ATB constructions are derived in the same way as *same* constructions, by variable binding and an ordinary movement operation. Therefore, there is no forking movement in the derivation of ATB constructions, and thus no special syntactic operation in the derivation of coordinate complexes.

In short, I argued against any special syntax for coordination. Coordination has no special status in syntax, but falls out automatically from structures, categories, constraints, and operations that are already used in non-coordinate constructions.

References

Abbott, Barbara 1976. "Right Node Raising as a test for constituenthood," *Linguistic Inquiry* 7: 639–642.

Abels, Klaus 2003. "Successive cyclicity, anti-locality, and adposition stranding," PhD diss., Storrs: University of Connecticut.

Abney, Steven 1991. "Syntactic affixation and performance structures," in Katherine Leffel and Denis Bouchard (eds.), *Views on Phrase Structure*, Dordrecht: Kluwer, pp. 215–227.

Aboh, Enoch Oladé 2009. "Clause structure and verb series," *Linguistic Inquiry* 40.

Adger, David 2003. *Core Syntax: A Minimalist Approach*. Oxford: Oxford University Press.

Adger, David and Gillian Ramchand 2005. "Merge and move: wh-dependencies revisited," *Linguistic Inquiry* 36: 161–193.

Agbayani, Brian and Ed Zoerner 2004. "Gapping, pseudogapping, and sideward movement." *Studia Linguistica* 58: 185–211.

Alexiadou, Artemis, Paul Law, Andre Meinunger, and Chris Wilder 2000. "Introduction," in Artemis Alexiadou, Paul Law, Andre Meinunger, and Chris Wilder (eds.), *The Syntax of Relative Clauses*, Amsterdam: John Benjamins, pp. 1–51.

Amfo, Nana Abe Appiah 2007. "Clausal conjunction in Akan," *Lingua* 117: 666–684.

Amritavalli, R. 2003. "Question and negative polarity in the disjunctive phrase," *Syntax* 6: 1–18.

Anandan, K. N. 1993. "Constraints on extraction from coordinate structures in English and Malalylam," PhD diss., Central Institute of English and Foreign Languages, Hyderabad, India.

Anderson, Carol 1983. "Generating coordinate structures with asymmetrical gaps," *Chicago Linguistic Society (CLS)* 19: 3–14.

Androutsopoulou, Antonia 1994. "The distribution of the definite determiner and the syntax of Greek DPs," in *Proceedings of the 30th regional meeting of the Chicago Linguistic Society*, Chicago: University of Chicago Press, pp. 16–29.

Aoun, Joseph and Elabbas Benmamoun 1999. "Further remarks on first conjunct agreement," *Linguistic Inquiry* 30: 669–681.

Aoun, Joseph and Yen-hui Audrey Li 2003. *Essays on the Representational and Derivational Nature of Grammar: The Diversity of Wh-constructions*. Cambridge, MA: MIT Press.

Aoun, Joseph, Elabbas Benmamoun, and Dominique Sportiche 1994. "Agreement and conjunction in some varieties of Arabic," *Linguistic Inquiry* 25: 195–220.

Artstein, Ron 2005. "Coordination of parts of words," *Lingua* 115 (4): 359–393.

Bach, Emmon 1964. *An Introduction to Transformational Grammars*. New York: Holt, Rinehart & Winston.

Baker, Mark 1988. *Incorporation*. Chicago and London: University of Chicago Press.

   1992. "Unmatched chains and the representation of plural pronouns," *Natural Language Semantics* 1: 33–73.

   1997. "Thematic roles and syntactic structure," in L. Haegeman (ed.), *Elements of Grammar*, Dordrecht: Kluwer Academic Publishers, pp. 73–137.

Baltin, Mark 2002. "Movement to the Higher V is Remnant Movement," *Linguistic Inquiry* 33: 653–658.

   2006. "The nonunity of VP-preposing," *Language* 82: 734–766.

Bánréti, Zoltán 1994. "Coordination," in Ferenc Kiefer and Katalin É. Kiss (eds.), *Syntax and Semantics 27: The Syntactic Structure of Hungarian*, San Diego: Academic Press, pp. 355–414.

   2003. "On the syntax of coordinate constructions," *Acta Linguistica Hungarica* 50(3–4): 265–340.

Barker, Chris 2007. "Parasitic Scope." *Linguistics and Philosophy* 30(4): 407–444.

Bar-Lev, Zev and Arthur Palacas 1980. "Semantic command over pragmatic priority," *Lingua* 51: 137–146.

Bayer, Samuel 1996. "The coordination of unlike categories," *Language* 72: 579–616.

Berchem, Jörg 1991. *Referenzgrammatik des Somali*. Köln: Rüdiger Köppe.

Besten, Hans den and Gert Webelhuth 1990. "Stranding," in Günther Grewendorf and Wolfgang Sternefeld (eds.), *Scrambling and Barriers*, Amsterdam: Benjamins, pp. 77–92.

Bever, Thomas G., C. Carrithers, W. Cowart, and D. J. Townsend 1989. "Language processing and familial handedness," in A. Galaburda (ed.), *From Reading to Neurons*, Cambridge, MA: MIT Press, pp. 331–357.

Bianchi, Valentina 1999. *Consequences of Antisymmetry: Headed Relative Clauses*. Berlin: Mouton de Gruyter.

Blakemore, Diane and Robyn Carston 2005. "The pragmatics of sentential coordination with *and*," *Lingua* 115(4): 569–589.

Blass, Regina 1989. "Pragmatic effects of coordination: the case of 'and' in Sissala," *UCL Working Papers in Linguistics 1*, University College, University of London, pp. 32–52.

Bloomfield, Leonard 1933. *Language*. New York: Holt, Rinehart & Winston.

Blümel, Rudolf 1914. *Einführung in die Syntax*. Heidelberg: C. Winter.

Bobaljik, Jonathan David and Sam Brown 1997. "Inter-arboreal operations: head-movement and the Extension Requirement," *Linguistic Inquiry* 28: 345–356.

Boeckx, Cedric 2003. "(In) direct binding," *Syntax* 6: 213–236.

   2007. "Review of linearization of chains and sideward movement," *Language* 83: 895–899.

Boeckx, Cedric and Norbert Hornstein 2005. "The status of D-structure: the case of binominal each," *Syntax* 8: 23–43.

Booij, Geert 1985. "Coordination reduction in complex words: a case for prosodic phonology," in Harry van der Hulst and Norval Smith (eds.), *Advances in Non-linear Phonology*, Dordrecht: Foris, pp. 143–160.

Borsley, Robert D. 1983. "A note on preposition stranding," *Linguistic Inquiry* 14: 338–343.

1994. "In defense of coordinate structures," *Linguistic Analysis* 24: 218–246.

2005. "Against ConjP," *Lingua* 115(4): 461–482.

Bošković, Željko 2006. "Case checking versus case assignment and the case of adverbial NPs," *Linguistic Inquiry* 37(3): 522–533.

Bošković, Željko and Steven Franks 2000. "Across-the-Board Movement and LF," *Syntax* 3: 107–128.

Bowers, John 1993. "The syntax of predication," *Linguistic Inquiry* 24: 591–656.

2001. "Predication," in M. Baltin and C. Collins (eds.), *The Handbook of Contemporary Syntactic Theory*. Malden, MA: Blackwell. 299–333.

2002. "Transitivity," *Linguistic Inquiry* 33: 183–224.

Bresnan, Joan and Höskuldur Thráinsson 1990. "A note on Icelandic coordination," in Joan Mailing and Annie Zaenen (eds.), *Syntax and Semantics 24: Modern Icelandic Syntax*, San Diego: Academic Press, 355–365.

Bruening, Benjamin 2001. "QR obeys superiority: frozen scope and ACD." *Linguistic Inquiry* 32: 233–273.

Büring, Daniel 2002. "2 × Singular ≠ plural," *Snippets* 6: 6–7.

Burton, Strang and Jane Grimshaw 1992. "Coordination and VP-internal subjects," *Linguistic Inquiry* 23: 305–313.

Camacho, José 1997. "The syntax of NP coordination," PhD diss., University of Southern California.

2003. *The Syntax of Coordination*. Dordrecht: Kluwer Academic Publishers.

Caponigro, Ivano 2003. "Unbalanced coordination in Maasai," UCLA *Working Papers in Linguistics* 9: 1–16.

Carlson, Greg 1987. "Same and different: some consequences for syntax and semantics," *Linguistics and Philosophy* 10: 531–565.

Carlson, Katy 2002. *Parallelism and Prosody in the Processing of Ellipsis Sentences*, New York and London: Routledge.

Carston, Robyn 1993. "Conjunction, explanation and relevance," *Lingua* 90: 27–48.

2002. *Thoughts and Utterances: The Pragmatic of Explicit Communication*. Oxford: Blackwell.

Castillo, Juan Carlos 2001. "Thematic relations between nouns," PhD diss., University of Maryland at College Park.

Chametzky, Robert 1987. "Coordination and the organization of a grammar." PhD diss., University of Chicago, Chicago.

Chang, Chia-Hao, Frank 2006. "Gapless Relative Clause Constructions in Mandarin Chinese," MA thesis, National Chung Cheng University.

Chao, Yuen Ren 1968. *A Grammar of Spoken Chinese*, Berkeley: University of California Press.

Chapman, Carol 1995. "A subject–verb agreement hierarchy," *Historical Linguistics* 2: 35–44.

Chaves, Rui Pedro 2007. "Coordinate structures: constraint-based syntax–semantics processing," PhD diss., Universidade de Lisboa.

Chen, Qitong, Qingyan Chen, Xuanrong Chen, *et al.* (eds.) 1982. *Xiandai Hanyu Xuci Lishi* [Examples of Functional Words in Modern Chinese], Beijing: Shangwu Press.

Cheng, Lisa Lai Shen 1986. "*De* in Mandarin," *Canadian Journal of Linguistics* 31(4): 313–326.

1988. "Transitive alternations in Mandarin Chinese," Talk presented at the Ohio State University Conference on Chinese Linguistics, May 1988.

Cho, Sunggeun and Xuan Zhou 2000. "The interpretations of wh-elements in conjoined wh-questions," in Noriko Akatsuka, Susan Strauss, and Bernard Comrie (eds.), *Japanese/Korean Linguistics 10*, CSLI publications, Stanford University, pp. 522–531.

Chomsky, Noam 1957. *Syntactic Structures*. The Hague: Mouton and Co.

1964. *Current Issues in Linguistic Theory*, Mouton, The Hague.

1965. *Aspects of the Theory of Syntax*. MIT Press, Cambridge, MA.

1968. *Language and Mind*. Harcourt, Brace, and World, New York.

1975. "Questions of form and interpretation," *Linguistic Analysis* 1: 75–109.

1977. "On wh-movement," in Peter Culicover, Thomas Wasow and Adrian Akmajian (eds.), *Formal Syntax*, New York: Academic Press, pp. 71–132.

1981. *Lectures on Government and Binding*. Dordrecht: Foris.

1993. "A Minimalist Program for Linguistic Theory," in K. Hale and S. J. Keyser (eds.), *The View from Building 20*, Cambridge, MA: MIT Press, pp. 1–52.

1994. "Bare phrase structure." *MIT Occasional Papers in Linguistics 5*. (Also in G. Webelhuth [ed.], [1995] *Government and Binding Theory and the Minimalist Program*, Oxford: Blackwell.)

1995. *The Minimalist Program*. Cambridge, MA: MIT Press.

2000. "Minimalist inquiries: The framework," in Roger Martin, David Michaels, and Juan Uriagereka (eds.), *Step by Step: Essays on Minimalist Syntax in Honor of Howard Lasnik*, Cambridge, MA: MIT Press, pp. 89–155.

2002. *On Nature and Language*. Cambridge: Cambridge University Press.

2007. "Approaching UG From Below," in Uli Sauerland and Hans-Martin Gärtner (eds.), *Interfaces + Recursion = Language?* Berlin: Mouton de Gruyter, pp. 1–29.

2008. "On Phases," in Robert Freidin, Carlos Otero, and Maria-Luisa Zubizarreta (eds.), *Foundational Issues in Linguistic Theory*, Cambridge, MA: MIT Press, pp. 133–166.

Chung, Sandra and William Ladusaw 2003. *Restriction and Saturation*, Cambridge, MA: MIT Press.

Citko, Barbara 2003. "ATB wh-questions and the nature of Merge," in Makoto Kadowaki and Shigeto Kawahara (eds.), *The Proceedings of NELS 33*, Umass, Amherst: GLSA Publications, pp. 87–102.

Cole, Peter, Gabriella Hermon, and Li-May Sung 1993. "Feature Percolation," *Journal of East Asian Linguistics* 2: 91–118.

Collins, Christopher 1988a. Part 1. "Conjunction adverbs." ms., MIT.

1988b. "Part 2. Alternative analysis of conjunction." ms., MIT.

1997. *Local Economy*. Cambridge, MA: MIT Press.

2002a. "Eliminating Labels," in S. Epstein and D. Seely (eds.), *Derivation and Explanation in the Minimalist Program*, MA: Blackwell, pp. 42–64.

2002b. "Multiple Verb Movement in ≠ Hoan," *Linguistic Inquiry* 33: 1–29.

Cormack, Annabel and Neil Smith 2005. "What is coordination," *Lingua* 115: 385–418.

Cowart, Wayne and Dana McDaniel 2008. "What kind of thing is a coordination?: qualitative comparisons of agreement relations in coordinate and subordinate sentences," ms. University of Southern Maine.

Cowper, Elizabeth and Daniel Hall 2000. "Intransitive and: locality, movement, and interpretation," in J. T. Jensen and G. Van Herk (eds.), *Proceedings of the 2000 Annual conference of the Canadian Linguistics Association*, Ottawa: Cahiers Linguistiques d'Ottawa, pp. 25–36.

Culicover, Peter W. 1990. "Strange extractions," ms., Center for Cognitive Science, the Ohio State University, Columbus.

Culicover, Peter W. and Ray Jackendoff 1997. "Semantic subordination despite syntactic coordination," *Linguistic Inquiry* 28: 195–217.

Dalrymple, Mary and Irina Nikolaeva 2006. "Syntax of natural and accidental coordination: evidence from agreement," *Language* 82: 824–849.

Davies, William D. and Stanley Dubinsky 2003. "On extraction from NPs," *Natural Language and Linguistic Theory* 21: 1–37.

de Vos, Mark Andrew 2005. "The syntax of verbal pseudo-coordination in English and Afrikaans," PhD diss., Leiden University.

de Vos, Mark and Luis Vicente 2005. "Coordination under Right Node Raising," in John Alderete, Chung-hye Han, and Alexei Kochetov (eds.), *Proceedings of the 24th West Coast Conference on Formal Linguistics*, Somerville, MA: Cascadilla Proceedings Project, pp. 97–104.

Déchaine, Rose-Marie and Martina Wiltschko 2002. "Decomposing Pronouns," *Linguistic Inquiry* 33: 409–442.

Dik, Simon C. 1968. *Coordination: Its Implications for the Theory of General Linguistics*. Amsterdam: North-Holland publishing company.

Dikken, Marcel den 2001. "Pluringulars, pronouns and quirky agreement," *The Linguistic Review* 18: 19–41.

2006. *Relators and Linkers*. Cambridge, MA: MIT Press.

Dikken, Marcel den and Rint Sybesma 1998. "Take serials light up the middle," talk presented at at GLOW 21, Tilburg University, April 15, 1998.

Dougherty, Ray C. 1969. "Review of *Coordination: Its Implications for the Theory of General Linguistics* by Simon C. Dik," *Language* 45: 624–636.

1970a. "Review of universals in linguistic theory," *Foundations of Language* 6: 505–561.

1970b. "A grammar of coordinate conjoined structures: I," *Language* 46: 850–898.

Dowty, David 1987. "Collective predicates, distributive predicates, and all," *The Proceedings of Eastern States Conference on Linguistics (ESCOL)* '86: 97–115.

Eggert, Randall 2000. "Grammaticality and context with respect to *and . . .* and *or . . . respectively*," *Chicago Linguistic Society* 36: 93–107.

Elbourne, Paul 2005. *Situations and Individuals*. Cambridge, MA: MIT Press.

Embick, David and Rolf Noyer 2007. "Distributed Morphology and the syntax/morphology interface," in G. Ramchand and C. Reiss (eds.), *The Oxford Handbook of Linguistic Interfaces*, Oxford: Oxford University Press, pp. 289–324.

Emonds, Joseph 1972. "Evidence that indirect object movement is a structure-preserving rule," *Foundations of Language* 8: 546–561.

Evans, Gareth 1980. "Pronouns," *Linguistic Inquiry* 11(2): 337–362.

Fitzpatrick, Justin Michael 2006. "Two types of floating quantifiers and their A/A-bar Properties," C. Davis, A. Deal and Y. Zabbal (eds.), *Proceedings of NELS* 36, pp. 253–265.

Fox, Danny 2000. *Economy and Semantic Interpretation*, Cambridge: MIT Press.

Frank, Anette 2002. "A (discourse) functional analysis of asymmetric coordination," in Miriam Butt and Tracy Holloway King (eds.), *Proceedings of the LFG02 Conference*, Athens: CSLI Publications, pp. 174–196.

Franks, Steven 1992. "A prominence constraint on null operator constructions," *Lingua* 87: 35–54.

1993. "On Parallelism in Across-the-Board Dependencies," *Linguistic Inquiry* 24(3): 509–529.

Frazier, Lyn and Charles Clifton 2001. "Parsing coordinates and ellipsis: copy α," *Syntax* 4: 1–22.

Frazier, Lyn, Jeremy M. Pacht, and Keith Rayner 1999. "Taking on semantic commitments, II: collective versus distributive readings," *Cognition* 70: 87–104.

Frazier, Lyn, Alan Munn and Charles Clifton 2000. "Processing coordinate structures," *Journal of Psycholinguistic Research* 29: 343–370.

Fromkin, Victoria, Robert Rodman, Nina Hyams 2007. *An Introduction to Language*. 8th edition, Boston, MA: Thomson Wadsworth.

Fu, Jingqi 1994. "On deriving Chinese derived nominals: evidence for V-to-N raising," PhD diss., University of Massachusetts.

Gawron, Jean Mark and Andrew Kehler 2004. "The semantics of respective readings, conjunction, and filler-gap dependencies," *Linguistics and Philosophy* 27: 169–207.

Gazdar, Gerald 1981. "Unbounded dependencies and coordinate structure," *Linguistic Inquiry* 12: 155–183.

Gazdar, Gerald, Geoffrey K. Pullum, Ivan A. Sag, and Thomas Wasow 1982. "Coordination and transformational grammar," *Linguistic Inquiry* 13: 663–676.

Gazdar, Gerald, Ewan Klein, Geoffrey Pullum, and Ivan Sag 1985. *Generalized Phrase Structure Grammar*. Oxford: Basil Blackwell.

George, Leland 1980. "Analogical generalization in natural language syntax," PhD diss., MIT.

Gleitman, Lila 1965. "Coordinating Conjunctions in English," *Language* 41: 260–293.

Godard, Danièle 1989. "Empty categories as subjects of tensed Ss in English or French?," *Linguistic Inquiry* 20: 497–506.

Goldsmith, John 1985. "A principled exception to the Coordinate Structure Constraint," in *Papers from the Twenty-First Annual Regional Meeting of the Chicago Linguistic Society*, Chicago: Chicago Linguistic Society, pp. 133–143.

Goodall, Grant 1987. *Parallel Structures in Syntax: Coordination, Causatives and Restructuring*. Cambridge: Cambridge University Press.

Gracanin-Yuksek, Martina 2007. "About sharing," PhD diss., MIT.

Grice, Paul 1967. "Logic and conversation: the William James Lectures," in H. P. Grice (1989), *Studies in the Way of Words*, Cambridge, MA: Harvard University Press, pp. 22–40.

Grimshaw, Jane 1981. "Form, function, and the Language Acquisition Device," in C. L. Baker and John J. McCarthy (eds.), *The Logical Problem of Language Acquisition*, Cambridge, MA: MIT Press, pp. 165–182.

1991. "Extended Projection," ms., Brandeis University.

Groot, A. W. De 1949. *Structurele Syntaxis*. The Hague: Servire.

Grootveld, Marjan 1994. "Parsing coordination generatively," HIL diss., Leiden University.

Grosu, Alexander 1972. "The strategic content of Island Constraints," PhD diss., Ohio State University.

1973. "On the nonunitary nature of the coordinate structure constraint," *Linguistic Inquiry* 4: 88–92.

1981. *Approaches to Island Phenomena*. Amsterdam: North-Holland.

1985. "Subcategorization and parallelism," *Theoretical Linguistics* 12: 231–240.

Hagstrom, Paul 1998. "Decomposing questions," PhD diss., MIT.

Haïk, Isabelle 1985. "The syntax of operators," PhD diss., MIT.

Hankamer, Jorge 1973. "Unacceptable ambiguity," *Linguistic Inquiry* 4: 17–68.

Hankamer, Jorge and Ivan. Sag 1976. "Deep and surface anaphora," *Linguistic Inquiry* 7: 391–428.

Harley, Heidi 2005. "One-replacement, unaccusativity, acategorial roots, and bare phrase structure," in Slava Gorbachov and Andrew Nevins (eds.), *Harvard Working Papers in Linguistics* 11, pp. 59–78.

Hartmann, Katharina 2000. *Right Node Raising and Gapping*. Amsterdam: John Benjamins.

Haspelmath, Martin 2002. *Understanding Morphology*. New York: Oxford University Press.

2004. "Coordinating constructions: an overview," in M. Haspelmath (ed.) *Coordinating Constructions, Typological Studies in Language 58*, Amsterdam: John Benjamins, pp. 3–39.

2007. "Coordination," in T. Shopen (ed.), *Language Typology and Syntactic Description*, vol. II: *Complex Constructions*, 2nd edn. Cambridge: Cambridge University Press, pp. 1–51.

Hegarty, Michael 2003. "Semantic types of abstract entities," *Lingua* 113: 891–927.

Heim, Irene 1982. "The semantics of definite and indefinite noun phrases," PhD diss., University of Massachusetts, Amherst.

Heim, Irene and Angelika Kratzer 1998. *Semantics in Generative Grammar*. MA: Blackwell Publishers.

Heim, Irene, Howard Lasnik and Robert May 1991. "Reciprocity and Plurality," *Linguistic Inquiry* 22: 63–101.

Hendriks, Petra 1991. "Deletion in coordinate structures: the parallelism requirement," in Mark Kas, Eric Reuland and Co Vet (eds.), *Language and Cognition 1*, Yearbook 1991 of the research group for Linguistic Theory and Knowledge Representation of the University of Groningen, pp. 99–110.

2002. "'*Either*' as a focus particle," ms., University of Gronigen.

2004. "Coherence relations, ellipsis, and contrastive topics," *Journal of Semantics* 21(2): 133–153.

Hernández, Ana Carrera 2007. "Gapping as a syntactic dependency," *Lingua* 117: 2106–2133.

Heycock, Caroline and Anthony Kroch 1994. "Verb movement and coordination in a dynamic theory of licensing," *The Linguistic Review* 11: 257–283.

Heycock, Caroline and Roberto Zamparelli 2000. "Friends and colleagues: plurality and NP-coordination," *NELS* 30, pp. 341–352.

2002. "Conjunction and plurality: a case study in the integration of syntax and semantics." Project Proposal, University of Edinburgh.

2003. "Coordinated Bare Definites," *Linguistic Inquiry* 34: 443–469.

2005. "Friends and colleagues: plurality, coordination, and the structure of DP," *Natural Language Semantics* 13: 201–270.

Higginbotham, James 1987. "Indefiniteness and predication," in Eric Reuland and Alice ter Meulen (eds.), *The Representation of (In)definiteness*, Cambridge, MA: MIT Press, pp. 43–70.

Hinds, John 1986. *Japanese*. London and New York: Routledge.

Hockett, Charles Francis 1958. *A Course in Modern Linguistics*. New York: The Macmillan Company.

Hoeksema, Jack 1983. "Plurality and conjunction," in A. ter Meulen (ed.) *Studies in Modeltheoretic Semantics*. Dordrecht: Foris.

Hoekstra, Eric 1994. "Expletive replacement, verb-second and coordination," *The Linguistic Review* 11: 285–297.

Hoh, Pau-San and Wen-yu Chiang 1990. "A focus account of moved wh-phrases at S-structure in Chinese," *Lingua* 81:47–73.

Höhle, Tilman 1990. "Assumptions about asymmetric coordination in German," in Joan Mascaró and Marina Nespor (eds.), *Grammar in Progress: A Festschrift for Henk van Riemsdijk*. Dordrecht: Foris, pp. 221–235.

Hornstein, Norbert 2001. *Move! A Minimalist Theory of Construal*. Malden, MA: Blackwell Publishers.

Hornstein, Norbert and Hirohisa Kiguchi 2003. "PRO gate and movement." Proceedings of the 25th annual Penn Linguistics Colloquium. *University of Pennsylvania Working Papers in Linguistics* 8(1): 33–46.

Hornstein, Norbert and David Lightfoot 1987. "Predication and PRO," *Language* 63: 23–52.

Hornstein, Norbert and Jairo Nunes 2002. "On asymmetries between parasitic gap and Across-The-Board constructions," *Syntax* 5: 26–54.

Huang, Cheng-teh James 1982. "Logical relations in Chinese and the theory of grammar," PhD diss., MIT.

1988a. "Hanyu zhengfanwenju de mozuyifa" [Chinese A-not-A questions: a modular approach], *Zhongguo Yuwen* 205: 247–264.

1988b. "Shuo shi he you" [On *Be* and *Have* in Chinese], *The Bulletin of the Institute of History and Philology* 59: 43–64.

1993. "Reconstruction and the structure of VP: some theoretical consequences," *Linguistic Inquiry* 24: 103–138.

Huang, Chu-Ren 1989. "Mandarin Chinese NP de – a comparative study of current grammatical theories." Nankang, Taipei (PhD diss., Cornell University 1987).

Huddleston, Rodney and Geoffrey Pullum 2002. *The Cambridge Grammar of the English Language*. Cambridge: Cambridge University Press.

Hudson, Richard A. 1972. *Systemic Generative Grammar*. Mimeo, London: University College.

1976. *Arguments for a Non-transformational Grammar*. Chicago: Chicago University Press.

Humphreys, Karin R. and Kathryn Bock 2005. "Notional number agreement in English," *Psychonomic Bulletin & Review* 12(4): 689–695.

Huttar, George 2003. "Sum: discourse-initial 'and'," *Linguist List* 14–1163.

2004. "Summary on Latin preposition and conjunction order," *Linguist List* 15–541.

1977. *X' Syntax: A Study of Phrase Structure*. Cambridge, MA: MIT Press.

Jackendoff, Ray 1997. *The Architecture of the Language Faculty*. Cambridge, MA: MIT Press.

Jacobson, Pauline 1987. "Review of G. Gazdar, E. Klein, G. Pullum, and I. Sag, *Generalized Phrase Structure Grammar*," *Linguistics and Philosophy* 10: 389–426.

Jaeggli, Osvaldo and Nina M. Hyams 1993. "On the independence and interdependence of syntactic and morphological properties: English aspectual *come* and *go*," *Natural Language and Linguistic Theory* 11: 313–346.

Jayaseelan, Karattuparambil A. 2001. "Questions and question-word incorporating quantifiers in Malayalam," *Syntax* 4: 63–93.

2008. "Question particles and disjunction." *LingBuzz/000644*.

Jensen, John Thayer 1977. *Yapese Reference Grammar*. Honolulu: University Press of Hawaii.

Jespersen, Otto 1924. *Philosophy of Grammar*, New York: Norton (1965 edn.).

Johannessen, Janne Bondi 1996. "Partial agreement and coordination," *Linguistic Inquiry* 27: 661–676.

1998. *Coordination*. Oxford: Oxford University Press.

Johnson, Kyle 1991. "Object positions," *Natural Language and Linguistic Theory* 9: 577–636.

1996. "Gapping. Ch. 2 of: *In search of the English Middle Field*," ms., University of Massachusetts–Amherst.

2002. "Restoring exotic coordinations to normalcy," *Linguistic Inquiry* 33: 97–156.

2007. "LCA + alignment = RNR. Workshop on coordination, subordination and ellipsis," talk presented at University of Tübingen, June 2007.

2008. "The view of QR from ellipsis," in Kyle Johnson (ed.), *Topics in Ellipsis*, Cambridge: Cambridge University Press, pp. 69–94.

2009. "Gapping isn't (VP) ellipsis," *Linguistic Inquiry* 40: 289–328.

Kandybowics, Jason 2006. "Nupe coordinate structures: a syntactically heterogeneous class," in Rebecca Cover and Yuni Kim (eds.), *Proceedings of the 31st Annual Meeting of the Berkeley Linguistics Society* (Volume 31S: Special Session on Languages of West Africa), Berkeley: Berkeley Linguistics Society, pp. 53–64.

Karimi, Yadgar 2007. "Kurdish Ezafe construction: implications for DP structure," *Lingua* 117: 2159–2177.

Kasai, Hironobu 2002. "Some remarks on the Coordinate Structure Constraint," talk presented at the GLOW in Asia (3), National Tsing Hua University, Tsinchu, Jan. 4–7, 2002.

2004. "Two notes on ATB movement," *Language and Linguistics* 5(1): 167–188.

Kayne, Richard 1994. *The Antisymmetry of Syntax*. Cambridge, MA: MIT Press.
    2002. "Pronouns and their Antecedents," in S. Epstein and D. Seely (eds.), *Derivation and Explanation in the Minimalist Program*, Malden, MA: Blackwell Publishers, pp. 133–166.
Keenan, Edward 1976. "Remarkable subjects in Malagasy," in Charles Li (ed.), *Subject and Topic*, New York: Academic Press, pp. 247–301.
Kehler, Andrew 2002. *Coherence, Reference, and the Theory of Grammar*. Stanford, CA: CSLI Publications.
Kitagawa, Chistato and Claudia Ross 1982. "Prenominal modification in Chinese and Japanese," *Linguistic Analysis* 9: 19–53.
Koizumi, Masatishi 1995. "Phrase structure in minimalist syntax," PhD diss., MIT.
Kolb, Hans-Peter and Craig Thiersch 1991. "Levels and empty categories in a principles and parameters approach to parsing," in Hubert Haider and Klaus Netter (eds.), *Representation and Derivation in the Theory of Grammar*, Dordrecht: Kluwer, pp. 251–302.
Koopman, Hilda and Anna Szabolcsi 2000. *Verbal Complexes*. Cambridge, MA: MIT Press.
Koutsoudas, Andreas 1968. "The A over A convention," *Linguistics* 46: 11–20.
Kratzer, Angelika 2009. "Building a pronoun: fake indexicals as windows into the properties of bound variable pronouns," *Linguistic Inquiry*, to appear.
Krifka, Manfred 1990. "Boolean and Non-Boolean 'and'," in *Papers from the Second Symposium on Logic and Language*, Budapest: Akademiai Kiado, pp. 161–188.
Kuno, Susumu 1973. *The Structure of the Japanese Language*. Cambridge, MA: MIT Press.
    1987. *Functional Syntax – Anaphora, Discourse and Empathy*. Chicago and London: The University of Chicago Press.
Laka, Itziar 1994. *On the Syntax of Negation*. New York: Garland Publishing Inc.
Lakoff, George 1986. "Frame semantic control of the coordinate structure constraint," in Anne M. Farley, Peter T. Farley, and Karl-Erik McCullough (eds.), *Chicago Linguistic Society* 22, Part 2*: Papers from the Parasession on Pragmatics and Grammatical Theory*, Chicago: CLS, pp. 152–167.
Lakoff, George and Stanley Peters 1966. "Phrasal conjunction and symmetric predicates." *Mathematical Linguistics and Automatic Translation*, Harvard Computation Laboratory, Report No. NSF-17, VI, pp. 1–49 (reprinted in 1969).
    1969. "Phrasal Conjunction and Symmetric Predicates," in David A. Reibel and Sanford A. Schane (eds.), *Modern Studies in English*, Englewood Cliffs, NJ: Prentice-Hall, pp. 113–142.
Landau, Idan 1999. "Possessor raising and the structure of VP," *Lingua* 107: 1–37.
Lang, Ewald 1984. *The Semantics of Coordination*. Amsterdam: John Benjamins.
Larson, Richard 1988. "On the double object construction," *Linguistic Inquiry* 19: 335–391.
    1990. "Double objects revisited: reply to Jackendoff," *Linguistic Inquiry* 21(1): 589–632.
Lasersohn, Peter 1995. *Plurality, Conjunction and Events*. Dordrecht: Kluwer Academic Publishers.

2000. "*Same*, models and representation," *Proceedings of SALT X*, Ithaca, NY: CLC Publications, pp. 83–97.

Law, Paul 2002. "Adjunct relative clauses in Chinese," in Zoe Wu (ed.) *Proceedings of the 13th Annual Meeting of the North American Conference on Chinese Linguistics*. Los Angeles: University of Southern California, pp. 80–97.

Lawler, John 1974. "Ample negatives," *Papers from the Tenth Regional Meeting (CLS)*. Chicago: Chicago Linguistic Society, pp. 357–377.

Legate, Julie 2008. "Morphological and abstract case," *Linguistic Inquiry* 39: 55–101.

Levin, Beth 1993. *English Verb Classes and Alternations: A Preliminary Investigation*, Chicago: University of Chicago Press.

Levin, Nancy and Ellen Prince 1986. "Gapping and Causal Implicature," *Papers in Linguistics* 19(3): 351–364.

Levine, Robert D. 2001. "The extraction riddle: just what are we missing?," *Journal of Linguistics* 37: 145–174.

Li, Charles and Sandra Thompson 1981. *Mandarin Chinese: A Functional Reference Grammar*. Berkeley: University of California Press.

Li, Ya-fei 1990. "On V–V compounds in Chinese," *Natural Language and Linguistics Theory* 8: 177–207.

Li, Yen-hui Audrey 1998. "Argument determiner phrases and number phrases," *Linguistic Inquiry* 29: 693–702.

2007. "De: adjunction and conjunction," talk presented at NACCL-19/IACL 15, Columbia University, May 25–27, 2007.

Lin, Chien-Jer Charles 2007. "Processing (in)alienable possessions at the syntax–semantics interface," talk presented at the conference On Linguistic Interfaces, University of Ulster, Northern Ireland, June 1–3, 2007.

Lin, Jo-Wang 2003. "On restrictive and non-restrictive relative clauses in Mandarin Chinese," *Tsinghua Journal of Chinese Studies*, New Series, 33(1): 199–240.

Lin, Jo-Wang and Chih-Chen Jane Tang 1996. "Modals as verbs in Chinese: a GB perspective," in *The Bulletin of the Institute of History and Philology*, Taipei: Academia Sinica, vol. 66, pp. 53–105.

Lin, Vivian 2001. "A way to undo A-movement," in K. Megerdoomian and L. A. Barel (eds.), *WCCFL 20 Proceedings*, Somerville, MA: Cascadilla Press, pp. 358–371.

2002. "Coordination and sharing at the interfaces." PhD diss., MIT, Cambridge, MA.

Link, Godehard 1983. "The logical analysis of plurals and mass terms: a lattice-theoretical approach," in R. Bäuerler, Chr. Schwarze, A. von Stechow (eds.), *Meaning, Use and Interpretation of Language*, Berlin and New York: De Gruyter, pp. 303–323.

1984. "Hydras: on the logic of relative constructions with multiple heads," in Fred Landmann and Frank Veltmann (eds.), *Varieties of Formal Semantics*, Dordrecht: Foris, pp. 245–257.

Liu, Jian and Alain Peyraube 1994. "History of some coordinative conjunctions in Chinese," *Journal of Chinese Linguistics* 22(2): 179–201.

Lobeck, Anne 1987a. "Syntactic constraints on ellipsis," PhD diss., University of Washington.

1987b. "VP ellipsis in infinitives: infl as a proper governor," in J. McDonough and B. Plunkett (eds.), *Proceedings of NELS* 17, GLSA, University of Massachusetts, Amherst, pp. 425–441.

1990. "Functional heads as proper governors," in *Proceedings of the North East Linguistic Society*, vol. 20, Amherst: GLSA, University of Massachusetts, pp. 348–362.

López, Luis 2001. "Head of a projection," *Linguistic Inquiry* 32: 521–532.

Lorimor, Heidi 2007. "Conjunctions and grammatical agreement," PhD diss., University of Illinois at Urbana-Champaign.

Lü, Shuxiang 1979. *Hanyu yufa fenxi wenti* [Issues in the analysis of Chinese grammar]. Beijing: Shangwu Press.

Lü, Shuxiang, Linding Li, Jian Liu, *et al.* 1999. *Xiandai Hanyu Babai Ci* [800 Words in Chinese]. Beijing: Shangwu Press (1st edition, 1980).

Lubbe, Henricus Franciscus Alphonsus Van Der 1958. "Woordvolgorde in het Nederlands; een synchrone structurele beschouwing," diss. Utrecht. Assen [summary in English].

Luka, Barbara and Lawrence Barsalou 2005. "Structural facilitation: mere exposure effects for grammatical acceptability as evidence for syntactic priming in comprehension," *Journal of Memory and Language* 52: 436–459.

Marantz, Alec 1997. "No escape from syntax: don't try morphological analysis in the privacy of your own lexicon," *U. Penn Working Papers in Linguistics* 4(2): 201–225.

Martin, Samuel Elmo and Yong-Sook C. Lee 1986. *Beginning Korean*. Tokyo: Tuttle.

Marušic, Franc Lanko, Andrew Nevins, and Amanda Saksida 2007. "Last-conjunct agreement in Slovenian," in Richard Compton, Magdalena Goledzinowska, Ulyana Savchenko (eds.), *Formal Approaches to Slavic Linguistics 15*: *The Toronto Meeting 2006*. Ann Arbor: Michigan Slavic Publications, pp. 210–227.

Massey, Gerald J. 1976. "Tom, Dick, and Harry, and all the king's men,' *American Philosophical Quarterly* 13: 89–107.

Matushansky, Ora 2006. "Head movement in linguistic theory," *Linguistic Inquiry* 37: 69–109.

May, Robert 1985. *Logical Form: Its Structure and Derivation*. Cambridge, MA: MIT Press.

McCawley, James 1968. "The role of semantics in grammar," in Emmon Bach and Robert Harms (eds.), *Universals in Linguistic Theory*. New York: Holt, Rinehart and Winston, pp. 124–169.

1988a. *The Syntactic Phenomena of English*, Chicago: Chicago University Press.

1988b. "The comparative conditional constructions in English, German and Chinese," in *Proceedings of the 14th Annual Meeting of the Berkeley Linguistics Society*, Berkeley: BLS, pp. 176–187.

McCloskey, James 1986. "Inflection and conjunction in modern Irish," *Natural Language and Linguistic Theory* 4: 245–281.

1991. "There, it, and agreement," *Linguistic Inquiry* 22: 563–567.

1999. "Embedding the root," talk presented at MIT, Nov. 12, 1999.

McCloskey, James and Ken Hale 1984. "On the syntax of person number marking in modern Irish," *Natural Language and Linguistic Theory* 1: 487–533.

McFadden, Thomas 2004. "The position of morphological case in the derivation: a study on the syntax–morphology interface," PhD diss., The University of Pennsylvania.

McNally, Louise 1992. "VP-coordination and the VP-internal subject hypothesis," *Linguistic Inquiry* 23: 336–341.

    1993. "Comitative coordination: a case study in group formation," *Natural Language and Linguistic Theory* 11: 347–379.

Merchant, Jason 2001. *The Syntax of Silence*. New York: Oxford University Press.

Mithun, Marianne 1988. "The grammaticalization of coordination," in J. Haiman and S. A. Thomson (eds.), *Clause Combining in Grammar and Discourse*, Amsterdam: John Benjamins, pp. 331–360.

Mittwoch, Anita 1979. "Backward anaphora in utterances conjoined with *but*," ms., The Hebrew University.

Moltmann, Friederike 1992a. "Coordination and comparatives," PhD diss., MIT.

    1992b. "Reciprocals and same/different: towards a semantic analysis," *Linguistics and Philosophy* 16: 411–462.

    1997. *Parts and Wholes in Semantics*. New York, Oxford: Oxford University Press.

Moro, Andrea 1997. *The Raising of Predicates*. Cambridge: Cambridge University Press.

    2000. *Dynamic Antisymmetry*. Cambridge, MA: MIT Press.

Morrill, Glyn 1990. "Grammar and logical types," *Proceedings of the Seventh Amsterdam Colloqium*, pp. 429–450.

Muadz, Husni 1991. "Coordinate structure: a planar representation," PhD diss., University of Arizona.

Müller, Gereon 1998. *Incomplete Category Fronting: A Derivational Approach to Remnant Movement in German*. Dordrecht: Kluwer.

Munn, Alan 1987. "Coordinate structure and X-bar theory," *McGill Working Papers in Linguistics* 4.1: 121–140.

    1992. "A null operator analysis of ATB gaps," *The Linguistic Review* 9: 1–26.

    1993. "Topics in the syntax and semantics of coordinate structures," PhD diss., University of Maryland, College Park.

    1996. "Some problems of coordination," talk presented at Max-Planck Gesellschaft ASG, Berlin, June 5, 1996.

    1999. "On the identity requirement of ATB extraction," *Natural Language Semantics* 7: 421–425.

    2001. "Explaining parasitic gap restrictions," in P. Cullicover and P. Postal (eds.), *Parasitic Gaps*, Cambridge, MA: MIT Press, pp. 369–392.

Myers, James 2009. "The design and analysis of small-scale syntactic judgment experiments," *Lingua* 119: 425–444.

Napoli, Donna Jo 1993. *Syntax: Theory and Problems*. New York: Oxford University Press.

Neijt, Anneke 1979. *Gapping: A Contribution to Sentence Grammar*. Dordrecht: Foris Publications.

Nida, Eugene A. 1949. *Morphology: The Descriptive Analysis of Words*. Ann Arbor: University of Michigan Press.

Ning, Chunyan 1993. "The overt syntax of relativization and topicalization in Chinese," PhD diss., University of California, Irvine.

Nunes, Jairo 2001. "Sideward movement," *Linguistic Inquiry* 32: 303–344.

2004. *Linearization of Chains and Sideward Movement*, Cambridge, MA: MIT Press.

Nunes, Jairo and Juan Uriagereka 2000. "Cyclicity and extraction domain," *Syntax* 3(1): 20–43.

Ochi, Masao 1999. "Some consequences of Attract F," *Lingua* 109: 81–107.

Ogawa, Yoshiki 2001. "The stage/individual distinction and (in)alienable possession," *Language* 77.1: 1–25.

Oirsouw, Robert van 1987. *The Syntax of Coordination*. New York: Croom Helm.

Panagiotidis, Phoevos 2007. "Determiner spreading as DP-predication." Ms. University Of Cyprus.

Partee, Barbara H. 1970. "Negation, conjunction, and quantifiers: syntax vs. semantics," *Foundations of Language* 6: 153–165.

2005, "Reflections of a formal semanticist as of Feb 2005," ms., University of Massachusetts, Amherst.

Payne, John 1985. "Complex Phrases and Complex Sentences," in Timothy Shopen (ed.), *Language Typology and Syntactic Description*, Cambridge: Cambridge University Press, pp. 3–41.

Pesetsky, David 1982. "Paths and categories," PhD diss., MIT.

2000. *Phrasal Movement and its Kin*, Cambridge, MA: MIT Press.

Peterson, Peter G. 2004. "Coordination: consequences of a lexical–functional account," *Natural Language and Linguistic Theory* 22: 643–679.

Peterson, David A. and Kenneth VanBik 2004. "Coordination in Hakha Lai (Tibeto-Burman)," in Martin Haspelmath (ed.), *Coordinating Constructions, Typological Studies in Language 58*, Amsterdam: John Benjamins, pp. 333–356.

Phillips, Colin 2003. "Linear order and constituency," *Linguistic Inquiry* 34: 37–90.

Platzack, Christer 2008. "Parametrized argument structure," ms., Lund University.

Pollard, Carl and Ivan Sag 1994. *Head-Driven Phrase Structure Grammar*. Chicago: University of Chicago Press.

Postal, Paul Martin 1972. "The two remarks on dragging," *Linguistic Inquiry* 3: 130–136.

1974. *On Raising: One Rule of English Grammar and its Theoretical Implications*, Cambridge, MA: MIT Press.

1998. *Three Investigations of Extraction*, Cambridge, MA: MIT Press.

Potts, Christopher 2002. "The syntax and semantics of as-parentheticals," *Natural Language and Linguistic Theory* 20: 623–689.

Progovac, Ljiljana 1998a. "Structure of coordination, Part 1," *GLOT International* 3(7): 3–6.

1998b. "Structure of coordination, Part 2," *GLOT International* 3(8): 3–9.

Pullum, Geoffrey and Arnold Zwicky 1986. "Phonological resolution of syntactic feature conflict," *Language* 62: 751–773.

Radford, Andrew 1997. *Syntactic Theory and the Structure of English: A Minimalist Approach*. Cambridge: Cambridge University Press.

Rebuschi, Georges 2005. "Generalizing the antisymmetric analysis of coordination to nominal modification," *Lingua* 115(4): 445–459.

Reinhart, Tanya 2002. "The theta system: an overview," *Theoretical Linguistics* 28: 229–290.

Reinhart, Tanya and Mats Rooth 1991. "Bare argument ellipsis." ms. Tel-Aviv University and University of Stuttgart.

Richards, Norvin 1997. "What moves where when in which language?," PhD diss., MIT.

Riemsdijk, Henk van and Edwin Williams 1986. *Introduction to the Theory of Grammar*, Cambridge, MA: MIT Press.

Roberts, John R. 1988. "Amele switch-reference and the theory of grammar," *Linguistic Inquiry* 9: 45–63.

Rögnvaldsson, Eiríkur 1982. "We need (some kind of) a rule of conjunction reduction," *Linguistic Inquiry* 13: 557–561.

1993. "Coordination, ATB-extraction, and the identification of pro," *Harvard Working Papers in Linguistics* 3: 153–180.

Ross, John Robert 1967. "Constraints on variables in syntax," PhD diss., MIT.

Ross, John Robert and David Perlmutter 1970. "Relative clauses with split antecedents," *Linguistic Inquiry* 1: 350.

Rothstein, Susan D. 1991a. "Heads, projections and category determination," in K. Leffel and D. Bouchard (eds.), *Views on Phrase Structure*, Dordrecht: *Kluwer*, pp. 97–112.

1991b. "Syntactic licensing and subcategorization," in S. Rothstein (ed.), *Syntax and Semantics*, vol. XXV, Academic Press, Inc., pp. 139–157.

Rubin, Edward J. 2002. "The structure of modifiers," ms., University of Utah.

2003. "Determining pair-merge," *Linguistic Inquiry* 34: 660–668.

Rudin, Catherine 1988. "On multiple questions and multiple wh-fronting," *Natural Language and Linguistic Theory* 6: 445–501.

Runner, Jeffrey T. 1995. "Noun phrase licensing and interpretation," PhD diss., University of Massachusetts at Amherst.

Ruys, Eddy 1992. "The scope of indefinites," PhD diss., Utrecht: OTS dissertation series.

Sabbagh, Joseph 2007. "Ordering and linearizing rightward movement," *Natural Language and Linguistic Theory* 25: 349–401.

Sabel, Joachim 2002. "A minimalist analysis of syntactic islands," *Linguistic Review* 19: 271–315.

Sadler, Louisa 1999. "Non-distributive features and coordination in Welsh", in Miriam Butt and Tracy Holloway King (eds.), *Proceedings of the LFG '99 Conference*, Stanford, CA: CSLI Publications. http://cslipublications.stanford.edu/LFG/4/lfg99-toc.html.

2003, "Coordination and asymmetric agreement in Welsh," in Miriam Butt and Tracy Holloway King (eds.), *Nominals: Inside and Out*, CSLI Publications, pp. 85–118.

Sag, Ivan 1982. "Coordination, extraction, and generalized phrase structure grammar," *Linguistic Inquiry* 13: 329–336.

1997. "English relative clause constructions," *Journal of Linguistics* 33(2): 421–484.

2000. "Another argument against wh-trace," http://ling.ucsc.edu/Jorge/sag.html.

Sag, Ivan, Gerald Gazdar, Thomas Wasow, and Steven Weisler 1985. "Coordination and how to distinguish categories," *Natural Language and Linguistic Theory* 3: 117–171.

Saiki, Mariko 1985. "On the coordination of gapped constituents in Japanese," *CLS* 21, pp. 371–387.

Saito, Mamoru and Keiko Murasugi 1999. "Subject predication within IP and DP," in K. Johnson and I. Roberts (eds.), Beyond Principles and Parameters, Dordrecht: Kluwer, pp. 167–188.

Saito, Mamoru, T.-H. Jonah Lin, Keiko Murasugi 2008. "N-ellipsis and the structure of noun phrases in Chinese and Japanese." *Journal of East Asian Linguistics* 17: 247–271.

Sauerland, Uli 2003. "A new semantics for number," in R. Young and Y. Zhou (eds.), *Semantics and Linguistic Theory XIII*, Ithaca: Cornell University, pp. 258–275.

Scha, Remko 1981. "Distributive, collective and cumulative quantification," in J. Groenendijk, T. M. V. Janssen, and M. Stokhof (eds.), *Formal Methods in the Study of Language*, Part 2, vol. 136 of *Mathematical Centre Tracts*, Amsterdam: Mathematisch Centrum, pp. 483–512.

Schachter, Paul 1977. "Constraints on coordination," *Language* 53: 86–103.

1985. "Parts-of-speech systems," in Timothy Shopen (ed.), *Language Typology and Syntactic Description*, vol. I, Cambridge: Cambridge University Press, pp. 3–61.

Schein, Barry (forthcoming). *Conjunction Reduction Redux*, Cambridge, MA: MIT Press.

Schmerling, Susan 1975. "Asymmetric conjunction and rules of conversation," in P. Cole and J. L. Morgan, (eds.), *Syntax and Semantics* 3: Speech Acts, New York: Academic Press, pp. 210–231.

Schütze, Carson 2001. "On the nature of default case," *Syntax* 4(3): 205–238.

Schütze, Carson and Edward Gibson 1999. "Argumenthood and English prepositional phrase attachment," *Journal of Memory and Language* 40: 409–431.

Schwarz, Bernhard 1999. *On the Syntax of Either . . . Or. Natural Language and Linguistic Theory* 17, 339–370.

Schwarzschild, Roger 1996. *Pluralities*. Dordrecht: Kluwer Academic Publishers.

2001. "Review of Winter (1998) *Flexible Boolean Semantics: Coordination, Plurality and Scope in Natural Language*," *Glot International* 5(4): 141–149.

2002. "The grammar of measurement," ms., Rutgers University.

Seiler, Hansjakob 1974. "The principle of concomitance: instrumental, comitative, and collective," *Foundations of Language* 12(2): 215–247.

Shaer, Benjamin 2003. "'Manner' adverbs and the association theory: some problems and solutions," in Ewald Lang, Claudia Maienborn and Cathrin Fabricius-Hansen (eds.), *Modifying Adjuncts*, Berlin: Mouton de Gruyter, pp. 211–259.

Shao, Jingmin and Chunhong Rao 1985. "On the conjunction *you*," *Yuyan Jiaoxue yu Yanjiu* [Language teaching and studies] 2: 4–16.

Shen, David Ta-Chun and Jen Ting 2008. "Morphological status of *de* in the V-*de* constructions in Mandarin Chinese: a study of interface between syntax and morphology." Paper presented at the 11th International Symposium on Chinese Language and Linguistics, National Chia Tung University, Hsinchu, Taiwan, May 23–25, 2008.

Shi, Youwei 1986. "Hanyu lianci de gongneng, jiexian he weizhi" [the functions, criteria and positions of conjunctions] *Zhongyang Minzu Xueyuan Xuebao*, 1986.3.

Shopen, Timothy 1971. "Caught in the act," in *Papers from the Seventh Regional Meetings of the Chicago Linguistic Society*, pp. 254–263.

Shyu, Shu-ing 1995. "The syntax of focus and topic in Mandarin Chinese," PhD diss., USC Los Angeles, CA.

Siloni, Tal. 2008. "The syntax of reciprocal verbs: an overview," in E. König and V. Gast (eds.), *Reciprocals and Reflexives: Theoretical and Typological Explorations, Trends in Linguistics*, Berlin: Mouton de Gruyter.

Simpson, Andrew 2003. "On the status of 'modifying' *de* and the structure of the Chinese DP," in Sze-Wing Tang and Chen-Sheng Liu (eds.), *On the Formal Way to Chinese Languages*. Stanford: CSLI, pp. 74–101.

Skrabalova, Hana 2003. "Coordination: some evidence for DP and NumP in Czech," paper presented at the Fifth European Conference on Formal Description of Slavic Languages (FDSL 5), University of Leipzig, Germany, November 26–28, 2003.

Sledd, James 1959. *A Short Introduction to English Grammar*. Chicago: Scott, Foresman and Co.

Sobin, Nicholas 2004. "Expletive constructions are not 'Lower Right Corner' movement constructions," *Linguistic Inquiry* 35: 503–508.

Speer, S. R. and C. J. Clifton 1998. "Plausibility and argument structure in sentence comprehension," *Memory and Cognition* 26: 965–978.

Sperber, Dan and Deirdre Wilson 1995. *Relevance: Communication and Cognition* (second edn). Oxford: Blackwell Publishers Ltd.

Sportiche, Dominique 1988. "A theory of floating quantifiers and its corrolaries for constituent structure," *Linquistic Inquiry* 19(3): 425–49.

Stassen, Leon 2000. "AND-languages and WITH-languages," *Linguistic Typology* 4: 1–54.

Steiner, Ilona 2008. "Partial agreement in German: a processing issue?," talk presented at Linguistic Evidence, Tübingen, Feb. 1, 2008.

Stepanov, Arthur 2001. "Late adjunction and minimalist phrase structure," *Syntax* 4: 94–125.

Stowell, Timothy 1981. "Origins of phrase structure," PhD diss., MIT.

Szabolcsi, Anna 1983. "The possessor that ran away from home," *The Linguistic Review* 3: 89–102.

   1994. "The noun phrase," in F. Kiefer and K. É. Kiss (eds.), *Syntax and Semantics 27: The Syntactic Structure of Hungarian*, San Diego: Academic Press, pp. 179–274.

   2001. "The syntax of scope," in M. Baltin and C. Collins (eds.), *The Handbook of Contemporary Syntactic Theory*, Malden and Oxford: Blackwell, pp. 607–633.

Szabolcsi, Anna and Marcel den Dikken 1999. "Islands," *Glot International* 4(6): 3–8.

Tai, James H.-Y. 1969. "Coordination reduction," PhD diss., Indiana University.

Takahashi, Daiko 1994. "Minimality of movement," PhD diss., University of Connecticut, Storrs.

Takano, Yuji 2002. "Surprising constituents," *Journal of East Asian Linguistics* 11: 243–301.

   2004. "Coordination of verbs and two types of verbal inflection," *Linguistic Inquiry* 35: 168–178.

Tang, Chih-Chen Jane 1990. "Chinese Phrase Structure and the Extended X'-theory," PhD diss., Cornell University.

Tang, Ting-chi 1979. *Studies in Chinese Syntax*. Student Book Co., Ltd.: Taipei.

Taylor, Heather 2006. "Moving out of if-clauses: If an if-clause is sentence-initial . . . ," talk presented at *GLOW* 29, Barcelona, April 5–8, 2006.

Teng, Shou-hsin 1970. "Comitative versus phrasal conjunction," *Papers in Linguistics* 2(2): 314–358.

Thiersch, Craig 1985. "VP and Scrambling in the German Mittelfeld," ms., University of Tilburg.

Tomioka, Satoshi 2003. "The semantics of Japanese null pronouns and its cross-linguistic implications," in Kerstin Schwabe and Susanne Winkler (eds.), *The Interfaces: Deriving and Interpreting Omitted Structures*, Amsterdam: John Benjamins, pp. 321–339.

Tsai, Wei-tien Dylan 1994. "On economizing the theory of A-bar dependencies," PhD diss. MIT.

Tsao, Feng-fu 1996. "hanyu de tisheng dongci" [Chinese raising verbs], *Zhongguo Yuwen* 1996(3): 172–182.

Ura, Hiroyuki 2000. *Checking Theory and Grammatical Functions in Universal Grammar*. New York: Oxford University Press.

Vergnaud, Jean Roger 1974. "French relative clauses," PhD diss., MIT. (Revised version in 1985, *Dépendances et niveaux de représentation en syntaxe*. Amsterdam: John Benjamins.)

Vicente, Luis to appear. "On the syntax of adversative coordination," *Natural Language and Linguistic Theory*.

Vries, Mark de 2002. "The syntax of relativization," PhD diss., Universiteit van Amsterdam.

   2005. "Coordination and syntactic hierarchy," *Studia Linguistica* 59: 83–105.

   2006. "The syntax of appositive relativization: on specifying coordination, false free relatives, and promotion," *Linguistic Inquiry* 37(2): 229–270.

Wälchli, Bernhard 2003. "Co-compounds and natural coordination," PhD diss., University of Stockholm.

   2005. *Co-Compounds and Natural Coordination*. Oxford: Oxford University Press.

Webelhuth, Gert 1989. "Syntactic saturation phenomena and the modern Germanic languages," PhD diss., University of Massachusetts, Amherst.

   1992. *Principles and Parameters of Syntactic Saturation*. Oxford: Oxford University Press.

Welsche, Birgit 1995. *Symmetric Coordination*. Tübingen: Max Niemeyer.

Whitman, Philip Neal 2002. "Category neutrality: a type-logical investigation," PhD diss., The Ohio State University.

   2004. "Semantics and pragmatics of English verbal dependent coordination," *Language* 80: 403–434.

Wilder, Chris 1994. "Coordination, ATB and ellipsis," in Cornelius Jan-Wouter Zwart (ed.), *Minimalism and Kayne's Asymmetry Hypothesis*, Groningen [*Groninger Arbeiten zur Germanischen Linguistik* 37], pp. 291–331.

  1997. "Some properties of ellipsis in coordination," in Artemis Alexiadou and T. Alan Hall (eds.), *Studies on Universal Grammar and Typological Variation*, Amsterdam: John Benjamins, pp. 59–107.

  1999. "The syntax of coordination," Handout of Linguistic Summer School, Potsdam University.

  2008. "Shared constituents and linerarization," in Kyle Johnson (ed.), *Topics in Ellipsis*, Cambridge: Cambridge University Press, pp. 229–258.

Williams, Edwin S. 1977. "Across-the-Board application of rules," *Linguistic Inquiry* 8: 419–423.

  1978. "Across-the-Board rule application," *Linguistic Inquiry* 9: 31–43.

  1980. "Predication," *Linguistic Inquiry* 11: 203–238.

  1989. "Maximal projections in words and phrases," in Mark Baltin and Anthony Kroch (eds.), *Alternative Conceptions of Phrase Structure*, Chicago: The University of Chicago Press, pp. 280–291.

Winter, Yoad 2001. *Flexibility Principles in Boolean Semantics: The Interpretation of Coordination, Plurality, and Scope in Natural Language*. Cambridge, MA: MIT Press.

  2006. "Multiple coordination: meaning composition vs. the syntax–semantics interface," ms., Technion/NIAS.

Woolford, Ellen 1987. "An ECP account of constraints on Across-The-Board extraction," *Linguistic Inquiry* 18: 166–171.

Wu, Jianxin 1999. "Syntax and semantics of quantification in Chinese," PhD diss., University of Maryland at College Park.

Wurmbrand, Susi 2001. "Agree: the other VP-internal subject hypothesis," in K. Megerdoomian and L. A. Barel (eds.), *Proceedings of WCCFL 20*, Somerville, MA: Cascadilla Press, pp. 635–648.

  2008. "Nor: neither disjunction nor paradox," *Linguistic Inquiry* 39: 511–522.

Yamada, S. and I. Igarashi 1967. "Co-ordination in transformational grammar," *Zeitschrift für Phonetik, Sprachwissenschaft und Kommunikationsforschung* 20: 143–156.

Yngve, Victor H. 1960. "A model and a hypothesis for language structure," *Proceedings of the American Philosophical Society* 104: 444–466.

Yoon, James Hye and Wooseung Lee 2005. "Conjunction reduction and its consequences for noun phrase morphosyntax in Korean," in John Alderete, Chung-hye Han, and Alexei Kochetov (eds.), *Proceedings of the 24th West Coast Conference on Formal Linguistics*, Somerville, MA: Cascadilla Proceedings Project, pp. 379–387.

Yu, Chiung-Yi 2008. "The processing of natural and accidental coordination," MA thesis, National Chung Cheng University.

Yuasa, Etsuyo and Jerry M. Sadock 2002. "Pseudo-subordination: a mismatch between syntax and semantics," *Journal of Linguistics* 38: 87–111.

Zagona, Karen 1988a. "Proper government of antecedentless VPs in English and Spanish," *Natural Languages and Linguistic Theory* 6: 95–128.

1988b. *Verb Phrase Syntax: A Parametric Study of English and Spanish.* Dordrecht: Kluwer.

Zepeda, Ofelia 1983. *A Papago Grammar.* Tucson: University of Arizona Press.

Zhang, Niina Ning 1999. "Chinese *de* and the *de*-construction," *Syntaxis* 2, 27–49.

2004a. "Move is remerge," *Language and Linguistics* 5(1): 189–209.

2004b. "Against Across-the-Board Movement," *Concentric: Studies in Linguistics* 30, 123–156.

2006. "On the configuration issue of coordination," *Language and Linguistics* 7(1): 175–223.

2007a. "The syntax of English comitative constructions," *Folia Linguistica* 41: 135–169.

2007b. "The syntactic derivations of two paired dependency constructions," *Lingua* 117: 2134–2158.

2007c. "A syntactic account of the direct object restriction in Chinese," *Language Research* 43 (1): 53–75.

2008a. "Repetitive and correlative coordinators as focus particles parasitic on coordinators," *SKY Journal of Linguistics* 21: 295–342.

2008b. "The syntactic derivations of split variable constructions," ms. *National Chung Cheng University*.

2008c. "Gapless relative clauses as clausal licensers of relational nouns," *Language and Linguistics* 9(4): 1003–1026.

2009. "Explaining the immobility of conjuncts," *Studia Linguistica* 63(3).

Zhou, Gang 2002. *Lianci yu xiangguan wenti* [Coordinators and the relevant issues] Hefei: Anhui Jiaoyu Press.

Zhu, Dexi 1982. *Yufa Jiangyi* [Lectures on grammar], Beijing: Shangwu Press.

Zoerner, Cyril Edward, III. 1995. "Coordination: the syntax of andP," PhD diss., University of California, Irvine.

Zwart, C. Jan-Wouter 1995. "Review of Johannessen, J. B., *Coordination: A Minimalist Approach*," *Glot International* 1: 11–13.

2000. "A head raising analysis of relative clauses in Dutch," in A. Alexiadou, A. Meinunger, C. Wilder, and P. Law (eds.), *The Syntax of Relative Clauses*, Linguistik Aktuell 32, Amsterdam: John Benjamins, pp. 349–385.

Index

Subjects